The Empire Unpossess'd

An Essay on Gibbon's *Decline and Fall*

FRONTISPIECE

Silhouettes of Gibbon and Lord Sheffield, taken in 1791, and preserved by Maria Josepha Holroyd among her souvenirs of the visit to Lausanne. Reproduced on the cover of Maria Josepha Stanley, *The Girlhood of Maria Josepha Holroyd. Recorded in Letters of a hundred years ago, from 1776 to 1796*, ed. J. H. Adeane (London: Longman, Green and Co., 1896).

THE EMPIRE UNPOSSESS'D

An Essay on Gibbon's
Decline and Fall

LIONEL GOSSMAN

Department of Romance Languages and Literatures
Princeton University

CAMBRIDGE UNIVERSITY PRESS
CAMBRIDGE
LONDON   NEW YORK   NEW ROCHELLE
MELBOURNE   SYDNEY

Published by the Press Syndicate of the University of Cambridge
The Pitt Building, Trumpington Street, Cambridge CB2 1RP
32 East 57th Street, New York, NY 10022, USA
296 Beaconsfield Parade, Middle Park, Melbourne 3206, Australia

First published 1981

Printed in the United States of America
Typeset by Graphic Composition Inc., Athens, Georgia
Printed and bound by Halliday Lithograph Corp., West Hanover,
Massachusetts

Library of Congress Cataloging in Publication Data
Gossman, Lionel.
    The Empire unpossess'd.
    Includes bibliographical references and index.
    1. Gibbon, Edward, 1737–1794. History of the decline
and fall of the Roman Empire.   2. Rome – History – Empire,
30 B.C.–476 A.D.   3. Byzantine Empire – History.
I. Title
DG311.G57G67   937'.06'072   80–24008
ISBN 0 521 23453 0

"Is the chair empty? Is the sword unsway'd?
Is the King dead, the empire unpossess'd?"

Shakespeare, *Richard III*

"Il n'y a plus qu'un sexe, et nous sommes tous femmes par
l'esprit."

Montesquieu

"En véritable élève du XVIIIᵉ siècle, il se plaisait surtout au
laisser-aller d'un pouvoir absolu, et jugeait que le plus agréable
des gouvernemens, c'est celui dont on peut se moquer tout bas,
sans risquer de le renverser."

Barante

Contents

Preface

IN THE 1930s the literature on Gibbon took the form of biography. The historian and his age, it appears, fascinated the men of that troubled time as much as did the History itself. We may speculate that they were disturbed by the destructiveness of the Great War, bewildered by intractable social, economic, and international problems, and apprehensive for the future of civilization as they knew it, and that they looked back for inspiration as well as for relief to the rationalism, the cosmopolitanism, the decorum, and the modest personal courage of the Age of Enlightenment. Whatever the reasons, we shall not see the like of their work again. The books they wrote are not scholarly, in our contemporary sense, though they are grounded in solid scholarship and research. Mingling interpretation freely with biographical narrative, they are far closer in spirit and style than any contemporary study to Gibbon himself and seem still to belong to that liberal belletristic tradition of which Gibbon is one of the chief ornaments. To write about Gibbon, one suspects, was in large measure, for G. M. Young, R. B. Mowat, and D. M. Low, to reaffirm the values Gibbon stood for.[1]

The student of Gibbon in our own time, professional and academic, has generally abandoned the biographical mode in favor of scholarly analysis of Gibbon's place in the history of ideas and the history of historiography and of the rhetoric and narrative art of the *Decline and Fall*. Gibbon and his time no longer represent a set of values to which the critic looks back with sympathy and respect. The text of the *Decline and Fall* itself, the intellectual and ideological context in which it was produced, and the literary conventions by which it was shaped are now the focus of interest.[2]

I could not hope to match the achievement of Young or Low, and I have not attempted to do over what has been very well done in the last two decades by Giarrizzo, Jordan, Bond, Brady, and Baridon, to mention only a few of the recent Gibbon scholars from whom the reader of Gibbon has much to learn. Biography, history of ideas, rhetoric, and narrative strategy are by no means ignored in the following pages, but my business has not been with any of these exclusively or principally.

The main thesis of my study is that Gibbon's essential concern in the *Decline and Fall* is with authority – with political authority in the first instance, but also with other kinds of authority, including that of language, of narrative, and of the historical text itself. Indeed, I believe Gibbon's grappling with a problem that presses heavily on the modern consciousness may well save his work, in our time, from exile to the narrow province of the antiquarian or the academic.

Throughout the *Decline and Fall*, it is argued, the highest value is placed upon what is original, undivided, one with itself, as the only possible foundation of authority. Whatever marks a rupture with the origins – interpretation, which takes the place of immediate understanding; rhetoric, which exploits the autonomy of language and the fateful gap between sign and thing; history itself, which Gibbon so readily associates with "intrigue" – is nearly always denounced and deplored. The reader of the *Decline and Fall* is clearly expected to accept the outlook of the narrator. This is not surprising, since it is a persistent feature of the tradition they both share not only to perceive the world in terms of the original or unitary versus the derived or alienated but to privilege the first of these terms absolutely over the second. Even in the century of Enlightenment disputes were most often conducted with reference to competing origins or sources – Revelation on the one hand, Nature or Reason on the other.

In Gibbon, however, as in some other eighteenth-century writers, accompanying the theme of origins and threatening to undermine it there is also a repeated suggestion that civilization is possible only because the supposed origin, the point of absolute presence, is in fact an empty space, an erasure. The "vacant space" at the heart of the Empire, in Gibbon's words, is what makes the substitution of humanly devised meanings and orders possible and necessary. It is both a scandal and an opportunity. The attempt to refound authority in the absence of origins and to discover an acceptable middle ground between what Gibbon and his contemporaries readily thought of as the "extremes" of anarchy and despotism, each of which involves a breakdown of social order and communication, appears in the *Decline and Fall* as a political problem in the narrative and as a rhetorical and esthetic problem of the narrative – one for which a solution is sought above all in a redefinition of the relation of reader and narrator and the adoption of an ingratiating yet decorous discourse equally remote from the playful conceits of libertines and the sublime enthrallment of metaphysicians and divines. There seems no doubt that Gibbon's solution of the esthetic problem went far to ensure the literary success of the *Decline and Fall*, its appeal to an audience that was at once feminine ("feathered ladies") and masculine ("judges"), and its ability to function simultaneously as literature, stimulating the imagination, and as history, limiting and restraining it.

The possible relation between Gibbon's perception of the problem of authority and response to it and the ideological requirements of a particular social group in eighteenth-century England is sometimes hinted at but has not been an object of investigation in the present study. Such an investigation, it seemed, was best left to a trained historian competent to handle the methodological issues involved. On the other hand, it is suggested in the first chapter that the problem of authority, which is found to be central to the *Decline and Fall*, was experienced in a variety of contexts by Gibbon himself as a human being – as a son, as a man, and as a friend – or at the very least was again projected, after the completion of the *Decline and Fall*, onto the historian's narrative of his life. The intention here is not to offer a psychoanalytical interpretation of Gibbon's achievement as a writer and a historian in terms of his family relations and early experience. It is simply to point out that Gibbon might have discovered the problem that preoccupied him in his great work not only in his reflection on the State and the Empire but also in the humbler situations of everyday life. In the historian's relation to his father, to his mother, to Aunt Kitty Porten, to his friends Deyverdun, the Holroyds, the Neckers, the de Séverys, it is almost impossible not to discern the same difficulties and the same strategies for dealing with them that we find in his work as an artist. No causal chain need link the man to the historian and the artist, but the same pattern of unmasking, veiling, and substitution is characteristic of all three.

Countless strands connect a reader and a text and most, no doubt, must remain concealed, especially from the reader himself. I think, however, that I may be able to identify three conscious experiences or concerns which converged, in my case, on Gibbon and his History.

The first and most obvious is the decline and fall of the British Empire, which still astonishes me even though it is now past history. No doubt it was already visible, by the 1920s, not only to those on the Left who wished for it but to many upper-class people who had much to fear from it. To a child of modest background, however, as I was, born and raised in a grimy industrial metropolis, which consoled itself for its many miseries with the sobriquet "Second City of the Empire" (after Calcutta, it was conceded), it came as a completely unexpected and disorienting experience. Everything in my education had encouraged me to believe in the miraculous and providential character of the process by which the inhabitants of a small group of islands off the coast of northwestern Europe had made themselves the center of a universal Empire and the custodians of world order. The war years intensified the feeling of being at the world's center in a crucial and heroic role, even though mine, as a schoolboy, was limited to helping with the annual potato harvest and running occasional errands on my bicycle for the Home Guard.

Perhaps no one who did not live through that time can understand how keen the communal commitment was, adroitly fostered as it was by government propaganda, and how bright the hope that a better social order would accompany the peace, not only at home but throughout the world, and especially in the territories under British administration. My growing up coincided with the end of the war. The euphoric expectations that swept the Labour government into office were extinguished not only by the Cold War and the sobering realization that the social order would not be easily or speedily renewed but by the transformation of the international order itself. Soon after the elation of victory, the extent of the decline of British power and influence became apparent. It gradually dawned on the young men and women of my generation that the destinies of the world would no longer be decided in Britain and that the seemingly vast power we had dreamed of turning to noble ends had been changed, in an astonishingly short time, into a kind of political Pantaloon, still commanding enough strength on the international stage to obstruct a few straggling opponents but devoid of grandeur, heroism, or dignity.

Everyone has to reappraise the values and authorities of his childhood, and it is not an easy thing to do. In my case, because of my experience as a British *subject* – a status I have retained out of piety, affection, and gratitude – that reappraisal assumed a more than personal or familial character. In Gibbon's time, the phase of Empire of which I observed the close was barely beginning. But he too stood close to the end of an international order, and the boyhood sweetheart of Suzanne Necker lived to see a large part of the world of his youth crash into the fires of the French Revolution. No one may claim to have heard everything Gibbon is saying, but I think my own experience may have made me particularly attentive to certain inflections of that voice "from the other shore."

To be raised in the United Kingdom, with its class distinctions and intense regional particularism, means to be especially sensitive to the forms and codes of communication and to be able to sympathize both with the desire to break them down in order to reach a more authentic, unmediated community with others – to build Jerusalem in England's green and pleasant land – and with the conviction that they are the indispensable means of any social communication and of any social order. It happens that the question of codes and masks has proved to be a central one for me also in my professional work as a teacher of French literature. It is especially important for understanding the eighteenth-century texts with which I most frequently have to concern myself professionally. Gibbon, as is well known, was by no means a stranger either to the French language or to French literature. It was inevitable, perhaps, that I should be drawn one day to a figure whose situation astride two cultures reminded me, *mutatis mutandis*, of my own.

Finally, because of my interest in masks and codes, I have long been intrigued by forms of writing in which the literary imagination appears to disguise itself and to submit to significant constraints – literary criticism, historiography, scholarship and erudition, natural history. As long as literary studies were dominated by rhetoric, the literary character of Buffon, Michelet, Carlyle, or Macaulay was recognized, and these authors were regularly studied as models of style to be followed or avoided. When rhetoric ceased to be the focus of interest in literary studies, however, such writers were most often quietly dropped from the literary canon and abandoned to students of biography and cultural history. I believe we are now ready to reread, reconsider, and, where appropriate, reinstate them. We now know that there are no firm boundaries separating literary from other forms of writing. Any text can be seen as a point of intersection of other texts, as a reorganization, revision, and redeployment of them for the purpose of generating new meanings, and as a stimulus to further reorganizations, revisions, and redeployments. At the same time, in its particularity, each text is a singular utterance, emitted at a specific point in time, the engagement of an individual user of language and of texts with the world. Gibbon's History, it seems to me, does not simply convey information. It utilizes other texts, other histories, to create meaning and to bear testimony. In trying to hear Gibbon's voice, to grasp his meaning, I stumbled, as a reader, on my own, and the movement of reading the History was continued for me, however modestly, in the act of writing this essay. A text that can unlock its reader's imagination and quicken his pen seems to deserve from him the gratitude and respect that readers usually accord to great works of literature.

Though I have been reading Gibbon and thinking about him for a number of years, I did most of the writing of this essay in 1978–9, during tenure of a fellowship from the National Endowment for the Humanities. I wish to express my gratitude to the Endowment. I am also indebted to Princeton

Preface

University for granting me a sabbatical leave that was largely earned at another institution. Finally, I would like to thank the Institute for Advanced Study at Princeton and its Director, Harry Woolf, for their generous hospitality.

Princeton, N.J.   L.G.
January, 1980

Historical note

E DWARD GIBBON WAS BORN in 1737 at Putney, near London, the
son of Edward Gibbon, member of Parliament for Petersfield (1734)
and Southampton (1741), and of Judith Porten, the daughter of a
London merchant. His childhood was sickly, and his formal education
suffered frequent interruptions. At the age of fifteen, he went up to Oxford
as a gentleman-commoner at Magdalen College, but he claims that the
time he spent there was "the most idle and unprofitable of my whole life."
In 1753, in the fortress of Anglicanism, he was converted to Roman Catholicism. His father immediately sent him to Lausanne in Switzerland, where
a local Calvinist minister, M. Pavilliard, was entrusted with completing his
general education and bringing him back to the Protestant fold. Pavilliard
executed both tasks with fair success. Gibbon read widely (Latin, some
Greek, logic, metaphysics, jurisprudence, French literature, and some
mathematics), and at the end of 1754 he received the sacraments in the
church at Lausanne. During this period he met Suzanne Curchod, the
daughter of another pastor, and the two young people planned to marry,
but Gibbon's father refused his consent and in 1758 recalled his son to
England. Gibbon gave up his matrimonial plans, and Suzanne Curchod
subsequently married Jacques Necker, the Genevan banker who became
French minister of finance in the last years of the *ancien régime*.

Gibbon spent the decade after his return to England serving in the
Hampshire militia, managing his father's dilapidated affairs, and tolerating
as best he could the tedium and dependency of his existence in the simple
old manor house at Buriton, Hampshire, which had been acquired by his
wealthy grandfather and to which his father had retired on Judith Porten's
death. This period was punctuated by the publication of his first book, an
Essai sur l'étude de la littérature, which appeared in French in 1761, by travel
abroad (between 1763 and 1765 he was on the Continent, with extended
stays at Paris, Lausanne, and Rome), and by some abortive literary projects: The first volume of a projected *Histoire générale de la République des
Suisses* was composed, again in French, in 1767, and in 1768 he began a

literary journal, *Mémoires littéraires de la Grande Bretagne*, which ceased publication, however, after the second volume. Above all, Gibbon read a great deal during this period and conceived the design of the *Decline and Fall of the Roman Empire*.

In 1770 Edward Gibbon Senior died, and the historian moved to London to pursue seriously his work on the *Decline and Fall*. The first volume appeared in 1776 and was an instant success. The others – six in all – followed at various intervals until 1788. In 1774 Gibbon was elected member of Parliament for Liskeard, but his parliamentary career was short (1774–83) and undistinguished. In 1779, at the request of the Secretary of State for the Southern Department, Lord Weymouth, he drew up for distribution to the courts of Europe a substantial and well-argued reply, in French, to a French government circular justifying the position taken by France in the American war. In return for this service, he was appointed to a sinecure at the Board of Trade, but the position disappeared when the Board of Trade was abolished in 1782. One year later, Gibbon began negotiations for the sale of all his property except his library, and left England to live with Georges Deyverdun, a Swiss friend of long standing, at Lausanne. Here he wrote the final volumes of the *Decline and Fall*.

With the publication of these in 1787 and the sale of Buriton to Lord Stawell in 1789, Gibbon's ties to England were further loosened. In May, 1793, however, he undertook an arduous journey back to his native country in order to be with his friend John Baker Holroyd, Lord Sheffield, who had just lost his wife. A few months later, in London, he underwent a series of operations for an ailment that had been with him for decades. An infection set in, and he died on January 16, 1794. He was buried in the village church at Fletching, Sussex, the Sheffield family burial place. An autobiography, on which he had been working before his death, was published posthumously by Sheffield in two volumes of *Miscellaneous Works*.

I

A name, a rank, a character, in the world

GIBBON EMERGES FROM THE PAGES of his Autobiography as a man with an unusually intense experience of the precariousness of identity. As he was a feeble child, he tells, and not expected to live, his father gave his name to several male children born after him;[1] at the height of adolescence he underwent a religious conversion that resulted in his being exiled from his native land for several years and almost forgetting his native tongue; and for a considerable time he hesitated between English and French as the language of his literary work. Throughout his life he spoke both tongues with equal facility, and although he was always a patriotic Englishman, he also liked to think of himself as a loyal Swiss. As his relation to his father was troubled and uncertain, and as he did not succeed in becoming a husband and father in his own right, he never felt he possessed a secure, solidly founded, native identity and authority, but was obliged always to resort to substitutes. The identity he finally established for himself, in his own eyes and in those of his contemporaries, as "the historian of the decline and fall,"[2] was not a native identity, but one he had invented through his writing and with the help of "my other wife, the decline and fall of the Roman Empire."[3] He himself acknowledged with great candor the important role writing played in his life as a substitute for native virtues and powers that he felt he lacked. "Twenty happy years have been animated by the labour of my history," he wrote, "and its success has given me a name, a rank, a character, in the World, to which I should not otherwise have been entitled."[4]

One of the first topics of the Autobiography is the hero's relation to his Aunt Catherine Porten, his mother's sister. His mother died when he was ten years old, the hero recounts, but as her place had always been filled by his Aunt Kitty – "the true mother of my mind as well as of my health"[5] – he was not much affected by his mother's death.[6] Aunt Kitty, not his mother, nursed him through a difficult childhood, consuming "many anxious and solitary days . . . in the patient tryal of every mode of relief and amusement" and "many wakeful nights . . . by my bedside in trembling expectation that each hour would be my last."[7]

Gibbon may well have had the early pages of Rousseau's *Confessions* in mind when writing this part of his autobiography. To Aunt Porten he ascribes a role very similar to that which Rousseau ascribed to Tante Suzon, and the portrait of Edward Gibbon senior also bears some resemblance to that of Isaac Rousseau in the *Confessions*. In both books the courtship and marriage of father and mother are likened to a "love tale,"[8] both men are said to have been passionately devoted to their wives, and both sons present themselves as having felt a kind of obligation to match these incomparable women in order to secure their father's affection. The famous scene in which Isaac Rousseau enjoins his son to take his mother's place for him is repeated in Gibbon's account of his first interview with his father after his mother's death:

> I can never forget the scene . . . ; the awful silence, the room hung with black, the midday tapers, his sighs and tears, his praises of my mother, a saint in heaven, his solemn adjuration that I would cherish her memory and imitate her virtues; and the fervour with which he kissed and blessed me as the sole surviving pledge of their loves.[9]

In the end, both Rousseau and Gibbon depict their fathers as erratic, impulsive, incapable of providing protection or security of affection, and in their very weakness obscurely menacing. As one would expect, however, Gibbon's autobiography is more "noble," more conventional than Rousseau's, and there is less material to define Aunt Kitty's precise place in his childhood than Rousseau provides for Tante Suzon. Gibbon, moreover, does not present himself as suffering the successive brother–sister *ménages* (Suzanne Rousseau and Isaac Rousseau, Pastor and Mademoiselle Lambercier) that must have introduced considerable confusion into Rousseau's conception of sexual roles and identities in general, and of his own place in the family configuration in particular.[10] Aunt Porten never completely displaced Gibbon's mother in his father's household, and even though his maternal grandfather's house at Putney appeared to him in later life "in the light of my proper and native home,"[11] he spent only part of the time there, during vacations or his parents' visits to London, prior to his mother's death.

Nevertheless, Gibbon unmistakably emphasizes Aunt Porten's crucial role in his life.[12] It is she, the maiden aunt and nurse, who is presented in the Autobiography as the center and focus of his affective life as a child, and not his natural mother, the younger and more attractive Judith, whose vivacity and worldliness he never fails to underline. "I was a puny child neglected by my Mother, starved by my nurse, and of whose being very little care or expectation was entertained," he wrote to Lord Sheffield on Kitty Porten's death; "without her maternal vigilance, I should either have been in my grave, or imperfectly lived a crooked ricketty monster a burthen to myself and others."[13] With Aunt Kitty, Gibbon achieved an intimacy that he never knew with his mother. "Like friends of an equal age," he tells, "we freely conversed on every topic, familiar or abstruse."[14] For the frail and sickly boy she was the perfect partner and playmate, as in later life she became the "faithful friend and agreeable companion,"[15] all the more so, perhaps, as the nephew she had raised had come in some ways to resemble her, being, like her, a victim of paternal improvidence and a bachelor, the fictitious parent of the children of others. Indeed, the price of intimacy with a spinster mother, for Gibbon as for Rousseau, was in all probability the strict suppression of sexuality.[16]

From earliest childhood, in sum, Gibbon seems to have experienced a division of woman into nurse and consoler on the one hand and sexual being on the other, into a sisterlike figure whose difference from him was outweighed by her closeness to him, and a creature whom he regarded with fear and anxiety as alien and even hostile. It is surely not without importance, moreover, that the foundation of his security was not the natural mother but the fictitious one, the substitute who made up for what the natural mother failed to provide. In his eyes, Aunt Kitty stood for the protection and contentment of a private and secluded world from which every menace of difference and disturbance had been eliminated, and throughout his life he was tempted by the idea of withdrawal to such a world. Thus he tells that he did not regret having to be removed – on grounds of poor health – from the society of his schoolfellows;[17] on the contrary, he was happy to be taken out of the rough and tumble of the competitive world of his peers. His mother, on the other hand, the siren whose charms had enslaved his father and brought the latter into conflict with *his* father, is associated in the hero's imagination with cruelty and deprivation:

> Every time I have . . . passed over Putney common I have always
> noticed the spot where my mother, as we drove along in the coach,
> admonished me that I was now going into the World, and [had]
> much [to] learn to think and act for myself. . . . There is not, in
> the course of life, a more remarkable change than the removal of a

child from the luxury and freedom of a wealthy house to the frugal diet and strict subordination of a school; from the tenderness of parents and the obsequiousness of servants to the rude familiarity of his equals, the insolent tyranny of his seniors, and the rod, perhaps, of á cruel and capricious pedagogue.[18]

The Horatian theme of withdrawal from the tumult of the city to an idyllic retreat "which should unite the society of the town with the beauties and freedom of the Country,"[19] in Gibbon's own words, was a common literary topos of the eighteenth century and probably a broadly shared ideal of life. It is important in the writings of Pope and Voltaire, and it also determined major decisions in their lives. Voltaire chose to live at the gates of Geneva, as his philosophically minded Quaker in the *Lettres philosophiques* had settled near London, his Oriental philosopher Zadig near Babylon, and his chastened and enlightened optimist Candide near Constantinople. In the same way, Pope settled at Twickenham and Gibbon at La Grotte, at the gates of Lausanne. Gibbon's description of Sheffield Place, the country seat of his friend John Holroyd, Lord Sheffield, as a "château . . . séjour du repos et de l'amitié,"[20] repeats a formula that Voltaire used frequently in his correspondence when referring to Mme. du Châtelet's residence at Cirey.

In Gibbon's case, the theme of withdrawal, the contrast of London and Lausanne developed in innumerable letters, seems to have been, in addition to a convenient epistolary topos, the expression of a deep-seated need. In Lausanne, he writes, he dominated and controlled his social environment as he could never do in London, and he remarks pointedly in a letter to his friend Sheffield that in England, when he was suffering from the gout, as he frequently was, "my confinement was sad and solitary; the many forgot my existence when they saw me no longer at Brookes's; and the few who sometimes cast a thought or an eye on their friend were detained by business or pleasure, the distance of the way or the hours of the house of commons." But at Lausanne, "the objects are nearer and more distinct, and I myself am an object of much larger magnitude. . . . During three months I have had round my chair a succession of agreeable men and women who came with a smile and vanished at a nod, and as soon as it was agreeable I had a constant party at cards which was sometimes dismissed to their respective homes, and sometimes detained by Deyverdun to supper without out the least trouble or inconvenience to myself."[21]

It is not surprising, perhaps, that as he came to acknowledge his preference for the order of Lausanne, in which he himself occupied a prominent and controlling place, over the free-for-all of London, where he was no more than "an obscure bachelor," he also modified his view of the Bernese government of Lausanne and of the relative value of liberty as opposed to a protective and paternalistic order. "That incessant hurry of Politicks," he wrote to his stepmother in 1785, "was indeed one of the things which disgusted me the most, and there is nothing pleases me so much in this Country as to enjoy all the blessings of a Good Government without ever talking or thinking of our Governors."[22] Two years later he told Catherine de Sévery that at Lausanne "la tranquillité du gouvernement dont vous ne sentez pas assez le prix . . . vaut mieux peut-être que notre liberté orageuse."[23] The growing conservatism of age in an increasingly restless world may have prompted these remarks,[24] but they are probably not inconsistent with Gibbon's deepest desires and memories throughout his life. No schoolboy adventures ever seemed more desirable to him than the protective care, the gentle society, and the "maternal vigilance" of his Aunt Kitty Porten, and in the History the happiest period in the history of man is not that of the virtuous Republic but the benevolent and paternalistic rule of the Antonines.

Yet Gibbon's withdrawal from the male world of competition and violence, from the "orageuse liberté" of politics and public life, was not a renunciation. It seems rather to have been a strategy of displacement or transposition. Even more than to Lausanne, it was to his library that the historian withdrew. "Though a lover of society my library is the room to which I am most attached," he wrote.[25] Impulses and desires that could not even be acknowledged at one level found release at another, and the pen, it seems, substituted for the native instruments through which Gibbon failed to assert himself. To this failure – to the "unmanly" detour by way of the pen – we owe *The Decline and Fall of the Roman Empire*. Gibbon, as we shall see, never gave up the ideal of direct engagement, of native authority, of the arms-bearing citizen; he did not draw the full lesson of his own history; nevertheless, his work bears important marks of his experience as a writer.

Gibbon provides several telling illustrations in the Autobiography of his inability or unwillingness to enter wholeheartedly into competition with his peers and of his adoption of the role of onlooker and recorder which was to serve him so well as a historian. In his account of the years he spent on his father's estate at Buriton after his return from exile in Lausanne, he emphasizes that, though by then a young man of twenty-one, he took no part in the manly activities indulged in by his father. "When he galloped away on a fleet hunter to follow the Duke of Richmond's foxhounds, I saw him depart without a wish to join in the sport; and in the command of an ample manour, I valued the supply of the kitchen much more than the exercise of the field. I never handled a gun, I seldom mounted a horse."[26] Even his service with the Hampshire militia appears to have been more notable for carousing and good companionship than for arduous military exercise. Later, as a member of Parliament, in a situation of considerable verbal violence and competition, Gibbon confesses that he was a very poor speaker and presents himself as an observer and judge of parliamentary action rather than a participant in it:

> After a fleeting illusive hope, prudence condemned me to ac-
> quiesce in the humble station of a mute. I was not armed by Na-
> ture or education with the intrepid energy of mind and voice –
> "Vincentem strepitus, et natum rebus agendis." – timidity was
> fortified by pride, and even the success of my pen discouraged the
> tryal of my voice. But I assisted at the debates of a free assembly
> . . . I listened to the attack and defence of eloquence and reason; I
> had a near prospect of the characters, views, and passions of the
> first men of the age.[27]

The hero's muteness – *mutus pecus*, he called himself – is the more strik-ing, as he appears from other evidence to have been a fluent conversation-alist, the only criticism being that his talk was somewhat composed,[28] and as we have his own word for it that eloquence and oratory determined the patterns of his written prose, his practice as an author being "to cast a long paragraph in a single mould, to try it by my ear, to deposit it in my memory" and "to suspend the action of the pen till I had given the last polish to my work."[29] It seems, therefore, that in Parliament it was the situation that intimidated and disarmed him, making him feel that before "the first men of the age" he somehow lacked the authority to speak. He certainly admired brilliant oratory, which he associated, traditionally enough, with manly energy and skill, and he paid tribute to "Mr. Sheridan's eloquence" at the famous impeachment trial of Warren Hastings before Parliament in 1788. In a curious note at this point in the Autobiography, which may well reflect a general anxiety about power and performance, Gibbon relates that, being struck – as indeed all those who heard him were – by Sheridan's "display of Genius, which blazed four successive days," he tried to find out how many words "a rapid and ready Orator might pro-nounce in an hour."[30] The hero of the Autobiography, moreover, himself suggests a connection between his lack of success and timidity in public oratory, his failure to perform as might have been expected of him, and his practice of the solitary and imaginative exercises of the pen: "even the success of my pen discouraged the tryal of my voice."[31] The sexual symbolism of the substitution of the artifice of the stylus for the tongue, the natural organ, was not lost, we may surmise, on a writer who so often reported the punishment of rebels by the tyrants' cutting off or pulling out of their tongues.

Timidity and withdrawal are thus presented as characteristic, throughout his career, of the hero's relation to the world of power and domination. Equally, identification with women and friendship with the wives of other men are recurrent features of his relations with others. All through his life, he was attracted by the friendship of married couples. With them he happily adopted the role of the son–brother–consort, who for all practical purposes agrees to be excluded from any relation to the woman that might disturb the male partner's exclusive possession of her. From the outset, in short, and by the nature of the role he adopts, the hero deliberately excludes himself from the exercise of power and refrains from directly challenging established authority. In this way Gibbon became the close friend and consort of his stepmother, his father's second wife, and in his letters to her he addresses her commonly as "My Dearest Friend." He had awaited her arrival with apprehension, he writes, but the imaginary monster turned out to be "an amiable and deserving woman" of "warm and exquisite sensibility." Like Aunt Kitty Porten, the second Mrs. Gibbon was a mother yet not a mother, a woman yet not a woman but a friend. "My suspicions . . . were gradually dispelled. . . . After some reserve on my side, our minds associated in confidence and friendship; and as Mrs. Gibbon had neither children nor the hopes of children, we more easily adopted the tender names and genuine characters of mother and son."[32]

The hero at this point had reached an age that "abolished the distance that might yet remain between a parent and a son"[33] and gave him virtual equality with his father, and the latter was "satisfied" by his son's behavior. The situation at Buriton thus anticipates others in which Gibbon was a friend to husband and wife alike. He was equally close, for instance, to Abigail Holroyd, the wife of his friend and protector Lord Sheffield – later the editor of the Autobiography – and he considered Sheffield Place as his home. "I have a very noble country seat about ten miles from East Grinstead in Sussex," he wrote playfully. "That spot is dearer to me than the rest of the three kingdoms."[34] The Holroyd children, likewise, he treated as no family member and no stranger, but only an intimate friend of the family could – with a mixture of affection, indulgence, playfulness, and protectiveness. To the children, in short, he was at once a father and a brother, a superior and an equal, a father relieved of the weight – or the burden – of authority, just as to the wife he was a male without designs of possession.

At Lausanne, after he settled there, he became a close friend of Catherine de Sévery, the aunt of Benjamin Constant, and her husband Salomon de Sévery, a dignified member of the Grand and the Petit Conseils of Lausanne, whom young Maria Holroyd, on a visit to Gibbon in Lausanne, described as "a very friendly, good kind of man; but a little *ennuyeux*."[35] Gibbon had known Catherine before her marriage; she appears to have been beautiful but cold. She "is called Mont Blanc, and I cannot give you a better Idea of her,"[36] Maria Holroyd wrote her aunt in England. With this gracious but reserved woman and her solid, reliable husband, Gibbon found "the most perfect system of domestic happiness,"[37] a family in which he felt himself at home, and whose children he regarded as his own.[38] In general, it seems, the role of the adopted father, son, consort, brother, suited Gibbon well.[39]

Of marriage there was a question only once in the hero's life. At the age of twenty-one, he tells, he wanted to marry Suzanne Curchod, the daughter of a protestant minister of the Pays de Vaud – later Madame Necker, wife of the famous banker and minister of finance under Louis XVI and mother of the redoubtable Madame de Stael. His father forbade the match, however, and the hero acquiesced with hardly a murmur. As his own historian, he distilled the episode into a characteristically memorable parallelism: "I sighed as a lover; I obeyed as a son." The affair is recounted briefly in the Autobiography:

> I hesitate, from the apprehension of ridicule, when I approach the delicate subject of my early love. By this word I do not mean the polite attention or the gallantry, without hope or design, which has originated from the spirit of chivalry, and is interwoven with the texture of French manners. [I do not confine myself to the grosser appetite which our pride may affect to disdain, because it has been implanted by Nature in the whole animal creation, "Amor omnibus idem." The discovery of a sixth sense, the first consciousness of manhood, is a very interesting moment of our lives; but it less properly belongs to the memoirs of an individual, than to the natural history of the species.] I understand by this passion the union of desire, friendship, and tenderness, which is inflamed by a single female, which prefers her to the rest of her sex, and which seeks her possession as the supreme or the sole happiness of our being. I need not blush at recollecting the object of my choice; and though my love was disappointed of success, I am rather proud that I was once capable of feeling such a pure and exalted sentiment. The personal attractions of Mademoiselle Susanne Curchod were embellished by the virtues and talents of the

mind. Her fortune was humble, but her family was respectable: her mother, a native of France, had preferred her religion to her country; the profession of her father did not extinguish the moderation and philosophy of his temper, and he lived content with a small salary and laborious duty in the obscure lot of Minister of Crassy, in the mountains that separate the pays de Vaud from the County of Burgundy. In the solitude of a sequestered village he bestowed a liberal, and even learned, education on his only daughter; she surpassed his hopes by her proficiency in the sciences and languages; and in her short visits to some relations at Lausanne, the wit and beauty and erudition of Mademoiselle Curchod were the theme of universal applause. The report of such a prodigy awakened by (*sic*) curiosity; I saw and loved. I found her learned without pedantry, lively in conversation, pure in sentiment, and elegant in manners; and the first sudden emotion was fortified by the habits and knowledge of a more familiar acquaintance. She permitted me to make her two or three visits at her father's house: I passed some happy days in the mountains of Burgundy; and her parents honourably encouraged a connection [which might raise their daughter above want and dependence]. In a calm retirement the gay vanity of youth no longer fluttered in her bosom; she listened to the voice of truth and passion, and I might presume to hope that I had made some impression on a virtuous heart. At Crassy and Lausanne I indulged my dream of felicity; but, on my return to England, I soon discovered that my father would not hear of this strange alliance, and that, without his consent, I was myself destitute and helpless. After a painful struggle I yielded to my fate.[40]

The reader of this narrative may be struck both by the narrator's diffidence on the subject of sex, under the guise of matter-of-factness, and by his apparent gratification that, thanks to Suzanne Curchod, his Autobiography will not lack the important ingredient of an affair of the heart, however brief and restrained. On her side, Suzanne appears to have sensed the literary character or inspiration of her romance with Gibbon. "Encore un mot sur notre roman," she writes as the affair was drawing to its inevitable conclusion, and in a later letter Gibbon is portrayed as having failed to live up to her "chymère céladonique."[41] Subsequently, and characteristically, the failed hero of the romance became the successful friend of the family. He visited the Necker couple in Paris, and especially after they returned to Switzerland to become virtually his neighbors, he was a frequent house guest at Coppet. During these years of renewed association, Suzanne Necker, who seems to have been strikingly close to her former lover temperamentally and who spent her later years, as he did, renouncing and repressing the impulses and fantasies of her youth, appears to have encouraged the rewriting of her early love for the historian as a Necker family legend. The most elaborate version of this legend was ultimately published as Madame de Stael's successful novel *Corinne*, but earlier versions of it are found among the juvenile writings of Suzanne Curchod's daughter. As the hero of the legend, the historian was finally united with his mistress in a way that left the rights of fathers and husbands unchallenged, almost exactly as the hero and heroine of that other Swiss romance, Rousseau's *La nouvelle Heloise*, were united in the second part of the novel in the family context of Clarens under the benevolent supervision of Julie's husband, Monsieur de Wolmar.

In general, Gibbon appears to have been satisfied with this kind of relation to women. He never wanted to marry and set up a family for himself, never sought to take on in earnest the role of husband or father, and hints that he was not much moved by sexual desire, his only "temptations" being those offered by a marriage of convenience.

> A matrimonial alliance has ever been the object of my terror rather than of my wishes. I was not very strongly pressed by my family or by my passions to propagate the name and race of the Gibbons, and if some reasonable temptations occurred in the neighborhood, the vague idea never proceeded to the length of a serious negociation.[42]

The historian's various "flirts" – with Madame de Cambis, Lady Elizabeth Foster, Eliza Hayley, Madame de Montolieu, Madame de Silva — have yielded nothing to the most careful investigation, and they all seem to have been harmless enough. Perhaps, as he wrote to Sheffield, his only passion was for "Fanny Lausanne."

The ideal relation, as the narrator of the Autobiography puts it himself, is that of brother and sister:

> It is a familiar and tender friendship with a female, much about our own age; an affection perhaps softened by the secret influence of sex, but pure from any mixture of sensual desire, the sole species of Platonic love that can be indulged in with truth and without danger.[43]

In this modified version of the mother–son relation, sexuality is transformed into a playful tenderness that never aspires to possession, which is accepted as the exclusive prerogative of the father. The "brother" acquires a privileged place, however, as mediator between his "sister" and the serious and responsible father, whose power and authority remain unchallenged. While he entertains a brotherly relation to the latter as to an alter ego, he tends, because of his renunciation of the goal of possession, to identify with his "sister." Gibbon liked to address Catherine de Sévery as his "soeur," and in many more-or-less humorous letters to Abigail Holroyd – "the respectable Matron, my dearest Mylady, whom I have now loved as a sister for something better or worse than twenty years" – he referred to her as his sister or to himself as her brother.[44] "I love her better than any woman in the world," he once wrote to her husband[45] – thus effectively guaranteeing the innocence of his attachment – and when he presumed to embrace her, it was only "autant qu'il m'est permis."[46]

Not surprisingly, the hero's rejection of the master's role and his predilection for the role of the son–brother–consort in his relations with women are complemented by a corresponding relation to his father and to other men. Indeed, it may well be that Gibbon's most essential relations were with men and that many of his friendships with women were elaborate though indispensable detours by which he hoped to reach the husband or father. "A Wife or a sister are, you know, most usefull and convenient things, to bring friends together," he once observed to his stepmother.[47] At the same time, association and even identification with the mother–wife–sister figure as against the father–husband figure, with the slave against the master, the victim against the oppressor, placed him in the role of the slave, and like her, he appears to have come at once to love, to desire, and to resent the power and authority the slave acknowledges in her master. One is tempted to say that the hero of the Autobiography is divided between longing and admiration for the ideal Father and master that he has failed to be or renounced being and that he did not find in his historical father, and desire to expose the fraudulent fathers, the tyrants, the castrators who are themselves castrated. The hero seems, in short, to be characterized by an ambivalence – male and female, victimizer and victim at once – to which, as the distinguished narrator of his own story, he gives appropriately dignified and discreet expression, but whose intensity the details and incidents he adduces allow the reader to surmise. Divided, uncertain of his identity, he presents himself as admiring in others an apparently natural integrity and authority that he cannot remember ever having possessed himself.

The historical fathers in the Autobiography are not, on the whole, very reassuring and hardly fill the role of the ideal one. Edward Gibbon, the historian's grandfather, is both a tyrant and a victim. As one of the directors of the South Sea Company, he amassed a fortune by "use or abuse" of his position, but it was a fortune that rested, characteristically for Gibbon, on shaky foundations, and with the collapse of the Company in 1719, it was "blasted in a single day."[48] The successful and influential director now became, in Gibbon's presentation of his case, the victim of "a popular and even a parliamentary clamour," and in a "pernicious violation of liberty and law" was stripped of his fortune in virtue of a hastily passed retroactive statute. On its ruins, however, he soon succeeded in "erecting the edifice of a new fortune," so that at the time of his death in 1736 the erstwhile victim of "violent and arbitrary proceedings" had been transformed back again into "the oracle and tyrant of a petty Kingdom" composed of his family and his neighbors at Putney.[49] Gibbon's own father soon felt the effects of grandfather Gibbon's return to power: The last will of "the old Tyrant" enriched, "at the expence of his only son, his two daughters, Catherine and Hester."[50] Recounting this episode, the historian recalls pointedly that the reason for his grandfather's displeasure was the love-match that brought his father and mother together, "by secret correspondence and stolen interviews," against the "harsh commands" of parental authority.[51]

About his maternal grandfather, the author of the Autobiography provides less information. His home, also at Putney, is where Gibbon remembers being happiest as a child, but he was a man of little substance, "slender fortunes and dubious credit."[52] In 1748 his financial ruin was complete and he "suddenly absconded," leaving his unmarried daughter Catherine, the historian's beloved Aunt Kitty, virtually penniless. The presentation of both grandfathers in the Autobiography anticipates the presentation of Gibbon's own father. In all three cases, authority is found to rest on a precarious foundation, and tyranny is the complement of weakness and victimization.

Edward Gibbon Senior emerges from the pages of his son's autobiography as something of a capricious oriental despot – amiable in some ways, yet unpredictably cruel on occasion, self-indulgent, vain, pleasure-loving, impulsive, an inveterate gambler who in his last years was totally dependent on his son to shore up his declining empire and put order in his sorry financial affairs.[53] To this son Mr. Gibbon often behaved harshly. The hero speaks of the decision to banish him to Lausanne following his conversion to Roman Catholicism as "my father's blind resolution";[54] he recalls the humiliating predicament he found himself in in Italy when his father suddenly and unaccountably cut off funds for him, leaving him unable to pay his bills; he tells how Mr. Gibbon remained deaf to his repeated entreaties to be allowed to return home from Switzerland until he found he needed his son back in England for financial reasons. The historian describes his sudden recall from Italy in order that he might break the entail on his grandfather's estate and make the resources available to his father, albeit with humor, as a victimization; his father immolating him on the altar of his own pleasures and requiring that his son sacrifice his patrimony to him. "The time of my recall had been so nicely computed that I arrived in London three days before I was of age: the priests and the altar had been prepared, and the victim was unconscious of the impending stroke."[55]

And yet, at the same time, the hero of the Autobiography, like the persona of the Correspondence, also appears as standing in awe of his father, eagerly seeking his approval and affection, and in the end willing to sacrifice his own establishment as a man – sexual, social, and financial – to his father. When Edward Gibbon Senior opposed his son's marriage to Suzanne Curchod, he did so not only because it was disadvantageous to Gibbon (Suzanne had no fortune), but also because it would be financially ruinous to him if his son were to claim full control of the family inheritance. "Il s'etendit sur la cruauté de l'abandonner, et de le mettre avant son temps dans le tombeau," Gibbon wrote to Suzanne.[56] Years later Gibbon still sees himself sacrificing his own establishment to his father's. "My views will never extend beyond the happiness of your life," he wrote, "that of Mrs. Gibbon, and of my own."[57] In other words, no desire for an establishment and a family of his own would be allowed to interfere with his management of the estate and his use of it to pay off his father's debts.

Throughout his life Gibbon continued to accept the role of the obedient and devoted son, never openly questioning his father's authority, steadfastly refusing to rebel, shrinking from the violence that would have been necessary for him to achieve his own freedom. He graduated from submission to his father not by revolt or resistance, but, too easily and too late, by his father's death. This event alone, he declares, released him from his filial position of respect and dependency. But such a release, coming when the hero was already thirty-three years of age, was at best incomplete, and in death as in life Mr. Gibbon continued to cast the shadow of a phantom authority over his son's existence. The hero's descriptions of his father's death are worth attending to. There is recognition that it gave him freedom and made him his own master, and he admits that this is what every man longs for, and that it was what he longed for.[58] "Domestic command, the free distribution of time and place, and a more liberal measure of expence, were the immediate consequences of my new situation,"[59] he declares. In other versions of the Autobiography he is more specific. His father's death, he says, referring to the elder Gibbon's spendthrift ways, "was the only event that could save me from an hopeless life of obscurity and indigence."[60] This statement is preceded by an avowal that would have been shocking without the classical nobility of diction and the universal character of the formulation that decorously remove it from any too-concrete reality: "Few, perhaps, are the children who, after the expiration of some months or years, would sincerely rejoyce in the resurrection of their parents."

It is understandable, given these expressions of joy at his release, that Gibbon, as though to conjure an unacknowledgable guilt, insisted obsessively on his piety and innocence. His father's death, he writes in another place, "was the only event that could have saved me from a life of obscurity and indigence; yet I can declare to my own heart that, on such terms, I never wished for a deliverance."[61] He did not dare to wish for it, perhaps, but he was glad when it came. "The tears of a son are seldom lasting." And he must have felt some prickings of conscience, for his grief, he says, "was soothed by the conscious satisfaction that I had discharged all the duties of filial piety."[62] The pattern here is characteristic of the hero of the Autobiography: desire for freedom ("Freedom is the first wish of our heart"), satisfaction at attaining it, and at the same time a sense of guilt at both the desire and the satisfaction. The pleasure of freedom has to be overlaid by the more acceptable and less disturbing pleasure of discharging "all the duties of filial piety."

The hero's fear of his own desire and his suppression or concealment of it appear to have governed all his relations. The Autobiography tells of several significant attachments to male friends. At puberty, around the age of twelve or thirteen, there is an intense friendship with a young schoolmate.[63] Not fortuitously perhaps, the conversion to Catholicism is associated with another, similar infatuation at Oxford.[64] And it was in Switzerland, during his first stay at Lausanne, as he was switching from English to French and thus once again struggling to define himself or perhaps to free himself from a certain definition of himself imposed by his father, that he "formed an intimate, lasting connection with M. Deyverdun, a young man of amiable temper and excellent understanding."[65] Deyverdun, according to Gibbon, like himself the son of "an improvident father," subsequently earned his living first as a tutor in Germany and then, thanks to Gibbon, as tutor to the sons of several English gentlemen.

Interestingly, the hero relates the beginnings of his friendship for Deyverdun at the same time as he tells of his love affair with Suzanne Curchod. And while he sacrifices the girl along with what she was to describe as a "passion travestie,"[66] he and Deyverdun never gave up planning their "final and inseparable union."[67] They saw each other regularly and this time there was no opposition from Mr. Gibbon Senior. "I was allowed to offer him the hospitality of the house at Buriton," the hero relates. "During four successive summers he passed several weeks or months at Buriton, and our free conversations on every topic that could interest the heart or understanding would have reconciled me to a desert or a prison."[68] With its faint allusion to the traditional images of the literature of love (desert, prison), this is warm language for the reticent author of the Autobiography, language reserved almost exclusively for Aunt Kitty Porten and Georges Deyverdun, the two principal affections of the hero's life.

In 1783, when Deyverdun, who had inherited a property at Lausanne, accepted Gibbon's proposal that they set up house together, the two faithful friends and inveterate bachelors were united in "a sort of Marriage," which proved remarkably happy for both.[69] "Two persons so perfectly fitted for each other were never created by Nature and education," Gibbon told both Mrs. Gibbon and Aunt Kitty.[70] Life at La Grotte appeared to him indeed as a veritable paradise harmoniously uniting the two essential elements of the eighteenth-century dream of happiness: the gardener and the philosopher, nature and education or culture, the active life and the contemplative life. "Le jardinier Georges et le philosophe Gibbon," as they referred to themselves, were at once two and one, different and yet the same.[71]

The account of Deyverdun's death in 1789 is marked in the Autobiography by a noticeable and, for Gibbon, rare heightening of the emotional tone and an exceptional resort, in one sentence, to the contemporary rhetoric of sentiment: "His health and spirits had long suffered a gradual decline; a succession of Apoplectic fits announced his dissolution and before he expired, those who loved him could not wish for the continuance of his life. The voice of reason might congratulate his deliverance, but the feelings of Nature and friendship could be subdued only by time: his amiable character was still alive in my remembrance; each room, each walk, was imprinted with our common footsteps, and I should blush at my own philosophy if a long interval of study had not preceded and followed the death of my friend."[72] Despite the improvements he made to Deyverdun's estate after his death, Gibbon went on to acknowledge, "I feel, and with the decline of years I shall more painfully feel, that I am alone in paradise."[73] That the historian's partner in paradise was no Eve but another Adam – the gardener to his philosopher – is a fact that surely deserves not to be disregarded.

The loss of Deyverdun was made more tolerable by another, in its way equally characteristic, relation. "Among the circle of acquaintances at Lausanne," the autobiographer relates, "I have gradually acquired the solid and tender friendship of a respectable family: the four persons of whom it is composed are all endowed with the virtues best adapted to their age and situation, and I am encouraged to love the parents as a brother, and the children as a father."[74] This is Gibbon's "chère famille," the de Séverys.

It would take too long to investigate in detail the historian's best-known friendship – the one that bound him until his death to John Baker Holroyd, Lord Sheffield, and his family. All the evidence of the Correspondence and the Autobiography points, however, to a confirmation of the patterns we have already discovered. Gibbon flirts with Abigail Holroyd, is playfully avuncular with the Holroyd children, and regards Sheffield – as he regarded Salomon de Sévery and Jacques Necker, Suzanne Curchod's husband – with respect and devotion.[75] Holroyd manages all the historian's business affairs for him and his advice is sought on all major decisions, such as the possible purchase of La Grotte after Deyverdun's death. As Gibbon himself declared, he is "always . . . directed by the advice of Mr. H."[76] This manly figure, who was so successful in all those areas of public life in which Gibbon had proved a failure,[77] was the historian's "best friend," the man he loved and esteemed the most, and whose "manly and vehement friendship" he treasured throughout his life.[78] Gibbon himself tells that he "sometimes wondered" – as well he might – "how two men so opposite in their tempers and pursuits should have imbibed so long and lively a propensity for each other."[79] If Georges Deyverdun was the historian's "standing dish," his "domestic friend,"[80] Holroyd perhaps occupied a more eminent place as his link to the larger world. The idyllic couple of "the gardener and the philosopher" became the nobler one of "the historian and the peer."[81] Rich, influential, a socially prominent public figure, Holroyd appears to have played the role of an alter ego, the ideal father, friend, and protector – "wise, active, indefatigable"[82] – that Gibbon never found in his own father, a figure similar in some respects to the one the hero of the *Confessions* unsuccessfully pursued in the Maréchal de Luxembourg and in George Keith. Whereas his own father had never been anything but a cause of anxiety and indebtedness, Holroyd worked tirelessly on Gibbon's behalf to ensure for him the security he longed for. Gibbon was grateful:

> I could not easily forgive myself for shutting you up in a dark room with parchments and attornies, did I not reflect that this probably is the last material trouble, that you will ever have on my account, and that after the labours and delays of near twenty years I shall at last obtain what I have always sighed for, a clear and competent income above my wants and equal to my wishes. – In this contemplation you will be sufficiently rewarded.[83]

If Holroyd can be thought of as a substitute father for Gibbon, it may be that his substitutive character was not a defect or a disability, but the very condition of the success of his relationship with the historian. Although Gibbon often takes the common seventeenth and eighteenth century view that signs and substitutes are inferior to the things they are signs of, and that the need for interpretation is the mark of a fall from grace, of a decadence or decline, there are also in the *Decline and Fall* many suggestions of a valorization of the sign precisely because it is not the thing itself and lacks its overwhelming authority, its annihilating presence. As Holroyd was but the sign of the father, not the father himself, his authority, however well founded in his character and behavior, was always subject to interpretation and reevaluation. The ideal father, in short, may well have been, for Gibbon, a substitute father, just as the ideal mother had been, with Kitty Porten, a substitute mother.

If the analyst might wish to identify Gibbon's uncertainty about his place in the family constellation as the crucial factor in his life and possibly in his work, the physician might well be intrigued by a peculiar physical disability that afflicted the historian. On November 11, 1793, shortly before he agreed to an operation from the consequences of which he subsequently died, Gibbon wrote to Sheffield: "Have you never observed through my inexpressibles a large prominency circa genitalia. It was a swelled testicle which as it was not at all painful, and very little troublesome I had strangely neglected for many years."[84] With this letter a hitherto unacknowledged element in the life of the "real" Gibbon was finally integrated into the persona which he projected to himself and to his friends and which, with the politeness of that age, the latter never attempted to dispute.[85] In fact the testicle in question had been sufficiently troublesome for Gibbon to consult a surgeon about it in 1761. The surgeon diagnosed either a hernia or a hydrocele and advised Gibbon to wait till it got larger and then come back. Gibbon did not return, but in the autumn of the same year he consulted another surgeon in Southampton about "a swelling in my left testicle which threatens being a serious effect."[86] It was also far more obvious than Gibbon was willing as yet to acknowledge, for although his friends were sufficiently civilized to connive in his disregard of it,[87] a Lausanne surgeon noticed it in 1786 and diagnosed it as a hydrocele, which might be reduced by a puncture, but which would recur, he thought, within six months.

Lady Holland, who did not like Gibbon and who therefore was not inclined to cooperate with him in maintaining his persona, has an unattractive description of him in her Journal dating from these last years in Lausanne: "He was a monster, and so filthy withal that one could not endure being close to him. He was buttoned up in the morning and never opened until he undressed at night; thus every besoin of nature was performed in his cloathes."[88] Whatever the real nature of Gibbon's malady – tumor, hydrocele, or inguinal hernia – it is almost impossible not to read the flaw at the heart of Gibbon's sexual being, at the heart of his identity as a man, the disease "circa genitalia," as the inscription upon the historian's own body of the flaw which in his work he discovered at the heart of all historical being and in consequence of which no authority could be fully and firmly founded. For Gibbon the phallus is the source of authority, but it is always flawed.

Gibbon's sense of a flaw at the source of being appears to have been both an opportunity and a limitation: an opportunity in that it led him to assume a critical stance with respect to the world, his own disability having made him no doubt uncommonly alert to the secret flaws of others; a limitation in that the absence of a ground or origin of authority seems still to have been thought of by him as a "flaw," a shame to be concealed, or at best shared only with an elite who would be unlikely to abuse the confidence, and a pathological rather than a normal condition. Wholeness, integrity, undividedness, and identity remain the ideal, if absent, standard by which all existence is measured. Piety and revolt, conservatism and criticism go hand in hand in Gibbon's writing: if there cannot truly be a firmly founded power or authority, he insinuates, let us act as if there were one, let us connive with the knowing and deceive the ignorant in order to preserve if not the substance of authority then at least its shadow.

Gibbon's linguistic ambivalence and his ambivalence in matters of religion would repay a more detailed study than they have yet received or can be given here. Religious fervor was not unfamiliar to the Gibbons. As tutor to his son, grandfather Gibbon had appointed one of the most devoutly religious men in England, the nonjuring William Law. Law was well known as the author of *A Serious Call to a Devout and Holy Life, Adapted to the State and Condition of all Orders of Christians* (1728), of an attack on Mandeville's *Fable of the Bees*, and of a defence of excess in matters religious in *An Earnest and Serious Answer to Dr. Trapp's Discourse of the Folly, Sin, and Danger of being Righteous Overmuch* (1740). A man whose profoundly devout nature and strong mystical leanings led him to Thomas à Kempis and then to Jakob Böhme, Law stood, in Leslie Stephen's words, "in opposition to the prevailing tendencies of his time" and was "the most thoroughgoing opponent of the dominant rationalism of which Locke was the great exponent, and which, in his view, could lead only to infidelity."[89] At Putney, this influential figure lived with the Gibbons as "the much honoured friend and spiritual director of the whole family," in Gibbon's own words,[90] and after grandfather Gibbon's death, he and Gibbon's aunt – "that holy Virgin who by Gods was Miranda called and by men Mrs. Hester Gibbon"[91] – moved to a small village in Northamptonshire where, along with another devout lady, they spent their lives in prayer and charitable exercises.

Of Hester Gibbon we have only the wonderfully sarcastic portraits of her that Gibbon drew long after he himself had come to look on religion with bitterness and distaste as a destructive and disruptive passion. Her career is evidence, however, that a longing for abnegation of self and for a more complete and satisfying order than any found in the historical world was not uncommon in the historian's immediate entourage. Unfortunately, we know little of Gibbon's conversion to Roman Catholicism at the age of sixteen but at the very least it indicates a strong desire for a more securely based and more authentic order and authority than any the historical world or the official church seemed likely to provide. Like his natural mother Judith Porten, Anglican Oxford had failed to provide Gibbon with the sustenance he needed. "Our venerable Mother had contrived to unite the opposite extremes of bigotry and indifference: an heretic or unbeliever was a monster in her eyes; but she was always, or often, or sometimes remiss in the spiritual education of her own children."[92] No doubt Edward Gibbon Senior correctly construed his son's flight into the arms of that other mother, the Church of Rome, when he read it as a rejection, but he might have recognized behind his son's dissatisfaction with the official religion of the day the lessons and the aspirations of his own tutor.

Gibbon's experience of religion was followed, however, unlike his Aunt Hester's, by a biting and sarcastic repudiation of religion, the place of which, in the Autobiography, is exactly analogous to that of sexual passion. Both religion and passion led him into conflict with his father, and both were renounced for ever for the sake of order and reason. The historian rarely let slip an opportunity to reaffirm, even on the most trivial occasions, his fear and distrust of violent emotional energies that threaten the boundaries of order. In the controversy over the merits of the French and the Italian theaters, for instance – one of many rehearsals of the debate between reason and passion in the eighteenth century – he unhesitatingly sided with the French; similarly, in the equally popular Parisian sport of comparing the two leading actresses of the French stage, he preferred "the consummate art of the Clairon to the intemperate sallies of the Dumesnil, which were extolled by her admirers as the genuine voice of nature and passion."[93]

It may be that from his later position of dispassionate neutrality the "historian of the Roman Empire" looked back on the religious episode of his youth with a sense of satisfaction at having been once capable of accepting an overwhelming and shattering experience, as he seems to have looked back on his affair with Suzanne Curchod, possibly even exaggerating its effect upon him. At all events, the nephew of Hester Gibbon remained throughout his career both fascinated and repelled by the power of religion to disrupt men's lives, make them transgress normally respected limits, and occasionally transcend themselves.[94]

Gibbon's linguistic ambivalence has not been much commented on, no doubt because it was not uncommon in an age when many educated people had two clearly distinct languages – a vernacular and a language of culture and cosmopolitan communication (Latin or French). By Gibbon's time, however, such bilingualism, which usually supposed a clearly defined sphere for each language, was becoming rare, in England at any rate,[95] and few English men of letters – William Beckford, the author of *Vathek*, whom Gibbon detested, might be one[96] – shared Gibbon's command of French. In Gibbon's case, English and French were not assigned each to its own proper sphere or context but competed for the same sphere. Gibbon's first published work, the *Essai sur l'étude de la littérature*, was written at Lausanne, he tells us, "in French, the familiar language of my conversation and studies in which it was easier for me to write than in my mother-tongue."[97] He continued the practice of writing in French after his return to England, he goes on, adding pointedly, "without any affectation or design of repudiating my vernacular idiom." Indeed, Gibbon did continue to write essays and letters and to make journal entries in French throughout his life, and he originally planned to use French for his historical writing as well, until he was dissuaded from this plan by Hume, but not before he had already composed the first volume of a projected *Histoire de la République des Suisses*.

Gibbon's linguistic situation is complex. The loss of his own tongue is attributable to his father; it was Edward Gibbon Senior who sent him into exile as a punishment for his conversion to Roman Catholicism. At the same time, Gibbon identified more completely with the language of his exile than one would expect of a seventeen-year-old man – to such an extent, indeed, that he practically forgot English. His letters from Lausanne to his father at this time are written in an incredible pidgin English, for which he soon substituted French.[98] Edward Gibbon Senior, however, did not look favorably on Gibbon's attempt to forge a new linguistic identity for himself. Having punished his son's rebellion by sending him into exile, he then reproached him with having lost his tongue and adopted an alien one. Gibbon's greater familiarity and identification with French was condemned both as a kind of betrayal and as a loss of manly virtue.[99] Apparently the father's tongue, even though denied to the son, was to remain the supreme value.

The structure of Gibbon's sexual dilemma thus recurs at the level of linguistic competence. Indeed, the correspondence between father and son suggests that the sexual symbolism of Edward Gibbon Senior's removal of his son from his native land and his native tongue and of Gibbon's attempt to deal with that situation by adopting a substitute tongue and a substitute linguistic identity may not have been lost on either the father or the son.

Gibbon appears to have achieved a more successful resolution of his linguistic ambivalence, however, than he achieved in the sphere of either sexuality or religion. On Hume's advice he undertook to write in English, to reappropriate his own tongue, and to establish himself, by common consent, as an incomparable master of it. He began writing the *Decline and Fall* immediately after his father's death, as though suddenly authorized to express himself in his native tongue, and within a short time he succeeded in establishing his identity as "the historian of the Roman empire." He finally achieved, in short, through his pen, the mastery and authority that eluded him in other areas. His victory was purchased at a price. To achieve this identity he was obliged to renounce many possibilities of existence and to devote himself single-mindedly to the accomplishment of his task. The composition of the *Decline and Fall* took up his whole life. Similarly, to become a great master of English, he felt he had to give up the ambition of establishing himself as a writer of French. When Suzanne Curchod, then Madame Necker, wrote him in 1776 suggesting that he himself undertake the French translation of his masterpiece, he answered that "on ne sait qu'une langue à la fois, et même en vous ecrivant je sens combien ma pensèe se courbe sous le poids de ces entraves etrangeres."[100] Nevertheless, Gibbon did not completely repudiate his other self, his French self. He continued to write and to speak French until the end of his life. Indeed, at the height of his fame he left London to settle in Lausanne, thus choosing freely his former imposed place of exile as his home – a gesture of withdrawal that he anticipated would be interpreted by the public and by many of his friends as a repudiation and a betrayal, rather as his father had once interpreted his adoption of the French language.[101]

Above all, Gibbon might have deduced from his linguistic experience that no "native" language is immediately or necessarily related either to its users or to the world and that all languages are systems of conventions that are translatable into or substitutable for each other – that the signs of one language, in other words, are not closer than those of any other either to the meanings and beings of speakers or to the world they designate. Languages, Gibbon might have concluded, are like other forms of social masks in this respect – or like historiographical works themselves, for that matter. Having no necessary relation to an already constituted and structured real world, they nevertheless claim to stand in some relation to the world and thus require that the nature and validity of that claim be continually reevaluated.

In the incidental portrait of a kinsman named Acton, who had studied medicine and attended Edward Gibbon Senior when the latter fell seriously ill at Besançon during his travels in France, Gibbon finally wrote his own rehabilitation into his Autobiography. Acton saved the historian's father, but "during the slow recovery of the patient, the Physician himself was attacked by the malady of love: he married his mistress, renounced his country and religion, settled at Besançon, and became the father of three sons, the eldest of whom, General Acton, is conspicuous in Europe as the principal minster of the King of the two Sicilies."[102] Gibbon may well have believed that, like Acton, he too could reasonably claim to have united in himself sickness and cure, the dissolution of certainties and the healing virtue of fictions, the renunciation of country and religion and the maintenance of filial piety and devotion.

Some of Gibbon's contemporaries are said to have observed maliciously that the portly, misshapen historian confused himself with the Roman Empire. They were not, perhaps, very wide of the mark. The *Decline and Fall* was the great and almost unique affair of Gibbon's existence, the cenotaph on which was inscribed a life that, from the point of view of worldly fortune, personal achievement, and political career, may well seem to have been a long renunciation and a kind of death. The image the historian traces of himself, "musing amidst the ruins of the Capitol and conversing with the dead," evokes those scenes in which writers of autobiography attempt to embrace their own death in the story of their life, as Montaigne did, for instance, in the essay "De l'exercitation," and Rousseau in the second of the *Rêveries d'un promeneur solitaire*. Viewed in this light, the Autobiography, begun some years after the completion of the *Decline and Fall*, can be thought of as renewing in a more direct manner a massive effort of self-definition and self-understanding that is already implicit in the History, in the way that Rousseau's *Confessions* and *Rêveries* have been seen as renewed attempts to achieve what the author had been working toward obscurely in his political, pedagogical, and fictional writings.

It need not be suprising, in sum, if the themes of Gibbon's Autobiography and of much of his correspondence – uncertainty and ambiguity, muted revolt, acceptance of an authority no longer believed in but not to be openly challenged – are also present in the *Decline and Fall*. In the history of Rome, as in the historian's history of his own life, the gesture of revolt – exposure of the weakness at the heart of all power, of the crack in every apparently self-contained being – is accompanied by fear of disintegration; and pious nostalgia for an original unity and integrity on which authority and order might have been securely founded but which cannot in fact be located anywhere in the world does not exclude glad acceptance of a substitute conventional order, an order based on the complicity of all who are party to the awful secret that no substantial foundation for authority or the legitimate exercise of power can be discovered. In the following two chapters I propose to pursue these themes in the *Decline and Fall*, and then, in Chapters 4 through 6, to argue that the relationship of the ironical, "neutral" narrator, the object of his irony, and the reader whom he seduces from respect for that object into complicity with himself, repeats at the level of the writer's strategies the power relations discovered in the subject matter of the narrative.

2

The plenitude of paternal power

GIBBON'S VIEW OF SOCIETY, though not his attitude toward it, bears some resemblance to that of Rousseau. On one or two occasions, the historian refers to what appears to be a kind of primitive anarchy, an original age of peace and mutual indifference in which men were scarcely bound to each other by the bonds of civil society but lived in relative autonomy, and in which power, institutions, and indeed the consciousness of freedom were unknown. With Tacitus, he declares, "We may allow with safety . . . that ancient Germany was not originally peopled by any foreign colonies already formed into a political society; but that the name and nation received their existence from the gradual union of some wandering savages of the Hercynian woods."[1] On the scale of Empire there was a brief and, of course, temporary return to an analogous state upon the death of Aurelian. As no successor could be agreed upon and no one would impose one, the senate deferring to the army and the army to the senate, every imperial administrator, cut off from the source of power at the center, peacefully pursued his own autonomous course. It was, says Gibbon, "an amazing period of tranquil anarchy, during which the Roman world remained without a sovereign, without an usurper, and without a sedition."[2] Where there is no power or authority, there is no revolt: Sovereignty, usurpation, and sedition belong together.

The binding together of men in civil society, however, involves the exercise of authority and of power. Inevitably, subordination is introduced, and with it, conflict and division. Union and division are thus different aspects of the same situation, as are law and violence, order and disorder. Civil freedom, as distinct from natural freedom, is defined by the unfreedom on which it exercises itself and in contrast with which it becomes a consciously held right of those who enjoy it.

As far as civil and historical society is concerned, therefore – and as a historian Gibbon is not concerned with any other kind – unity is not original and division a falling away from it, and authority is not prior to violence, or freedom to oppression. There is no original authority, no

25

power without a history of its coming-to-power and not, therefore, subject in turn to overthrow. Even in the golden age of the Republic, when virtue was synonymous with the possession by every citizen of his own weapon, the Romans were already divided into patricians and plebeians.[3] As Rome expanded and more people acquired citizenship, this repeated itself as a division between Romans and barbarians, citizens and slaves.[4] Even among some primitive peoples, freedom appears as the consequence of an act of violence against another. Among the Taifalae, allies of the Visigoths, every youth was subordinated, like a woman, to a free man – and had to win his freedom by an act of violence and subjugation.[5] Among the Franks, we are told, the love of freedom "was reduced to the contempt of order and the desire of impunity."[6] By qualifying the Franks as "licentious," Gibbon implies that the transformation of freedom into violent anarchy was a particular consequence of the Frankish character; in fact, however, his own analysis makes it clear that because freedom, in the state of society, is founded on violence, it is continually tending toward this kind of anarchy.

For Gibbon the ideal authority and the only true one is that which is absolutely original, self-authorizing, self-contained, indifferent to because independent of any other, requiring neither justification nor recognition of itself as dominion over another. Inevitably, it cannot be found in history, for it belongs only to God, or at best to individuals in the state of nature, prior to social and historical life. Surprisingly, however, this ideal occupies an important place in the *Decline and Fall* and is an essential point of reference in a wide range of arguments and narratives. As with Rousseau and Montesquieu, it seems, a condition which is acknowledged at times, implicitly at least, to be incompatible with any historical existence is projected on to an early moment of history and imparts to the historical narrative something of the character of a myth or fiction. Montesquieu's Roman history duplicates, in important respects, the myth of the Troglodytes in the *Persian Letters*; Rousseau's account of the economic and political evolution of society has an avowedly fictional aspect; and the story told by the President's British disciple often seems, in its turn, to illustrate a metaphysical adventure.

Division and multiplicity are always seen, in the *Decline and Fall*, as error, weakness, decline, decay.[7] The reader is not expected to question the commonplace that "the paths of error are various and infinite";[8] this is given as an explanatory maxim. One of the least attractive aspects of Christianity, for instance, and a sign, for Gibbon, of its lack of credibility, is its continual division of itself into innumerable sects. Difference seldom has a positive value. It is almost always defined as "faction,"[9] and it seems inevitably to involve violence and deceit, for wherever there is division, uniformity of belief and conduct has to be imposed. The contrast between the unitary, the self-sufficient and self-grounding, on the one hand, and the multiple, the differentiated and dependent, on the other, occurs in the *Decline and Fall* in a variety of guises: as the contrast between reality and appearance, substance and image, "nature" and "art," original genius and the art of commentary or interpretation, original text and "the dark and doubtful medium of translation,"[10] primitive virtue and constitutional liberty, the unadorned language of truth and the affectation of eloquence, the Republic and the Empire, and, in the end, the unchanging and the historical. In various ways, moreover, the opposition of nature and art, or substance and image, is associated with the categories of male and female, possession and dispossession (or lack). True authority, it is implied, would be exercised without violence, violence being, as in the seraglio of Montesquieu's *Lettres persanes*, the recourse of weakness, impotence, dispossession, alienation. The true father – reason, one is tempted to say – commands, in principle at least, without violence. Violence is always the work of tyrants or false fathers, men inwardly divided and separated from themselves, eunuchs, phallic mothers usurping a place and authority to which they have no title. The historical world, however, turns out to be preeminently the domain of such false fathers.

Gibbon's own father "renounced the tumult of London . . . , and buried himself in the . . . rustic solitude of Buriton," ostensibly because his heart was broken by the death of his wife but in large measure because "his fortune was impaired" and "his debts had multiplied."[11] The character of all the emperors, as Gibbon portrays them, is marked by duplicity and artfulness; indeed, this is the character of virtually all the personae of the *Decline and Fall*. Gallus is "deceived by the affected tranquillity of Constantine" and "seduced by the flattering assurances of the tribune Scudilo, who, under the semblance of a rough soldier, disguised the most artful insinuation."[12] Even in Julian, of the later emperors the one most sympathetically portrayed, "simplicity was not exempt from affectation."[13]

Julian, we are told, is "filled . . . with the noblest precepts and the most shining examples . . . animated . . . with the love of virtue, the desire of fame, and the contempt of death." "He derived from his philosophical studies an inflexible regard for Justice, tempered by a disposition to clemency, the knowledge of the general principles of equity and evidence."[14] Above all, he has a pristine quality, an appearance of being fresh, unused, ingenuous, unspoiled – "manly" as Gibbon puts it – that inspires respect. The soldiers, we read, "gazed on the manly countenance of Julian and observed with pleasure that the fire which sparkled in his eyes was tempered by a modest blush on being thus exposed for the first time to the public view of mankind."[15] Yet compared even with Alexander, who, in the first part of the third century "laboured to restore the glories and felicity of the age of the genuine Antonines,"[16] Julian, at the end of the fourth century, is a tarnished figure, lacking the original, native virtue of the true hero. The philosopher king and the "philosophic warrior"[17] are models for him, roles or parts that he tries to play. There is thus about his virtue some of that quality of comedy and representation, that lack of originality, naturalness, and immediacy, which for Gibbon characterizes the whole history of Rome since the Republic. Julian is not whole. He is divided, like Rome itself, self-consciously representing himself to himself in the theater of his mind in an effort at reappropriation which is the mark of alienation and loss. Hence his return to the ancient religion of Rome never really succeeds. Julian's religion is not that of the ancient Romans; it is a mimicry of it, "a relapse into the habits of superstition," and it is flawed by the "unnatural alliance of philosophy and superstition" characteristic of the neo-Platonists who were his friends.[18] Everything about Julian, in short, appears in a second-rate version or masquerade of the "original" glory that had preceded his time and that no effort seems able to recapture. "When we inspect with minute, or perhaps malevolent, attention the portrait of Julian, something seems wanting to the grace and perfection of the whole figure."[19]

It is not only history's subjects that are flawed, imperfect, ambiguous; the historian is himself separated from them by a thick layer of darkness – the accompaniment of his critical vision. He does not see clearly and he knows that the world does not present itself to him in a transparent and unmediated vision. Few works of history are as ridden with expressions of doubt and uncertainty as the *Decline and Fall*. To "the reluctance of Tacitus" is added, "and it might possibly be sincere." Probus is said to have "displayed the sentiments, or at least the language, of a Roman patriot." Diocletian is an abyss: "It is not improbable that motives of prudence might assist the humanity of the artful Dalmatian"; "the first considerable action of his reign seemed to evince his sincerity"; "whenever the provinces were invaded, [he] conducted himself with that calm dignity which he always affected or possessed." The Roman philosophers are "induced by reason or by vanity" to preserve their philosophical religion from the knowledge of the multitude. The motives of Constantine's conversion "may variously be deduced from benevolence, from policy, from conviction, or from remorse." Adopting "a generous but artful system of policy," Constantius restored the fortunes of the Sarmatians. Sapor, the successor of Cyrus and Artaxerxes, "condescended to make some artful or perhaps sincere over-

tures towards a negotiation of peace." Maximus "artfully or modestly refused to ascend the throne." Leovigild, the Gothic king, sentences his rebel
son to death "with apparent reluctance." Narses spares the lives of some
hostages out of "humanity or . . . prudence." The deputies of the Senate
"reported, or perhaps invented" Justinian's deathbed choice of a nephew to
succeed him.[20] Similar examples could be gathered from every page of
Gibbon's history.

Most often the historian's uncertainty reflects his conviction of the duplicity of the historical subjects themselves. We are told of Julian that "the
new emperor, overwhelmed with real or affected grief, retired into the
most secret recesses of his apartment." Gibbon adds that "the grief of Julian
could proceed only from his innocence; but his innocence must appear
extremely doubtful in the eyes of those who have learned to suspect the
motives and professions of princes."[21] Again, when we are told of Julian's
"real or affected humanity," of the love of virtue and of fame which "he
displayed, perhaps with some ostentation, in his last moments," and when
his throne is described as "the seat of reason, of virtue, and perhaps of
vanity,"[22] the uncertainty inheres both in the knower and in the object of
his knowledge.

In one sense, to be sure, the historian's uncertainty is itself a mask. Slyly
he insinuates to the polite few what he will not openly proclaim before the
unwashed multitude, namely that the august fathers of the Empire, the
heroes of history, are frauds. But Gibbon's mask may not be so easily
penetrable and his unwillingness to denounce the emperors may be more
than mere prudence. It is not unlikely that he wished at one and the same
time to unmask his heroes and to undo his unmasking, to discover their
secret and to preserve it by imparting to the reader a sense of the impossibility of ever fixing the meaning of the signs the historian has to decipher.
It is easier, he argues, to know principles than facts, for reason is clear and
constant, whereas history – which is precisely the domain of those things
that are not identical with themselves, but divided and alienated – is dark,
devious, and doubtful. Concluding his account of the career of Mohammed, Gibbon recognizes that historiographical convention requires an
obituary portrait. He provides one, but before doing so, warns that no
ordered and intelligible portrait is ever a faithful copy of reality:

> At the conclusion of the life of Mohammed it may perhaps be
> expected that I should balance his faults and virtues, that I should
> decide whether the title of enthusiast or impostor more properly
> belongs to that extraordinary man. Had I been intimately conver-
> sant with the son of Abdallah, the task would still be difficult, and

the success uncertain: at the distance of twelve centuries I darkly contemplate his shade through a cloud of religious incense; and could I truly delineate the portrait of an hour, the fleeting resemblance would not equally apply to the solitary of Mount Hera, to the preacher of Mecca, and to the conqueror of Arabia.[23]

For Gibbon, it would seem, history and civilization are in themselves a process of alienation and dispossession by which an original, closed, and self-contained being – a being that can never be found in history, however, since it is already divided by the very fact of being historical – extends outward, multiplies, enters into contact with others, and is altered by this contact. And it is this very process that produces not only doubt and un-certainty but ever more desperate and despotic attempts to resolve them. As the one disintegrates and transforms itself into the many, unity ceases to be "natural"; it must be contrived by art and protected from dissolution by unrelenting vigilance. Having been extended outward to the four corners of the world, the Roman Empire was held together by roads and posts.

> But these beneficial establishments were accidentally connected with a pernicious and intolerable abuse. Two or three hundred *agents* or messengers were employed, under the jurisdiction of the master of the offices, to announce the names of the annual consuls, and the edicts or victories of the emperors. They insensibly as-sumed the licence of reporting whatever they could observe of the conduct either of magistrates or of private citizens; and were soon considered as the eyes of the monarch and the scourge of the people. Under the warm influence of a feeble reign, they multi-plied to the incredible number of ten thousand.[24]

The passage from the one to the many, from the identical to the different, from truth to eloquence, from simplicity to art, from "originality" to com-mentary parallels the historical passage of Rome from virtuous Republic to Empire. The Republic is characterized by unity and compactness: It is a community of equals. Gibbon's version of it anticipates Niebuhr's ideal community of independent freeholders. Every citizen "had a country to love, a property to defend, and some share in enacting those laws, which it was their interest, as well as duty, to maintain,"[25] and every citizen bears his own arms in defense of the state, being "trained from his earliest youth in the discipline and exercise of a soldier."[26] The history of Rome, as told in the *Decline and Fall* – a history whose basic program strikingly recalls that of Rousseau's First Discourse – is the story of the progressive alienation of the citizen from his property, from his arms, from his government, and from the laws.

Similarly, although ancient Athens at her most flourishing is said to have been relatively poor compared to Constantinople in the last moments of her decay – "a scanty sum of six thousand talents, or twelve hundred pounds sterling, was possessed by twenty-one thousand male citizens of an adult age" – each citizen of Athens "was a freeman who dared to assert the liberty of his thoughts, words, and actions; whose person and property were guarded by equal law; and who exercised his independent vote in the government of the republic," and the small number of the citizens appeared "to be multiplied by the strong and various discriminations of character," whereas "the subjects of the Byzantine empire, who assume and dishonour the names both of Greeks and Romans, present a dead uniformity of abject vices."[27] At Rome, there was increasing division of labor: "the powers of the human mind were contracted by the irreconcilable separation of talents as well as of professions."[28] Soldiering became a career, not a citizen's duty: "in proportion as the public freedom was lost in extent of conquest, war was gradually improved into an art, and degraded into a trade."[29] Finally, the old Roman freeholders were expropriated from their land: "The lands of Italy, which had been originally divided among the families of free and indigent proprietors, were insensibly purchased or usurped by the avarice of the nobles; and in the age which preceded the fall of the republic, it was computed that only two thousand citizens were possessed of any independent substance."[30]

As one would expect of an eighteenth-century Englishman, Gibbon places the Republic, as a compact of free and independent individuals, at the origin of Roman history and says little or nothing about the Rome of the Kings, in which certain nineteenth-century scholars were later to discover a more closely knit tribal community. Nevertheless, he still considers the Republic single and undivided, as all its members are seen as identical with each other in their very independence. Its decline is attributed directly or indirectly to the opening up and expansion of the state, the dissemination and dispersal of Roman strength, the intermingling of the original Roman population with alien populations, and the process of change itself – "an immense and tumultuous capital, a wide extent of empire, the servile equality of despotism, an army of four hundred thousand mercenaries, and the experience of frequent revolutions."[31] Trade and exchange are explicitly associated with pestilence and disease: "No restraints were imposed on the free and frequent intercourse of the Roman provinces: from Persia to France the nations were mingled and infected by wars and emigrations; and the pestilential odour which lurks for years in a bale of cotton was imported, by the abuse of trade, into the most distant regions."[32] In the end,

> the nation of soldiers, magistrates, and legislators, who composed the thirty-five tribes of the Roman people, was dissolved into the common mass of mankind and confounded with the millions of servile provincials, who had received the name without adopting the spirit of Romans.[33]

To Gibbon the decline of Rome seems to have been exemplary – the most striking of all manifestations of a general law of development. In Chapter XLIV the theme of Roman decline is interwoven, on the occasion of a discussion of Roman law, with a theory of the origin of property and of the rise and development of civil society that owes an obvious debt to Locke but is also, somewhat surprisingly, reminiscent of Rousseau:

> The original right of property can only be justified by the accident or merit of prior occupancy; and on this foundation it is wisely established by the philosophy of the civilians. The savage who hollows a tree, inserts a sharp stone into a wooden handle, or applies a string to an elastic branch, becomes in a state of nature the just proprietor of the canoe, the bow, or the hatchet. The materials were common to all; the new form, the produce of his time and simple industry, belongs solely to himself. His hungry brethren cannot, without a sense of their own injustice, extort from the hunter the game of the forest overtaken or slain by his personal strength and dexterity. If his provident care preserves and multiplies the tame animals, whose nature is tractable to the arts of education, he acquires a perpetual title to the use and service of their numerous progeny, which derives its existence from him alone. If he encloses and cultivates a field for their sustenance and his own, a barren waste is converted into a fertile soil; the seed, the manure, the labour, create a new value, and the rewards of harvest are painfully earned by the fatigues of the revolving year. In the successive states of society, the hunter, the shepherd, the husbandman, may defend their possessions by two reasons which forcibly appeal to the feelings of the human mind: that whatever they enjoy is the fruit of their own industry; and that every man who envies their felicity may purchase similar acquisitions by the exercise of similar diligence. Such, in truth, may be the freedom and plenty of a small colony cast on a fruitful island. But the colony

32

multiplies, while the space still continues the same; the common rights, the equal inheritance of mankind, are engrossed by the bold and crafty; each field and forest is circumscribed by the landmarks of a jealous master. . . . In the progress from primitive equity to final injustice, the steps are silent, the shades are almost imperceptible, and the absolute monopoly is guarded by positive laws and artificial reason."[34]

The evolution of Rome from Republic to Empire is at the same time a movement from simplicity to ostentation, from natural eloquence to sophistry and rhetoric, from substance to image, from the rule of men to that of women and eunuchs, from the "manly" Occident to the "effeminate" Orient. "The manly pride of the Romans, content with substantial power, had left to the vanity of the East the forms and ceremonies of ostentatious greatness."[35] But with the spread of Christianity – in itself a divisive religion, which, unlike the primitive religion of Rome, does not confirm and support the laws of the state but sets itself up in opposition to the state[36] and is for this reason associated with women, eunuchs, slaves, all the dispossessed, the humiliated, the resentful – simplicity is overwhelmed by declamation and show: "When he harangued his people from the pulpit, Paul affected the figurative style and the theatrical gestures of an Asiatic sophist, while the cathedral resounded with the loudest and most extravagant acclamations in the praise of his divine eloquence."[37] By the time of Diocletian and Constantine, antique simplicity has become profusion, variety, multiplicity; everything is signs, images, appearances. With Constantine, we are told, the Asiatic pomp of Diocletian's reign "assumed an air of softness and effeminacy. . . . He is represented with false hair of various colours, laboriously arranged by the skilful artists of the times; a diadem of a new and more expensive fashion; a profusion of gems and pearls, of collars and bracelets; and a variegated flowing robe of silk, most curiously embroidered with flowers of gold."[38]

Gibbon consistently equates the arts of eloquence and rhetoric with falsehood: they are always "fallacious," "corrupt."[39] The historian loses no opportunity of asserting his own pious respect – specifically as an historian – for the manly virtue and the simplicity of which his narrative traces the decline. As a historian, he repeatedly deplores the concealment of simple truth beneath the "gaudy colours" of rhetoric.[40] "The simple circumstantial narrative (did such a narrative exist) of the ruin of a single town, of the misfortune of a single family, might exhibit an interesting and instructive picture of human manners, but the tedious repetition of vague and declamatory complaints would fatigue the attention of the most patient reader."[41] The contrast between the historian's discourse – associated with judgment, philosophy, and truth – and the discourse of the poet and rhetorician is a recurrent theme of the *Decline and Fall* and helps to define, as we shall see again later, the persona – the values and loyalties – of the narrator as well as that of the implied reader. "We should vainly search for the pure and spontaneous sentiments of the barbarian amid the declamation and learning of a sophist," the narrator observes of an epistle written by Cassiodorus in the name of Theodoric.[42] "Instead of the simplicity of style and narrative which wins our belief," he confides to the reader, Anna Comnena's life of her father, the Emperor Alexis, is marred by "an elaborate affection of rhetoric and science," that "betrays on every page the vanity of a female author."[43] Authorship, it appears, like authority, is properly masculine; commitment to truth and unadorned simplicity of discourse are the signs of its masculine character. In general, while Gibbon liked to think of himself as steering a middle course between "the dry annalist, and the tumid and flowery orator,"[44] it is the "tumid and flowery," with its unmistakable sexual connotations, that he finds most threatening and disturbing and that he repudiates most vehemently. Although he thought of himself, as we shall see later, as a writer and as continuing an epic tradition, he differentiates himself scrupulously, as a historian, from "authors of epic poetry and romance," as well as from dramatic writers, such as Corneille, scolded for having Attila speak "in bombast lines . . . with ridiculous fury."[45]

From the simplicity of the Republic to the complicated and unwieldy multiplicity of the Empire, from the virtue of the founding families to the corruption of those who have taken their place (and who, Gibbon takes care to observe, have no direct connection at all with those virtuous beginnings), from silence or the noble frugality and austerity of words that directly designate the things they signify to the artfulness of eloquence that revels in its own profusion, from truth to fiction and fraud, the decline is nowhere, perhaps, so vehemently denounced by Gibbon as in relation to the law.

Gibbon's comments on Roman law in the *Decline and Fall* are marked by a profound and characteristic ambivalence. On the one hand, the historian denounces the corruption of the law as it falls into the hands of interpreters and acquires "an obscurity, a prolixity and an uncertainty which . . . at last render the priests of Themis the sole interpreters of her oracles," in the words he once used of the English common law so ardently defended by Blackstone. Like a true *philosophe*, anticipating Bentham, he indicates a clear preference for a completely original, rational code of laws over continual rearrangements and modifications of the tradition. On the other hand, however, he came in time to defend the value of existing laws and of the veneration paid to them, even though he acknowledged that they neither were nor had to be divinely or rationally authorized. The laws deserve the respect of the sage, he came to believe, even though they are the product of men acting in history and responding to historical needs and problems, because they have proved capable of holding society together and of promoting its well-being. As they clearly do not promote the well-being of all in equal measure, however, Gibbon believed that such a plain justification of the law must remain the secret doctrine of an elite of magistrates and other philosophical spirits. The rest may respect the law for an authority it does not possess. Gibbon himself thus came finally to share that "becoming tenderness of a pious son who would wish to conceal the infirmities of his parent," for which he had once – gently and with understanding – chided Blackstone.[46]

Early in the *Decline and Fall* criticism and commentary are reproved as secondary, parasitic activities in relation to the original genius that inspired the early poets and orators. "A cloud of critics, of compilers, of commentators," we are told – and Gibbon's phrase lets us hear the continuous clacking of their tongues – "darkened the face of learning, and the decline of genius was soon followed by the corruption of taste."[47] Subsequently, the neo-Platonists – "these sophists," as they are described in a note that underlines their distance from the original they professed to follow[48] – are attacked for their interpretations of Greek and Roman myth:

> This freedom of interpretation, which might gratify the pride of the Platonists, exposed the vanity of their art. Without a tedious detail the modern reader could not form a just idea of the strange allusions, the forced etymologies, the solemn trifling, and the impenetrable obscurity of these sages, who professed to reveal the system of the universe. As the traditions of Pagan mythology were variously related, the sacred interpreters were at liberty to select the most convenient circumstances; and as they translated an arbitrary cipher, they could extract from *any* fable *any* sense which was adapted to their favorite system of religion and philosophy. The lascivious form of a naked Venus was tortured into the discovery of some moral precept, or some physical truth; and the castration of Atys explained the revolution of the sun between the tropics, or the separation of the human soul from vice and error.[49]

It is not only the art of interpretation as practised by the neo-Platonists that Gibbon deplores, however; it is the interpretation as such, and ultimately the ambivalence and uncertainty that make it necessary in the first place. More precisely, it is the essential character of the sign, which the act of interpretation reveals: "laws and language are ambiguous and arbitrary; where reason is incapable of pronouncing, the love of argument is inflamed by the envy of rivals, the vanity of masters, the blind attachment of their disciples."[50] Like Rousseau, Gibbon imagines a time or place, a point of origin outside of history, where the sign is undivided and inseparable from the meaning or intention of its users. The ambivalence of law and language, he implies, is indissolubly linked to historicity. The study of law begins as an attempt to repair the ravages of time, to restore contact with origins and foundations that are perpetually receding, becoming less and less legible, to establish fixed points in a world of change:

> The alteration of the idiom and manners of the Romans rendered the style of the Twelve Tables less familiar to each rising genera-tion, and the doubtful passages were imperfectly explained by the study of legal antiquarians. To define the ambiguities, to circum-scribe the latitude, to apply the principles, to extend the conse-quences, to reconcile the real or apparent contradictions, was a much nobler or more important task; and the province of legisla-tion was silently invaded by the expounders of ancient statutes.[51]

But just as "the abuse of philosophy"[52] – which produced wasteful and destructive debates such as the Trinitarian controversy – seems inseparable from its use, so the consequences of interpretation appear to be contrary to those originally intended. Interpretation inevitably shifts attention from the laws themselves, insofar as they are embedded in a particular context and inseparable from a particular situation, to the principles underlying them, in order that these may be applied to altered contexts and situations. In this way, law is divorced from customs, manners, and particular needs and institutions and ultimately becomes a means of subverting these – becomes itself an instrument of change: The "subtle interpretations" of the legal scholars

> concurred with the equity of the praetor to reform the tyranny of the darker ages; however strange or intricate the means, it was the aim of artificial jurisprudence to restore the simple dictates of na-ture and reason, and the skill of private citizens was usefully em-ployed to undermine the public institutions of their country.[53]

At first "the freedom of inquiry," which "in more enlightened times . . .established the general principles of jurisprudence," simply tore aside "the veil of mystery" that had long protected the instrumentalities of power – "the patrician arts" of arms, eloquence, and the law – but did not affect the institutions of the state.

> Subtle and intricate cases were elucidated by the disputes of the forum; rules, axioms, and definitions were admitted as the genuine dictates of reason; and the consent of the legal professors was interwoven into the practice of the tribunals. But these interpreters could neither enact nor execute the laws of the republic.[54]

Later, however, with Augustus and Tiberias, "the science of the civilians" was put to use to "accommodate the old system to the spirit and views of despotism." And at the same time, "the judges were enjoined to obey the comment as well as the text of the law; and the use of codicils was a memorable innovation, which Augustus ratified by the advice of the civilians."[55]

From having been in some way prior to history, a kind of extrahistorical foundation of the state, law is now launched, along with everything else, on the sea of historical change. There are different schools – traditionalist and liberal in their interpretations – and there are eclectics, notably under the Antonines, who "like the contemporary philosophers . . . adopted from every system the most probable doctrines." But even the eclectics do not agree among themselves. "Their writings would have been less voluminous, had their choice been more unanimous" is Gibbon's characteristically formulated judgment. The consequence is that law has become increasingly incomprehensible, its "original" meaning obscured by layers of commentary, compilation and interpretation. "The conscience of the judge was perplexed by the number and weight of discordant testimonies, and every sentence that his passion or interest might pronounce was justified by the sanction of some venerable name."[56] By the time of Justinian, "the infinite variety of laws and legal opinions had filled many thousand volumes, which no fortune could purchase and no capacity could digest."[57] Reform was urgently necessary. In his discussion of Justinian's *Institutes*, Gibbon's persistent preference for the simple, unitary, and unchanging and his fear of multiplicity and of time, which is its medium and agent, are unmistakable.

Ideally, reform should have been a cutting back, through the accretions of ten centuries of interpretation, to native origins. Such a reform might perhaps have been carried out by an original genius – a genius in immediate contact with origins. "If Caesar had achieved the reformation of Roman law, his creative genius . . . would have given to the world a pure and original system of jurisprudence." Lacking this genius, Justinian "bor-

rowed the aid of time and opinion" – that is, of the absolute enemies of
truth and law: "his laborious compilations are guarded by the sages and
legislators of past times. Instead of a statue cast in a single mould by the
hand of the artist, the works of Justinian represent a tesselated pavement of
antique and costly, but too often of incoherent fragments."[58] The authority
of original texts was thus overthrown or violated. The scholars' commentaries "on the Twelve Tables, the Perpetual Edict, the laws of the people,
and the decrees of the senate, succeeded to the authority of the text; and
the text was abandoned, as a useless, though venerable, relic of antiquity."[59]
This disrespect for the founding text – for the word of the founding fathers
and their earlier interpreters – is compounded by a thoroughly irreverent
attempt to appropriate their authority.

> The writings of the old republicans, however curious or excellent,
> were no longer suited to the new system of manners, religion, and
> Government. . . . As the legislator of the empire, Justinian might
> repeal the acts of the Antonines, or condemn as seditious the free
> principles which were maintained by the last of the *Roman* law-
> yers. But . . . the emperor was guilty of fraud and forgery when he
> corrupted the integrity of their text, inscribed with their venerable
> names the words and ideas of his servile reign, and suppressed by
> the hand of power the pure and authentic copies of their senti-
> ments.[60]

Respect for tradition was thus as much an appearance as the piety with
which Justinian "ascribed the consummation of this great design to the
support and inspiration of the Deity."[61] In reality, the "passive and dutiful
submission" of Justinian and his principal legal advisor Tribonian masked
the emperor's opportunism, and this commitment to time and change in
the end determined the fate of the Institutes and the Pandects themselves.[62]
Physically, the text, like other ancient manuscripts, has been subjected to
continual renewal and revision by "sacrilegious scribes."[63] But even in Justinian's own time, despite his efforts to fix and guarantee the text of the
Pandects, the Institutes, and the Code by proscribing the use of ciphers
and abbreviations by the scribes as well as all attempts to "interpret or
pervert" his intention, "the emperor was unable to fix his own incon-
stancy":

> Six years had not elapsed from the publication of the Code before
> he condemned the imperfect attempt by a new and more accurate
> edition of the same work which he enriched with two hundred of
> his own laws and fifty decisions of the darkest and most intricate

points of jurisprudence. Every year, or, according to Procopius, each day of his long reign was marked by some legal innovation. Many of his acts were rescinded by himself; many were rejected by his successors; many have been obliterated by time.[64]

Once the original authority has been lost, in other words, no attempt to establish a new one can succeed, for every authority born of time and change is subject to them, and the strenuousness of men's efforts to make their timebound institutions perdure is only another testimony to their impotence and to the hopelessness of the task.

The development of Roman jurisprudence thus parallels fairly closely that of the Roman state: It is a passage from a self-authorizing law, in which authority and law are one and undivided, to a condition of division, in which authority is alienated from law in the form of a tradition, a past, an original text that has become undecipherable. In the first condition, authority is immediately assumed and cannot even be discussed, since it is one with those who exercise it – the free citizens of the Republic; in the second, since the power to make laws is no longer vested in the citizens – since sovereignty, in other words, has been alienated – authority must seem to be borrowed from a source external to it. Moreover, as power, in the Empire, is exercised in the context of a vast and complex state with innumerable conflicting private interests, the appropriation of the authority for exercising it often is and always can be seen as an attempt to provide a mask of disinterestedness for an interested action. The passage is therefore from unity to multiplicity, from compactness to extension and ramification, from the center to the periphery, from the Republic, as a single sphere of public life in which all participate fully, to the Empire with its lack of public life and its myriad private relations.

> Our duties to the state are simple and uniform; the law by which he is condemned is inscribed not only on brass or marble, but on the conscience of the offender. . . . But our relations to each other are various and infinite; our obligations are created, annulled, and modified by injuries, benefits, and promises; and the interpretation of voluntary contracts and testaments, which are often dictated by fraud or ignorance, affords a long and laborious exercise to the sagacity of the judge. The business of life is multiplied by the extent of commerce and dominion, and the residence of the parties in the distant provinces of an empire is productive of doubt, delay, and inevitable appeals from the local to the supreme

magistrate. Justinian, the Greek emperor of Constantinople and the East, was the legal successor of the Latin shepherd who had planted a colony on the banks of the Tiber. In a period of thirteen hundred years the laws had reluctantly followed the changes of government and manners; and the laudable desire of conciliating ancient names with recent institutions destroyed the harmony, and swelled the magnitude, of the obscure and irregular system. The laws which excuse on any occasions the ignorance of their subjects, confess their own imperfections; the civil jurisprudence, as it was abridged by Justinian, still constituted a mysterious science and a profitable trade, and the innate perplexity of the study was involved in tenfold darkness by the private industry of the practitioners.[65]

It is consistent with Gibbon's account of Roman jurisprudence that "laws," "arts," and "vices" are associated syntactically: in a memorable phrase in Chapter XVII the corruption of a great empire is attributed to "the multiplicity of laws, of arts, and of vices."[66]

The preference for the unitary over the multiple, for the entire over the divided, the closed over the open, the original over the historical has, of course, a significant social dimension. The degradation and corruption of the law is also its appropriation by the dispossessed – by those who were not originally and, as it were, by nature in possession of it. "The noble art which had once been preserved as the sacred inheritance of the patricians, was fallen into the hands of freedmen and plebeians who, with cunning rather than with skill, exercised a sordid and pernicious trade."[67] The opposition here is crude – and the obvious class values it rests on and supposes to be shared by the reader define the role Gibbon ascribed to his reader – but it could hardly be clearer. Positive values are defined as inheritance, preservation, nobility, the sacred, patricians; negative values are trade (which we already saw identified with disease), hands (i.e., manual labor), cunning, the sordid and pernicious, freedmen and plebeians. If the patrician is situated in the sphere of the sacred, the freedman is located in history; he is a constant reminder of the reality of change, the instability of the social order, and the unfoundedness of sovereignty. In the ideal citizen or the Roman patrician freedom is identical with the bearing of arms, the original possession of a weapon: It is, as Gibbon likes to say, "manly." But in the freedman, civil rights are acquired and they substitute for a fundamental and original lack. Moreover, the freedman's freedom is seen by Gibbon usually as negative – the right not to be subjected to various forms of oppression, rather than positive – the right to make and impose laws.

By the time freedmen are a significant element in the Roman population, the original law-making Roman people has already been displaced and its sovereignty has been alienated from it.

> As long as the people bestowed by their suffrages the honours of the state, the command of the legions, and the administration of wealthy provinces, their conscious pride alleviated in some measure the hardships of poverty. . . . But when the prodigal commons had imprudently alienated not only the *use* but the *inheritance*, of power, they sunk, under the reign of the Caesars, into a vile and wretched populace, which must, in a few generations, have been totally extinguished, if it had not been continually recruited by the manumission of slaves and the influx of strangers.[68]

The opposition between the unitary and the multiple, the original and the derived, the Republic and the Empire, has a sexual aspect as well as a social one.[69] Alongside the freedman and the plebeian, and closely associated with them in Gibbon's writing as beings marked by lack rather than possession, the eunuch and woman serve to offset the manly virtues of the Republic. As cunning is the dispossessed and impotent freedman's substitute for the power he lacks and the weapon he does not bear, intrigue is the resort of both women and eunuchs. We hear much of "female intrigues" and of "the ensnaring subtleties of the eunuchs," who are "skilled in the arts of flattery and intrigue."[70] Both women and eunuchs are agents of division, and both have division inscribed on their bodies: the constant association of women and eunuchs leaves little doubt that woman, in the *Decline and Fall*, is a castrated male. Castration, real or symbolic (amputation of tongues, noses, hands, putting out of eyes), recurs throughout the History as a common form of punishment. People may at any time be "deprived of their titles and noses," in Gibbon's compact phrase, and the threat of castration hangs over everyone. Justinian II has his nose and "perhaps his tongue," amputated by his father's general Leontius, whom he had previously jailed, but the "mutilated tyrant," as Gibbon calls him, had only to wait out three years in exile to learn that "Leontius in his turn had been dethroned and mutilated by the rebel Apsimar."[71]

The horror of this mutilation, which is often explicit in Gibbon's text, should not be seen as incidental or picturesque. Castration or unmanning is the most vivid form of that alienation of sovereignty, that loss of oneness and identity that seems to be a major theme of Gibbon's work. Like women and religion, which we shall discover again and again as powerful unmanning or alienating agents, eunuchs are associated, from the beginning, with the Orient – "the production of Oriental jealousy . . . the contagion of Asiatic luxury"[72] – in that mythical struggle of Occident and Orient, reason and sense, spirit and matter that is familiar to readers of nineteenth-century histories and that one is somewhat surprised to find so clearly sketched out in the greatest historiographical work of the Enlightenment. The appropriation of Rome by the Empire, of the original city by her conquered slaves, is also the insinuation of eunuchs into positions of power and authority, the substitution of false and cruel fathers for true ones: "Abhorred," in the time of Augustus, as "the monstrous retinue of an Egyptian queen," eunuchs "were gradually admitted into the families of matrons, of senators, and of the emperors themselves. . . . Reduced to an humble station by the prudence of Constantine, they multiplied in the palaces of his degenerate sons, and insensibly acquired the knowledge, and at length the direction, of the secret councils of Constantius." "If we examine the general history of Persia, India, or China," Gibbon notes, "we shall find that the power of the eunuchs has uniformly marked the decline and fall of every dynasty."[73]

The historian's horror at the infestation of the Empire by swarms of eunuchs reaches a climax in his account of the career of Eutropius. The eunuch and the freedman, so often associated, here come together. Under the predecessors of the Emperor Arcadius, "the reign of the eunuchs had been secret and almost invisible," for "though they insinuated themselves into the confidence of the prince," they were officially confined to "the menial service of the wardrobe and Imperial bedchamber. They might direct in a whisper the public counsels, and blast by their malicious suggestions the fame and fortune of the most illustrious citizens; but they never presumed to stand forward in the front of empire, or to profane the public honours of the state. Eutropius was the first of his artificial sex who dared to assume the character of a Roman magistrate and general."[74] Moreover, "this deformed and decrepit eunuch, who so perversely mimicked the actions of a man, was born in the most abject conditions of servitude."[75] It is a measure of the deformation of the Roman Empire from its original simple and manly virtue that Eutropius was not only hailed as a founder – the third founder of Constantinople – but "promoted to the rank of *patrician*, which began to signify, in a popular and even legal acceptation, the father of the emperor." The unfoundedness of authority and the falseness of the fathers is now, at last, fully manifest. Not surprisingly, it is the western part of the Empire that in the end refuses to be "polluted by the *consulship* of an eunuch and a slave" and that rejects "the effeminate consul . . . as an indelible stain to the annals of the republic."[76] Only in an exceptional case – that of Narses, the general of Justinian – does Gibbon moderate this language of horror and indignation.[77]

The plenitude of paternal power

The alienation of sovereignty and of manly virtue, which for Gibbon is inscribed on the body of the eunuch, is also the mark of the homosexual. Although the historian admits that this "odious vice, of which modesty rejects the name, and nature abominates the idea," was not unknown to the "primitive Romans," he implies that it was not original with them, but, like a disease, was introduced to Rome, as the eunuchs were, from the East: "The primitive Romans were infected by the example of the Etruscans and Greeks." To Gibbon, renunciation of manliness is a political renunciation of sovereignty, and "the voluntary and effeminate deserter of his sex" deserves to be "degraded from the honours and rights of a citizen."[78] One of the most striking images of the inner decay of the empire is provided by the inversion of Heliogabalus: "The master of the Roman world affected to copy the dress and manners of the female sex, preferred the distaff to the sceptre, and dishonoured the principal dignitaries of the empire by distributing them among his numerous lovers; one of whom was publicly invested with the title and authority of the emperor's or, as he more properly styled himself, of the empress's husband."[79]

Not surprisingly, the same language that is used of eunuchs and slaves who acquire or aspire to power is also used of women. The female virtues, according to Gibbon, are "mildness and fidelity."[80] He might have added renunciation and sacrifice, which he presents as the supreme expression of conjugal affection.[81] The ideal marriage is, indeed, in many respects, that of older woman and young man – of mother and son. Thus the single redeeming feature of Mohammed's otherwise almost comically excessive sexual life is his fidelity to Cadijah, the "rich and noble widow of Mecca" whom he married at the age of twenty-five. "During the twenty-four years of their marriage," the historian relates,

> her youthful husband abstained from the right of polygamy, and the pride or tenderness of the venerable matron was never insulted by the society of a rival. After her death he placed her in the rank of the four perfect women, with the sister of Moses, the mother of Jesus, and Fatima, the best beloved of his daughters. "Was she not old?" said Ayesha, with the insolence of a blooming beauty; "has not God given you a better in her place?" "No, by God," said Mohammed, with an effusion of honest gratitude, "there can never be a better! She believed in me when men despised me; she relieved my wants when I was poor and persecuted by the world."[82]

Woman, in sum, is ideally a nurse or nourisher, and her proper relation to man is that of a providing mother. "Elle pourvoit et prévoit," as Michelet

43

was to say half a century later. The courageous Amazonian women of the Germans do not win the historian's favor. "Heroines of such a cast may claim our admiration; but they were most assuredly neither lovely, nor very susceptible to love. Whilst they affected to emulate the stern virtues of *man*, they must have resigned that attractive softness in which principally consists the charm of *woman*. . . . Female courage, however it may be raised by fanaticism, or confirmed by habit, can be only a faint and imperfect imitation of . . . manly valour."[83] The phallus, in short, is exclusively male.

Above all, sexually active, desiring women – "agitated by female passions"[84] – are dangerous and must be controlled, for they are the enemies and destroyers of men, whose place and powers they seek to usurp. Theophano, the lubricious wife of Romanus, the son of Constantine VII, is a typical figure from a gallery of similar women – most of them princesses of Byzantium, that is, of the final decadence of the Empire. Suspected of having murdered her father-in-law, Theophano also does away with her husband. Gibbon is careful to identify "this impious woman" socially as well as sexually. She belongs to the dispossessed in both senses and is a usurper in both, being "of base origin" as well as "masculine spirit and flagitious manners."[85]

The account of the public indignation provoked by Eutropius's open assumption of political rank and status is repeated in the case of Procopia, the wife of Michael I. Michael's "mild virtues" did not fit him to lead his soldiers successfully against the Bulgarians. But "while his want of ability and success exposed him to the contempt of the soldiers, the masculine spirit of his wife Procopia awakened their indignation. Even the Greeks of the ninth century were provoked by the insolence of a female who, in the front of the standards, presumed to direct their discipline. . . ."[86] A still more "shameful and destructive" episode is the twenty-eight year reign of the daughters of Constantine IX, the "cold and pious" Theodora and the insatiable, murderous Zoe, a period "in which the Greeks, degraded below the common level of servitude, were transferred like a herd of cattle by the choice or caprice of two impotent females."[87] The female, it appears, represents the animal side of humanity, and the rule of women is marked by the bestialization of men.

These destructive "mothers," as the Greeks called them, according to Gibbon, have many counterparts in the History. Invariably, instead of educating their sons to assume their proper role as men and masters, they emasculate them. Several centuries before Theodora, Placidia, daughter of the great Theodosius II and mother of Valentinian III, is said to have been "jealous of the power she was incapable of exercising: she reigned twenty-five years in the name of her son; and the character of that unworthy emperor gradually countenanced the suspicion that Placidia had enervated his youth by a dissolute education, and studiously diverted his attention from every manly and honourable pursuit."[88] Among the Germans, the "innocent son" of Sigismond is "inhumanly sacrificed to the pride and resentment of a stepmother."[89] In this case both the son and the father, who is prevailed upon to do the deed, only to regret it later, are equally the victims of the castrating female. Like Placidia, the Empress Irene is an "unnatural mother" who has "studiously neglected" the education of her son, Constantine VI, and has secretly nourished his vices. The rivalry of mother and son lasts several years, until finally "it was decreed in her bloody council that Constantine should be rendered incapable of the throne." A symbolic castration is performed upon the sleeping prince. "Her emissaries . . . stabbed their daggers with such violence and precipitation into his eyes as if they meant to execute a mortal sentence."[90] Sophia, the wife of Justin, eager to "preserve her station and influence" after the death of her husband, develops designs on his successor, her adopted son Tiberius, "one of the tallest and most comely of the Romans" and a "wise and equitable" ruler who "reigned above twenty years over the East and over himself; expelling from his mind the wild democracy of passions and establishing (according to the quaint expression of Evagrius) a perfect aristocracy of reason and virtue." When her advances are repulsed by Tiberius, whose character is marked by "filial reverence and gratitude," she plots to have him destroyed.[91]

The most celebrated portrait in a gallery of incestuous and destructive mothers is probably that of Antonina, the wife of Belisarius. Gibbon attributes to her the temperamental and social characteristics the reader has come to expect: Her mother was "a theatrical prostitute"; her father and grandfather "exercised . . . the vile though lucrative profession of charioteers"; she herself is the favorite of the Empress Theodora, and these two "loose and ambitious females" were separated only "by the jealousy of vice" then "at length reconciled by the partnership of guilt." Her definition is thus to have no definition, to be pure lack or absence of identity, nothing but shifty appearance: of obscure birth, she is associated by the historian with the theater, the brothel, the showground, money, and unbridled sexuality. "In the autumn of her age" Antonina conceives a passion for a young Thracian whom she and Belisarius had adopted as their son. Her passion is discovered, the credulous Belisarius forgives her, but Photius, her son by a previous marriage, voices his indignation. Having destroyed the two witnesses who testified to Belisarius against her, "Antonina pursued her son with implacable hatred, and the gallant Photius was exposed to her secret persecutions in the camp beyond the Tigris." Photius turns to his stepfather

Belisarius for protection against his mother. The good father and the good son are thus again united in opposition to the lustful, scheming and destructive woman. At the end of this lively and colorful narrative Antonina tortures and kills, as if he were "a malefactor and a slave," the son whose filial piety stood in the way of her desire.[92]

Ambitious and desiring – in Gibbon's terms, "unnatural" – women are associated throughout the *Decline and Fall* not only with eunuchs and freedmen but with the Church, which is presented as the instrument of all the weak, the dispossessed, and the resentful – women, eunuchs, foreigners, and slaves. "Christianity," according to Hester Gibbon's nephew, "in every age has acknowledged its important obligation to female devotion," and religious motives, we are told, "acted most forcibly on the infirm minds of children and females."[93] In the household of Diocletian, it is his wife Prisca and his daughter Valeria, along with the principle eunuchs, Lucian, Dorotheus, Gorgonius, and Andrew, who "protected by their powerful influence the faith which they had embraced."[94] Functionally, moreover, women, eunuchs, and religion are equivalent as destroyers of manly virtue and power. "The eunuchs, the women, and the bishops," we are told, "governed the vain and feeble mind of the emperor."[95] Like the eunuchs who insinuated themselves into the domestic lives of Roman matrons and patricians, the monks "insinuated themselves into noble and opulent families" and won influence over them by "the specious arts of flattery and seduction."[96] In this way, they corroded the very center of power and authority, just as foreigners and slaves were undermining the origin and source of the Empire, Rome herself. "The freedom of the mind, the source of every generous and rational sentiment, was destroyed by the habits of credulity and submission."[97]

The unmanning that had been half accomplished by political tyranny was thus completed by religion. When Homer wrote " 'that on the first day of his servitude the captive is deprived of one half of his manly virtue,' " Gibbon observes, he could not have foretold "that the second moiety of manhood must be annihilated by the spiritual despotism, which shackles not only the actions but even the thoughts of the prostrate votary."[98] And like the castrating mother who sets father against son and son against father, religion, as Gibbon might well have concluded from his own experiences, teaches a man "to violate the duties of a son and a subject."[99] The Catholics of Spain applaud Hermengild's "pious rebellion against a heretical father,"[100] a rebellion that ends in a repetition of Sigismond's murder of his son. Reluctantly, after repeated provocations, Leovigild has his rebellious son executed. There can be little doubt that the reader is intended to perceive Hermengild's pious rebellion as a contradiction in terms. Nor is the raising of father against son and son against father accidental. It is an essential feature of a religion that "represents man as a criminal, and God as a tyrant."[101] Throughout the *Decline and Fall* Christianity appears as a powerful agent of dissolution. "The bonds of civil society," Gibbon frequently laments, "were torn asunder by the fury of religious factions."[102]

Like eunuchs and women, those other agents of dissolution and division, the missionaries of Christianity are at once alienated and alienating. "Unhappy exiles from social life," they are themselves marked by that "indelible stain of manhood" which they aim to impose on their victims, the manly and the strong. It comes as no surprise, therefore, that many of them are also described as socially alienated – "obscure and rigid plebeians, who gained in the cloister much more than they sacrificed in the world."[103] In the celebrated account of that day in October, 1764, when he supposedly first conceived the idea of the *Decline and Fall*, Gibbon concentrated in a simple but telling image one of the persistent themes of his work – the hollowing out of an integrative and "manly" system of manners and beliefs that served as the cornerstone of the state[104] by a divisive and "feminizing" religion alienated from and opposed to the state,[105] and the installation of that religion at the seat and source of authority. "In the close of the evening," as he sits musing, the owllike historian hears the Franciscan friars singing vespers "in the Temple of Jupiter on the ruins of the Capitol."[106]

3

The vacant space of the eternal city

ROMAN UNITY IS THE CRITERION by which all that follows it is measured, but from the beginning of the *Decline and Fall* – and the title itself indicates the scope of the work – Roman unity is already no more than an idea. By the time of the Antonines, what Gibbon calls the "free constitution" of the early citizen state was a mere memory, of which "the image . . . was preserved with decent reverence."[1] "The system of the Imperial government, as it was instituted by Augustus," we are told, "may be defined an absolute monarchy disguised by the forms of a commonwealth."[2] Even in "the most happy, most prosperous" period in the history of the world, it is the *forms* of the civil administration, "the image of liberty," that are carefully preserved by Nerva, Trajan, Hadrian, and the Antonines.[3] Virtually no direct and continuous connection can be established between the Empire and its origins in the old Republic.

> Where was the Roman people to be found? . . . Very few [patrician familes] remained who could derive their pure and genuine origin from the infancy of the city, or even from that of the republic, when Caesar and Augustus, Claudius and Vespasian, created from the body of the senate a competent number of new Patrician families, in the hope of perpetuating an order which was still considered as honourable and sacred.[4]

Augustus, the founding father of the Empire, is himself a model of the new state. "The obscure name of Octavianus he derived from a mean family in a little town of Aricia . . . and he was desirous . . . to erase all memory of his former life. . . . The illustrious surname of Caesar he had assumed as the adopted son of the dictator; but he had too much good sense, either to hope to be confounded, or to wish to be compared with that extraordinary man." In the end, the name of Augustus was chosen for him "as being the most expressive of the character of peace and sanctity, which he uniformly affected."[5] The very name of this unworthy son, who was linked to his

49

noble father by a legal fiction, was thus contrived to conceal beneath a pleasing and impressive image a mean and debased reality. The founder of the new system of government is not a true father but a scheming usurper – "at first the enemy, and at last the father of the Roman world" – who, at the age of nineteen, put on "the mask of hypocrisy, which he never afterwards laid aside."[6] With him the transparent virtues of the old republican city have disappeared; the new empire is marked instead by fraud and deceit. Appearance is divided from reality, image from substance, name from thing. "The system of the Imperial authority" is "artful," designed by Augustus "to deceive the people by an image of civil liberty."[7] As the Empire moves through its long "decline" toward its "fall," the distance between appearance and reality grows progressively greater: The prominence of fraud, duplicity, and deceit in Gibbon's History has already been amply illustrated.

The actual evolution described in the *Decline and Fall* is not, however, one from unity to multiplicity or from identity to duplicity. That break, as we observed, has already occurred before the book opens. The state under both Augustus and Diocletian is said to be "a theatrical representation," and the difference between the two reigns is one of degree, not of kind: "Of the two comedies the former was of a much more liberal and manly character than the latter. It was the aim of the one to disguise, and the object of the other to display"[8] the tyrannical power of the emperors. The story Gibbon has to tell is therefore that of the progressive enfeeblement of a center that is already attacked, of a source of energy that has already begun to dissipate itself. By the third century A.D., "the limits of the Roman Empire still extended from the Western Ocean to the Tigris, and from Mount Atlas to the Rhine and the Danube. To the undiscerning eye of the vulgar, Philip appeared a monarch no less powerful than Hadrian or Augustus had formerly been. The form was still the same, but the animating health and vigour were fled."[9] A little later, the weakness of the Roman senate is finally exposed under Tacitus: the armies and the provinces could not long obey the "luxurious and unwarlike nobles of Rome. On the slightest touch the unsupported fabric of their pride and power fell to the ground."[10] By the time the seat of the Empire was transferred to the East, the unity and strength of Rome had become a patently empty show: "The genius of Rome expired with Theodosius, the last of the successors of Augustus and Constantine who appeared in the field at the head of their armies, and whose authority was universally acknowledged throughout the whole extent of the empire."[11] At the end of the fourth century, it can be said of Arcadius, the son of Theodosius, only that he "appeared to reign over the provinces of the Eastern Empire." As he so often does, Gibbon concentrates the gradual hollowing out of the substance of the Empire into a striking individual image. At his death,

> the body of Constantine, adorned with the vain symbols of great-
> ness, the purple and diadem, was deposited on a golden bed in
> one of the apartments of the palace, which for that purpose had
> been splendidly furnished and illuminated. The forms of the court
> were strictly maintained. Every day, at the appointed hours, the
> principal officers of the state, the army, and the household, ap-
> proaching the person of their sovereign with bended knees and a
> composed countenance, offered their respectful homage as seri-
> ously as if he had been still alive. From motives of policy, this
> theatrical representation was for some time continued; nor could
> flattery neglect the opportunity of remarking that Constantine
> alone, by the peculiar indulgence of Heaven, had reigned after his
> death.
>   But this reign could subsist only in empty pageantry; and it was
> soon discovered that the will of the most absolute monarch is
> seldom obeyed when his subjects have no longer anything to hope
> from his favour, or to dread from his resentment.[12]

The history of Rome, in sum, seems to be initiated by a fall from grace whereby sovereignty was alienated from the citizenry in whom it was origi-nally vested, and political power was separated from authority, the real from the ideal, appearance from truth. The process of history is a growing distance between power and authority, the real and the ideal, appearance and truth. To Gibbon, it appears, the disease is incurable, but knowledge of the "dangerous secret" that political power is not legitimate, and of the even more terrible secret that it may be only an appearance, must at all costs be kept from the vulgar, because its divulgence would threaten the entire order of society. If justice is not eternal, Montesquieu's Usbek confides to his friend Rhedi, if it should turn out that, contrary to our deepest convic-tions, it is not independent of human conventions, "that would be a terrible truth that one would feel obliged to conceal even from oneself."[13] In the golden world of the Antonines, the imperial policy of preserving respect for traditional forms was "happily seconded by the reflections of the en-lightened, and by the habits of the superstitious, part of their subjects."[14] The fictions on which, in the eyes of philosophers, the traditional edifice of civil society rested were regarded by the people as true and respected by the magistrates as useful. The philosophers themselves "diligently practised the ceremonies of their fathers, devoutly frequented the temples of the gods;

and sometimes condescending to act a part on the theatre of superstition, they concealed the sentiments of an Atheist under the sacerdotal robes."[15] In contrast to the harmonious complicities of the Antonines, however, the Emperor Maximin, a Thracian, is equally cruel to those who had opposed him and to those who had assisted him to power, for they were all "guilty of the same crime, the knowledge of his original obscurity."[16] Instead of accepting, in other words, as the Antonines had done, the necessity of associating his friends with him in keeping the secret of the fatal disability of his reign – the fact that he had no authority to rule – and rewarding them in return with a pleasurable and civilized life, he tried vainly to blot it out, and this led him to make manifest what might otherwise have been decently concealed.

Once exposed, moreover, sustaining fictions are not easily restored.[17] For the peace of society, therefore, they should be preserved for as long as possible. Gibbon willingly recognizes their necessity and value. The philosopher may smile at the notion that

> on the father's decease, the property of a nation, like that of a drove of oxen, descends to his infant son, as yet unknown to mankind and to himself; and that the bravest warriors and the wisest statesmen, relinquishing their natural right to empire, approach the royal cradle with bended knees and protestations of inviolable fidelity. Satire and declamation may paint these obvious topics in the most dazzling colours, but our more serious thoughts will respect a useful prejudice, that establishes a rule of succession, independent of the passions of mankind; and we shall cheerfully acquiesce in any expedient which deprives the multitude of the dangerous, and indeed the ideal, power of giving themselves a master.[18]

No philosopher concerned for social order and well-being, Gibbon holds, would want to disturb the process by which "the generality of mankind" comes to believe that "the ideas of inheritance and succession," because of their familiarity, are "founded not only in reason but in nature itself."[19] No one, in other words, would do away with the fictions by which we overcome the fatal discontinuities afflicting all historical existence and succeed in establishing a sense of continuity and presence. To such fictions Byzantium, for instance, owes whatever periods of peace and prosperity it enjoyed, having been "most tranquil when it could acquiesce in hereditary succession."[20] Gibbon acknowledges that his concern for order is not compatible with the love he professes for liberty. "As the sense of liberty became less exquisite, the advantages of order were more clearly understood," he observes at one point in his History.[21] But the incompatibility of order and freedom is in itself a mark of the alienation of sovereignty. The free citizens of a Republic do not need to preserve fictions for the sake of order, because they are themselves the principle of order.

Yet, as the historian's gaze travels backward in time to those early ages of unity and manly simplicity, it continually discovers conflict, division, and alienation. The distinction between patricians and plebeians – "so incompatible with the spirit of a free people" – was "established in the first age of the Roman republic."[22] Freedom, it appears, is always, in history, defined by servitude, the possession of power by the ability to exercise it on others. "The constitution of civil society" is such, Gibbon concedes, "that whilst a few persons are distinguished by riches, by honours, and by knowledge, the body of the people is condemned to obscurity, ignorance, and poverty."[23] This is not, Gibbon insists, the "original" condition of mankind. "The common rights, the equal inheritance of mankind, are engrossed by the bold and crafty."[24] There is an original equity, in short, but it seems to be in some way prior to civil society, which is marked by the end of equity, by enclosure, property, violence done to the common share. This violence is then continued throughout history: "Most of the crimes which disturb the internal peace of society are produced by the restraints which the necessary, but unequal laws of property have imposed on the appetites of mankind, by confining to a few the possession of those objects that are coveted by many."[25]

There is no truly free and equal commonwealth in history, none that does not rest on some form of violence, oppression, or deceit. Even the ideal ages of apparent virtue and simplicity turn out to be flawed. "We are surprised to discover," Gibbon remarks in a discussion of murder by poison, "how such subtle wickedness had infected the simplicity of the republic and the chaste virtues of the Roman matrons."[26] At best, property will not imply violence where men rarely encounter each other and are not in competition with each other for scarce resources. "Such, in truth," says Gibbon cautiously, "*may be* the freedom and plenty of a small colony cast on a fruitful island."[27] What he appears to have in mind is less the state of nature itself than a very primitive social condition of the kind Rousseau outlines in the Second Discourse, a condition in which property can be said to exist, but only as "une espèce de propriété," in Rousseau's words – that is, as reflecting the laborer's transformation of nature and addition of value to it but not yet implying the exclusion of others, because abundance makes such exclusion unnecessary.

There is little doubt that history, as Gibbon presents it – and indeed as it appears in the work of most of the writers of the Enlightenment – is the realm of division, difference, the displacement of things themselves by images and substitutes.[28] That is why it can be related. It is because "the paths of error are various and infinite,"[29] because the "images" have an infinite variety of forms and are infinitely substitutable for each other, whereas the "reality" they substitute for is one and unchanging, that there is history, rather than an eternally unchanging state of being, or that there is a story rather than a simple word, the ultimate term of truth. The happy ages of history, according to Gibbon, are on its edges, eventless and unnarratable, like the hours of perfect contentment the historian himself claims to have spent with his Aunt Porten or the "studious social tranquillity of Lausanne" far from "the tumult of London and the house of Commons."[30] Silent and self-contained, they lack connection with the world of change and exchange and cannot be fitted into the narratives of the past. "In the placid course of our lives at Lausanne and Bath," he once wrote to his stepmother, "we have few events to relate and fewer changes to describe."[31] The reign of Antoninus is "marked by the rare advantage of furnishing very few materials for history; which is, indeed, little more than the register of the crimes, follies and misfortunes of mankind."[32] Similarly, the fortunate position of Spain, "separated on all sides . . . by the sea, by the mountains, and by intermediate provinces . . . secured the long tranquillity of that remote and sequestered country." It is for Gibbon "a sure symptom of domestic happiness, that in a period of four hundred years, Spain furnished very few materials to the history of the Roman empire."[33] Likewise the Ethiopians, for almost a thousand years, have no history. They "slept near a thousand years, forgetful of the world, by whom they were forgotten."[34] The "obscure felicity" of Damascus in its "pleasant vale," is directly related to its having "hitherto escaped the historian of the Roman empire."[35] The Vandals, to whom their conquered territories became a prison, lived to regret the banks of the Elbe and "the humble inheritance which, in a happier hour, they had almost unanimously renounced."[36]

For individuals, as for peoples, happiness is living in isolation on the periphery of history, avoiding entanglement with it. As a senator, Petronius Maximus was cited as a "rare example of human felicity." He came of a good family, enjoyed an adequate fortune, and lived a civilized and graceful life. "But the day of his inauguration was the last day of his happiness."[37] In an opposite movement, Gelimer, the defeated king of the Vandals, bursts into laughter when he encounters his conqueror Belisarius. "The crowd might naturally believe that extreme grief had deprived Gelimer of his senses; but in this mournful state unseasonable mirth insinuated to more intelligent observers that the vain and transient scenes of human greatness are unworthy of a serious thought." Gelimer received an estate in remote Galicia from the emperor whose general had defeated him, and thither he retired "with his family and friends, to a life of peace, of affluence, and perhaps of content."[38]

Historical existence is thus synonymous in the *Decline and Fall* with change, disturbance, disorder, division, unhappiness, and the pursuit of imaginary and illusory goals rather than real ones. While it is apparently impossible, as the Vandals discover to their chagrin, to recover the lost paradise of innocence, oneness with oneself, and contentedness with one's lot, there are palliatives, fictions that help to make life in history more tolerable. Thus the very evil of history – the substitution of appearances for reality, of ersatz goods for genuine ones, of images for things and fictions for truth – is also its remedy.

As we saw, fictions such as the "extensive consanguinity" of the Tartars, the belief that all the members of each tribe are descended from a single "great father" or "first founder of the tribe," are treated with respect in the *Decline and Fall*.[39] For the most part the function of such fictions is to patch up and cover over an emptiness without which they could not have arisen in the first place – to establish, for instance, a necessary relation between power and authority or justice by postulating a continuity between the successive historical manifestations of power and some original condition in which power and authority were one and the lawgivers and law enforcers gave laws to themselves. The sons of the Tartar "great father" could perceive themselves as identical with him, as being of his substance, and as following their own laws in following his. Awareness that the historical condition is the disruption of this unity, the alienation of power and authority, of lawgiver and subject, usually produces only further violence and unlawfulness, whereas a belief in the legitimacy of power and in its continuous transmission will at least ensure a degree of peace and order. For his part, the philosopher who sees through the fiction and recognizes the discontinuity will respect the historical lawgiver even though he is admittedly not what he claims to be. Gibbon thus advocates support for the fiction that there is a continuity of authority between the mundane historical order and an ideal order, which supposedly preceded it but which cannot really, by definition, be found in history. For the vast majority of mankind, this fiction of a continuity between the ideal and the real, or between the sacred and the profane, founds the legitimacy, according to Gibbon, of all historically wielded authority.[40] Gibbon himself remains vague on the status of the original, ideal order. On the one hand, by suggesting that the Republic was such an order, he implies that it has an historical reality; on the other, he appears to leave open the possibility that the community that relies for its cohesion on no founding fiction, that knows no alienations and is one with itself, undivided by a sense of its own historicity – indeed is out of history – might be itself a fiction, and indeed a founding fiction. "Such *may be*," he had said, "the freedom and plenty of a small colony on a fruitful island."[41]

Gibbon's account of the origin and development of society and of civil laws is quite similar to that of Rousseau. In Rousseau, however, the unmasking of the historical basis – the basis in violence and illegitimacy – of all positive law and authority led to the demand that the legitimacy of the law be restored by reinventing the power to legislate in all the members of society equally. In this way, as in Gibbon's ideal republic, each citizen, having the right to bear arms and the right to legislate, would be in himself at once the source and origin of law and of the power that enforces it, and the object on which it is exercised. Rousseau's ideal is nonhistorical: in order to avoid the alienation of the law from the lawgiver, it must presuppose a time made up of instants, each of which is complete in itself, a full present, open to neither past nor future, and a law that is, by implication, continually reenacted by the sovereign, as it were, in each successive instant of that time. There can be no question, for Rousseau, of interpreting the law, because the law is always freshly promulgated, freshly willed. Gibbon, on the other hand, is concerned for the maintenance and continuity of society and its institutions as these exist in history. He therefore advocates a different course, one that Rousseau came close to adopting in his more conservative moments, notably in the *Lettres écrites de la montagne*, where the antiquity of the law is itself an object of pious veneration and the making of new laws is discouraged. But whereas Rousseau's conservatism reflects his view that whatever is prior is less corrupt, Gibbon's conservatism is primarily aimed at veiling the origin of law in what Rousseau called "the mists of antiquity."[42] A custom, as Blackstone wrote succinctly, "if any one can show the beginning of it, . . . is no good custom."[43]

The alternative thus seems to be between an ideal, ahistorical condition, in which all men, as citizens, are at once makers and obeyers of the law and in which legislation is never alienated from the legislator, since it is always present legislation; and an actual historical condition, in which – since society is divided and all do not participate in the act of legislation or continually renew the act of legislation – the law is, from the beginning, an instrument used to manipulate some groups of people in the interest of others, and in which it is necessarily mystified and alienated from those who live under it, sustained only by the fiction of its ideal or sacred origin. The philosopher who perceives this fiction of the law may denounce it, or he may wish to conceal it; he may tear aside the veil, or he may try to hold it in place.

He may, in short, act the part of the champion of truth or that of the cynical hypocrite. Both positions – commitment to truth and hypocrisy – assume that the fictions by which the law is maintained and the alienation of the law from the lawmakers (in a written corpus, for instance) are incompatible with genuine law; both share the same idea of what genuine law must be. For Rousseau, for example, the fiction of the law generally disqualifies it as true law, because true law must be an immediate emanation from an original sovereign source, whether God or – as in Rousseau's own political writing – the citizen. But there is a third position, which mediates between commitment to truth and hypocrisy by altogether rejecting the criterion of truth in the sense of an absolute correspondence of sign and meaning or referent. Montesquieu had already sketched out such a position when he placed monarchy and the principle of honor between the heaven of the ideal but irretrievable republic, with its principle of virtue, and the hell of despotism, founded on violence and fear. It is possible to respect the law, in short, even while acknowledging its fictional basis, to the extent that it is discerned to be productive of social utility. "Instead of following this high priori road," Gibbon wrote in 1765 in his remarks on Blackstone – and it is hard not to recognize here the student of Montesquieu and the admirer of Hume – "would it not be better simply to investigate the desires, fears, passions and opinions of the human being; and to discover from thence what means an able Legislator can employ to connect the private happiness of each individual, with the observance of those laws which secure the well being of the whole."[44] As he grew older and more conservative, Gibbon did not alter fundamentally the position adopted here. He only came to believe that the wise legislator will work within the existing system of laws, altering or adding to it where necessary, and allowing equity to correct what is deficient, while always preserving his pious respect for it.[45] The alternative he presents is not between violence and the Utopian order of a revived social contract, but between violence and any order based on law, some being admittedly more conducive to human happiness than others.

In the world of history violence apparently begets violence: "almost every reign is closed by the same disgusting repetition of treason and murder."[46] The choice is between endlessly repeated struggles to impose or overthrow an authority that is only as lasting as the power that sustains it, between continually renewed conflicts of sons and fathers, or Jacks and their masters – with the sons inevitably becoming fathers and the Jacks masters in their turn – and the relative peace and continuity that can be obtained by respect for the law. Among the people, Gibbon implies, this respect will be based on belief in the legitimacy of the established order and in the union of power and authority. Hence the value of the principle of heredity. The enlightened, however, being aware of the alienation of power from authority and of the distance separating all historical regimes from the foundation and origin by which they claim to be authorized, will accept the commands of the established ruler and comply with the prescriptions of established law for the sake of the peace, order, and well-being of society. Thus, while the transcendental foundation of law and authority is undermined, a new foundation is found for them in practical utility. The evacuation of the "original" authority creates a space that can be filled only by substitute authorities, signs of authority, which by their very nature are not absolute, but always questionable and replaceable, yet at the same time respectable in virtue of the function they fulfill. Gibbon, in short, seems here to valorize those signs and substitutions that in so many places in his text he explicitly denounces.[47]

The condition of ironic detachment coupled with dutiful submission and respect is one that is privileged throughout the *Decline and Fall* – perhaps even above the condition of manly simplicity and virtue that is consistently maintained as an ideal. To look back upon the ideal, in other words, may be preferable to living with it; to maintain pious respect for an absent father may be better than living in the blinding light of his presence. While the Republic with its ideal virtue is never more than a remote and abstract point of reference, the age of the Antonines in which "philosophers . . . asserted the dignity of reason; but . . . resigned their actions to the commands of law and of custom" is described at length and with sympathy as "the period in the history of the World during which the condition of the human race was most happy and prosperous."[48] Indeed, the forces of corruption, to which the decline of virtue is ascribed, are all seen as producers of new values, human values of culture and civilization. The space vacated by the origin – the space of human history – is thus viewed ambiguously as estrangement or decline and as opportunity, just as the space between the signifier and the signified is lamented as the space of error and at the same time glorified as the occasion of the ingenuity and freedom of interpretation. To "the division of labour and the facility of exchange," which contributed to the decline of republican Rome is due the enrichment of society[49] and the tempering of "the spirit of rapine and revenge."[50] Trade, associated with corruption and disease, is also accompanied by knowledge and politeness. "The merchant," we are told, "is a friend of mankind."[51] The baleful image of the "bale of cotton" with its "pestilential odour"[52] has its corollary in the shimmering image of the

silkworm, the "first artificer of the luxury of nations." There is no suggestion of decline here. On the contrary, the original state is vile and the
subsequent one beautiful. Value lies not in what is given but in what is
added, in what supplements the original or the given. "I need not explain
that silk is originally spun from the bowels of a caterpillar and that it
composes the golden tomb from which a worm emerges in the form of a
butterfly."[53]

Even within the silkworm passage, Gibbon retains his characteristic ambiguity. Used by Heliogabalus, the "rare and elegant luxury" of silk is
condemned as an "effeminate habit" that "sullied the dignity of an emperor
and a man."[54] Admiration for the "simple judgment of unenlightened and
unprejudiced barbarians," who cannot discern the merit of "the theologian
profoundly skilled in the controversies of the Trinity and the Incarnation,"[55]
coexists with repeated disavowals of sympathy for "savage ancestors whose
imaginary virtues have sometimes excited the praise and envy of civilized
ages."[56] On the whole, however, although enlightenment and civilization
have their attendant evils – the "abuse" of eloquence or of philosophy[57] –
as a positive value Gibbon's savage state is never more than a typical eighteenth-century foil, in the manner of Voltaire's Candide or his Ingénu, to
be used against "prejudice." It is never more than an abstract zero point of
measurement: "*un*enlightened and *un*prejudiced." Gibbon's concrete de-
pictions of primitive life are as repellent as Voltaire's.[58] Similarly, although
Gibbon has some respect for the simplicity of pastoral tribes, who, being
"ignorant of the distinction of landed property, . . . disregarded the use as
well as the abuse of civil jurisprudence" and among whom the eloquence
of lawyers excited only "contempt . . . and abhorrence,"[59] the administration of justice among "savage" peoples leaves much to be desired. "The
fierce and illiterate chieftain was seldom qualified to discharge the duties of
a judge, which require all the faculties of a philosophic mind, laboriously
cultivated by experience and study."[60] The natural judgment alone, it seems,
is not enough. Gibbon's ambivalence about the nature and value of origins
is especially striking in his discussions of eloquence. On the one hand,
eloquence is said, like philosophy, to be "congenial to a popular state,
which encourages the freedom of inquiry, and submits only to the force of
persuasion."[61] Invested with the very spirit of the speaker, the spoken
word, in short, serves as the transparent vehicle of authentic communication among equal citizens in the virtuous republic. In this sense, it contrasts
with the written word, the instrument of culture and corruption, which, as
it is alienated from its origin, spreads doubt and uncertainty and serves as
a means of deception and domination. On the other hand, however, the
spoken word has itself all the features of the sign; and eloquence in the

Decline and Fall is as often associated with artifice as it is with the simplicity and directness of origins.[62]

The *Decline and Fall*, in sum, proposes the model of an absolutely simple, undifferentiated, "natural" community in which all decisions are obvious and immediate and no disagreement is possible because all are united as members of a single family. In this ideal state, nothing is concealed or mysterious; everything is known immediately as it is. Eloquence is unnecessary or at least natural; speech itself seems hardly useful, because everything is in principle perfectly and immediately clear. Similarly, law is not alienated in written codes that require to be deciphered and interpreted. It issues as a live and original utterance from its source. The judge is not an interpreter of the law; he promulgates it and is its origin – as Father, Chief, God.

At the same time, however, as this model is proposed and used as a stick to beat corruption with, it is also rejected. Those historical societies that appear to approximate it the most turn out on inspection to be unacceptably flawed. Nature, which ought to be complete and self-sufficient, seems everywhere to suffer from strange deficiencies and to require the corrective of culture. Above all, the unity that is an object of nostalgia is shown to be an imaginary identity of individual wills, for the only unity found in history results from the imposition of one will upon another. In the ideal republic, each citizen is his own master and is armed with his own weapon; but as the well-being of the individual is by definition indistinguishable from that of the community, all citizens seek identical and legitimate ends. In all historical communities, however – the Roman Republic being set aside as a special and unique case, uncertainly historical and ideal at the same time – unity is imposed by force, because will is informed by passion, not reason. In other words, division already exists, and passion and duty are already at loggerheads. History is the scene not of abstract reason and law, which are unified and general, but of real, unregulated, divisive ambitions and desires. Its true ruler is not the ideal, unchanging, austere yet protective father, but the false fathers, the eunuchs, the phallic mothers, all pursuing their own ends, and it is pointless to try to correct the violence and chaos of this world by calling upon an ideal father whose kingdom, whatever it might be, is not of this world. Effective remedies are better sought in the very ills they must cure, and the wise legislator will not seek to deduce his laws from the laws of nature or of God, but will try to turn "the desires, fears, passions, and opinions of the human being" into instruments of social preservation rather than of social disintegration. He will take the low road of history rather than the "high priori road" of abstract speculation.

The ideal founding father may be the source and support of certainty, truth, and order, but the historical fathers who appear in the pages of Gibbon's narrative bear little resemblance to that model. They are most often cruel and oppressive tyrants, whose authority is ungrounded, unoriginal, the fruit of violence and rapine. Nothing is clear and open in this world; concealment and deceit, intrigue and danger are everywhere. It is, as we saw, a world in which individuals vie with each other for a power that is not originally or properly theirs and abuse each other with the relics of a supposedly original authority. As a reality, the father, in the *Decline and Fall* as in the Autobiography, is a capricious tyrant who persecutes his son or at best affords him ineffectual protection. Indeed, in many cases, it is the son who becomes the champion and protector of a parent of whose infirmities he is sadly aware but unwilling to take advantage and whose standing and authority he chooses not to discredit or to undermine for the sake of the general order and well-being of society. In this way Blackstone tries, "with the becoming tenderness of a pious son," to conceal the defects of the English universities; Photius in the *Decline and Fall* rises to the defense of his affronted father Belisarius, as Belisarius stands always ready to defend his master Justinian; and Gibbon, in the Autobiography, devotes years of his life to propping up the tottering, debt-ridden figure of Edward Gibbon Senior.

Typically, fathers in the *Decline and Fall* are usurpers and tyrants, bad sons and bad fathers both, in thrall to seductive, corrupt, and scheming women whose designs they are impotent to thwart. Sons, however, are obstinately and unswervingly faithful to undeserving and ungrateful fathers. The emperor Justinian, born of "an obscure race of barbarians," owes his elevation to his cunning and his ambition.[63] Gibbon grants him none of the "manly" virtues: "timid," "ambitious," and "crafty," he achieves his ends by "flattery and falsehood,"[64] associates himself with religious orthodoxy and with women, and is disloyal to companions and superiors alike. Early in his career he is accused of assassinating his "spiritual brother," the Gothic chief Vitalian, who, like Justinian, had campaigned against the emperor Anastasius in defense of the orthodox faith and had been honored in consequence by the emperor Justin, Justinian's uncle and protector. In the first days of the latter's reign, moreover, Justinian "prompted and gratified the popular enthusiasm against the memory of the deceased emperor."[65] Much later, as a legal reformer, he again showed his impiety when he allowed the work of commentators to "succeed to the authority of the text," which was "abandoned as a useless, though venerable, relic of antiquity."[66] Above all, he "corrupted the integrity" of the text of the old

Roman lawyers and "inscribed with their venerable names the words and ideas of his servile reign."[67] Separated from the line of the father, to which he has acceded illegitimately by craft and cunning, concealing pride beneath his mask of piety, Justinian is an impostor, a bad son and a false father. His reign is notable not for the protection it affords his subjects, but as a "uniform yet various scene of persecution."[68] Toward his faithful "lieutenant" Belisarius, in particular, he shows only distrust and ingratitude.

Gibbon points out that the central theme of his version of the story of Belisarius is the piety of the son and the ingratitude of the father. The traditional story, which he rejects as "a fiction of later times," is popularly appreciated, he says, as "a strange example of the vicissitudes of fortune."[69] But the "simple and genuine narrative" in the *Decline and Fall* tells of "the fall of Belisarius and the ingratitude of Justinian."[70] Justinian's betrayal of the paternal role is confirmed by his marriage to Theodora, a well-known actress and prostitute, who is also believed to have murdered her only son.[71] Theodora is thus presented in Gibbon's narrative as a *hetaera* figure, evocative of the untrammelled lusts and orgiastic excesses of the mythical age of female dominance, and as in the myths, her husband appears as her consort rather than her master. Justinian insists that she be "seated . . . on the throne as an equal" with him, and as, in fact, "her dominion was permanent and absolute" over him, his reign is truly hers.[72] The false and tyrannical father here appears as the instrument of another nefarious power – the cruel and vengeful female,[73] the unnatural, castrating mother. Theodora, indeed, is the inveterate and irreconcilable enemy of the faithful Belisarius, and the opposition of these two figures in the *Decline and Fall* – the faithful son struggling to defend and sustain an order that has no absolute or authentic authority, and the ambitious, intriguing woman, whose only goal is the gratification of her own desires – opens up two visions of history and society: one in which human passions are turned toward the preservation of social order and one in which, unregulated and uncontrolled, they accomplish its destruction.

If Justinian represents the oppressive and cruel father, Belisarius is the supreme example in Gibbon of the pious son. He is brave, patient, temperate, self-sacrificing, and disdainful of luxury.[74] Above all, his loyalty is unshaken by either the ingratitude or the persecutions of his imperial master. In the unworthy figure of the tyrant, Belisarius continues to revere the faded image of the ideal of paternal authority. His filial piety is vividly illustrated in one of the most powerfully evocative scenes of the History. Having stayed the hand of the Gothic king Totila, who threatened to destroy Rome and turn it into a "pasture for cattle," Belisarius cannot prevent him from driving out all the city's inhabitants. Desolate and despoiled,

Rome nevertheless remains for Gibbon's hero the seat and origin of power and glory. "At the head of a thousand horse," he cut his way through the enemy and "visited with pity and reverence the vacant space of the eternal city."[75]

Belisarius, the pious son, is also a father, and in this role he manifests another aspect of the historical father. Like Justinian, he has succumbed to a scheming, Circe-like female who has "violated all the duties of a mother and a wife" but to whom he remains inescapably bound, as by a charm. The otherwise manly hero is unmanned by this enslavement and rendered incapable of protecting his son. The loyalty of Belisarius to Justinian is matched by the loyalty of Photius to Belisarius. And in both cases the father–son bond is clearly presented not as a blood bond – on the contrary, it is mother and son who are linked through the body – but a fictional spiritual bond, a bond freely assented to by the parties concerned. Photius is the son of Antonina, but he takes on himself the humiliations his mother inflicts on his stepfather and sides with paternal authority and law against his natural mother. Belisarius himself "adjured him to remember his obligations rather than his birth." But whereas Photius maintains both his resolve to punish his mother's crimes against paternal authority and his loyalty to the father (imprisoned by Antonina, he "sustained the torture of the scourge and the rack without violating the faith he had sworn to Belisarius") Belisarius succumbs to his wife's blandishments and weakly abandons the son to whom he had obligated himself by "holy vows of revenge and mutual defence." In both sets of relations, in sum, that of Justinian and Belisarius and that of Belisarius and Photius, the sons appear as pious and devoted, the fathers as false or impotent, empty temples of a vanished God, revered – like the ruins of Rome – not for what they are but as signs of what they are not.[76]

In a similar episode in Chapter XLV, the emperor Justin the Younger is described as impotent and ready to yield the diadem. His "artful" wife Sophia, whose son had "died in his infancy," selects as his successor Tiberius, "his faithful captain of the guards." Sophia then attempts to preserve her power and influence by exercising her charms on Tiberius. The faithful captain, however, maintains his "filial reverence and gratitude," even after the emperor's impotence is made complete by his death, and continues to treat Sophia with "the piety of an adopted son." This treatment "serves to exasperate rather than appease the rage of an injured woman," and Sophia plots his downfall. The three figures of the impotent father, the pious son, and the castrating mother are thus brought together once again in this episode.[77]

As signs of authority, the father figures in the *Decline and Fall* are revered; as weak, ineffectual men dominated by their wives or mistresses, they are pitied; as cruel and vengeful tyrants, they are feared and resented. The historian's discussion of the family provisions of Roman law, in particular of the famous *patria potestas* in Chapter XLIV, underlines the complexity and perhaps the ambivalence of the presentation of authority in the *Decline and Fall*. It also makes it clear that while the Empire may represent in Gibbon's history a decline from the earlier heroic age of Rome and the feminization of the manly Republic, the latter is by no means unequivocally presented as an ideal.

As Gibbon presents it, early Rome is characterized by the absolute authority of the fathers. This authority is such that no son, even after attaining manhood, achieves autonomous existence as a man. He is considered always part of the father, identical with him. As part of the father, he is the latter's property, along with the other things the father has acquired or produced. "In the forum, the senate, or the camp, the adult son of a Roman citizen enjoyed the public and private rights of a *person*: in his father's house he was a mere *thing*: confounded by the laws with the movables, the cattle, and the slaves, whom the capricious master might alienate or destroy without being responsible to any earthly tribunal. The hand which bestowed the daily sustenance might resume the voluntary gift, and whatever was acquired by the labour or fortune of the son was immediately lost in the property of the father."[78] The son might be sold into slavery by the father, he was subject to humiliations and punishments arbitrarily inflicted without inquiry into the validity of the charges, ranging from stripes to imprisonment, exile, or forced labor "in chains among the meanest of his servants" on his father's estates. "Examples of . . . bloody executions, which were sometimes praised and never punished, may be traced in the annals of Rome," Gibbon claims, "beyond the times of Pompey and Augustus."[79] A deep chord seems to have been struck in the historian's imagination by this "exclusive, absolute, and perpetual dominion of the father over his children," which Gibbon considers characteristic of Roman jurisprudence.[80] His normally measured language assumes the highly colored tones of indignation as he discusses the abuse of "domestic power" by the "unnatural father" in an oppressive system that sets Roman jurisprudence apart from both the law of nature and the law of reason. "The Roman empire," he concludes, "was stained with the blood of infants."[81]

Yet it is the Republic, virtuous and manly, that by Gibbon's account is most eminently the city of the fathers. Along with many vices, the historian points out, the emperors also introduced some relaxation of the laws governing paternal rights over children – since these were obstacles to their own pretensions – so that, characteristically, the historian finds himself applauding that decline of "manly" virtue which he elsewhere deplores: "The same crimes that flowed from the corruption were more sensibly felt by the humanity of the Augustan age; and the cruel Erix, who whipped his son till he expired, was saved by the emperor from the just fury of the multitude."[82]

One of the few specific cases mentioned by Gibbon in the section of Chapter XLIV dealing with *patria potestas* concerns the banishment by Hadrian, in order to mark his displeasure at the abuse of parental power, of a "jealous parent, who, like a robber, had seized the opportunity of hunting to assassinate a youth, the incestuous lover of his stepmother."[83] If the son is linked to the father by "the assurance that each generation must succeed in its turn to the awful dignity of parent and master,"[84] the status of victim associates him with women. As the man who has not yet attained the position of the father, the son is thus in an ambivalent position with respect to paternal power and authority. On the one hand, these are experienced as "oppression" and "abuse;" on the other, they must be defended against the schemes and intrigues of ambitious, uncontrolled women. It is not surprising that women are portrayed in the *Decline and Fall* at one and the same time with deep hostility and with warm sympathy. Gibbon's women are either cruel, castrating viragos or pathetic victims. In Chapter XLIV women are above all the victims of male tyranny, and their status is almost identical with that of children. All are alike the property of the father:

> A fiction of the law, neither rational nor elegant, bestowed on the mother of a family (her proper appellation) the strange characters of sister to her own children and of daughter to her husband or master, who was invested with the plenitude of paternal power. By his judgment or caprice her behaviour was approved, or censured, or chastised; he exercised the jurisdiction of life and death; and it was allowed that in the cases of adultery or drunkenness the sentence might be properly inflicted. She acquired and inherited for the sole profit of her lord; and so clearly was woman defined, not as a *person*, but as a *thing*, that, if the original title were deficient she might be claimed, like other movables, by the *use* and possession of an entire year. . . . In the first ages the father of a family might sell his children, and his wife was reckoned in the number of his children: the domestic judge might pronounce the death of the offender, or his mercy might expel her from his bed and house;

but the slavery of the wretched female was hopeless and perpetual, unless he asserted for his own convenience the manly prerogative of divorce. The warmest applause has been lavished on the virtue of the Romans, who abstained from the exercise of this tempting privilege above five hundred years; but the same fact evinces the unequal terms of a connection in which the slave was unable to renounce her tyrant, and the tyrant was unwilling to relinquish his slave.[85]

As in the case of the sons, the improvement of the social and civil condition of women coincides with the decay of the old republican virtues: "After the Punic triumphs the matrons of Rome aspired to the common benefits of a free and opulent republic . . . and their ambition was unsuccessfully resisted by the gravity of Cato the Censor." Subsequently the principle that women might divorce their husbands was recognized and "in three centuries of prosperity and corruption, this principle was enlarged to frequent practice and pernicious abuse."[86] In barely two pages, the historian shifts from deploring the humiliating subjection of women to denouncing the "abuse" of freedom and the threat that the emancipation of women poses to the order of society:

> The facility of separation would destroy all mutual confidence, and inflame every trifling dispute: the minute difference between a husband and a stranger, which might so easily be removed, might still more easily be forgotten; and the matron who in five years can submit to the embraces of eight husbands must cease to reverence the chastity of her own person.[87]

Confronted with clear evidence of tyranny, Gibbon sides with its victims and expects the complicity of his readers. In Chapter XXXV he tells with particular sympathy of Honoria, the sister of the emperor Valentinian, who, prevented from marrying for reasons of state, "no sooner attained the sixteenth year of age than she detested the importunate greatness which must forever exclude her from the comforts of honourable love" and "in the midst of vain and unsatisfactory pomp . . . sighed, yielded to the impulse of nature, and threw herself into the arms of her chamberlain Eugenius." The consequences were in due course apparent, but Gibbon, who had had personal experience, after all, of similar "reasons of state," who had also been excluded from the comforts of honorable love, and who may well have envied the princess's courage, sides unequivocally with the "unhappy princess" in whom nature had been violated. He refuses to acknowledge her "guilt and shame" and rejects the terms themselves as instruments of prejudice and tyranny, "the absurd language of imperious man."[88]

On the whole, however, Gibbon does not repudiate the principle of male authority. On the contrary, in proportion as she attempts to assume the authority that properly belongs to the father, the female is presented as the enemy of the son as well as of the father, and as the robber of the phallus, which is the source and symbol of power and authority. Sympathized with as a victim, as a rebel she is feared and reviled. It is thus not paternal authority itself that Gibbon questions but the abuse of it, the notion that it can inhere absolutely in anyone, and the failure to recognize that it depends in large measure on the belief or consent of those who are subject to it. The enemy of the son – and of the woman – is the bad father: From the good one, on the contrary, they may both expect love and protection. In Chapter XXXV a princess is falsely judged guilty of a crime and suffers a horrible mutilation as punishment, but it is not the true father who condemns her – in this case her natural father Theodoric, King of the Goths. It is the false one – her father-in-law Genseric, King of the Vandals, "a jealous tyrant whom she called her father."[89] In Christianity, likewise, it is the tyranny of the father and the concomitant imputation of guilt to the son – "the savage enthusiasm which represents man as a criminal and God as a tyrant"[90] – that Gibbon so vehemently rejects. But if the true father of Genseric's victim "was urged by the feelings of a parent and a king, to revenge such irreparable injuries," history, in the *Decline and Fall* at least, affords few examples of such good fathers and kings. Those who claim to be invested with authority in history almost invariably abuse it: Every historical father, it appears, is a tyrant.

Gibbon resolves the dilemma posed by the problematic character of authority in history in a manner not untypical of other eighteenth-century writers: by maintaining respect for the empty locus of authority – the word, the sign, the role, the form – while at the same time subjecting every concrete use of the sign or form to critical scrutiny and evaluating it in terms not of its proximity to an ideal original but of its success in promoting social order and well-being. The much-regretted separation of the sign or word from the thing it signifies thus provides the space of a limited freedom. The relation between word (signifier) and thing (referent), one might say, is not viewed as one of mere reflection, but is seen as mediated by a third term, the concept (signified), whose relation to the implied referent or the world of reality, far from being a necessary one, is highly problematic and dependent, in the end, on the consciously or – more commonly – unconsciously held beliefs and opinions of the users of the sign. The linguistic code does not reflect reality, in other words, but in large measure determines what we take reality to be. At the same time, the danger of anarchy is averted, for Gibbon, by the recognition on the part of those users of the sign who are aware of the problematic relation of signified and referent that social order and prosperity require them to abide by conventional codes as they would abide by divinely instituted or rationally deduced codes.

As the sign, throughout the *Decline and Fall*, of the authority of the father, Rome itself, the city of *patria potestas*, inspires respect and piety, even in decay. The terms used to describe the greatness and decline of the city are obviously phallic. In Chapter XLV Rome is "a lofty tree, under whose shade the nations of the earth had reposed" but at the close of the sixth century it was "deprived of its leaves and branches, and the sapless trunk was left to wither on the ground."[91] Like the image of the tree, the theme of depopulation developed in the same chapter is conventional, but it also is clearly related to the idea of impotence. Later still, when Pope Leo IV – "born a Roman" – briefly restores to Rome some of her former greatness, he is described as standing "amidst the ruins of his country . . . erect, like one of the firm and lofty columns that rear their heads above the fragments of the Roman forum."[92] The ruins of former grandeur themselves continue to inspire respect, as the historian obviously believes they should. The principal redeeming feature of Julian, for Gibbon, is that, although he is removed by time from virtues that he can at best attempt to imitate, he cherishes the vanished institutions and "[contemplates] with reverence the ruins of the republic."[93]

Two centuries later, the pious Belisarius stays the decree of Totila, by which Rome was to be "changed into a pasture for cattle." In striking contrast to the barbarian's efforts to desecrate the sacred ruins, Belisarius "visits with pity and reverence the vacant space of the *eternal* city."[94] The irony of the italicized *eternal* is perhaps tinged with pathos: While pointing to the liberating power of history – the authority that claimed to be eternal is now unmasked as ephemeral and insubstantial – the historian seems at the same time to wish to insinuate reverence for the sign itself. Social and political institutions are invested, it would seem, not with authority – for none is truly original – but with the sign of authority. Yet this sign of authority, Gibbon implies, is as respectable and awesome in its way as any real authority would be. It is not and ought not to be an object of contempt – *only* a sign – for there is no substantial or original authority in comparison with which it deserves to be regarded as *merely* an image. In other words, what men revere as authority is always the sign of authority. Though nothing now remains of the original founding authority of the fathers except the place of its absence, for Belisarius this very vacancy at the heart of the world is itself almost sacred. It stands for both the value of authority and law and their lack of any transcendental foundation or authority beyond history, for the value of order and the fact of freedom at the same time. It is understandable that Belisarius was appalled by Totila's attempt to erase the vacant space from the consciousness and memory of men.

Reverence for a "vacant space" is not, however, easily or commonly accorded. The vast majority of men will rather aim to unmask the vacancy, to expose the failure of authority by toppling whatever may be left of it in order to impose their own, and to seek their own freedom, not, like Belisarius, in the limited space between knowledge and respect, but, like Totila the barbarian, in the desecration of every mark of prior power and authority. "Where . . . will this tremendous inundation, this conspiracy of numbers against rank and property, be finally stopped?" Gibbon later wondered as he looked out anxiously from La Grotte in 1792 at the spectacle of a nation "gone mad."[95] For Gibbon, knowledge of the void at the heart of the world is something that not only is, but must remain, restricted to the few who, like Belisarius, have the wisdom to tolerate it; otherwise it will result in the destruction of all order and authority. Radical changes in laws and institutions must be sedulously avoided, and no true philosopher will desire them. It was "the perpetual revolutions of the throne," it will be remembered, "that erased every notion of hereditary right."[96]

In a much-quoted passage at the beginning of the *Decline and Fall* Gibbon describes the tolerant and easygoing age of the Antonines: "the various modes of worship, which prevailed in the Roman world, were all considered by the people, as equally true; by the philosopher, as equally false; and by the magistrate, as equally useful."[97] Like the author of the *Esprit des lois*,[98] to whom he frequently refers (albeit with the niggling criticism writers sometimes reserve for those to whom they are most indebted), Gibbon places the magistrate above both the multitude and the philosopher. The magistrate is the third term, the term that resolves the antithesis of belief and disbelief, credulity and incredulity, affirmation and negation. Whereas the assent of the populace is conditional on its belief in the objective truth of the various religions and that of the philosopher is an "external reverence" masking "inward contempt,"[99] the assent of the magistrate retains something both of the philosopher's detachment and incredulity and of the populace's blind belief. For the magistrates, who "are themselves philosophers" and enlightened,[100] recognize the hidden wisdom of that which reason at first despises. From the standpoint of pure reason, the altar is empty and the God a figure of clay. The philosopher delights in pointing out to all who are willing to listen that the emperor has no clothes; what prudence he preserves is determined only by his fear of irritating the fanatical and superstitious multitude. The magistrate, on the other hand, admires the positive function of the lie or fiction in maintaining complex social systems. His compliance with religion does not spring solely from fear of unleashing the passions of the ignorant; it rests on a positive evaluation of the necessity of myth in the foundation of any social order in which variety of individuals and classes prevents total identity of ideas and values.

In Montesquieu, the republic is situated in an ideal prehistorical or extrahistorical space. As it is characterized by the equality – that is, for Montesquieu, as for most other eighteenth-century thinkers, the identity – of its members, it has no inner dialectic propelling it continually from one historical state to another. Similarly, despotism knows no dialectic, only the successive acts of a single will. Each moment in a despotism is autonomous, unconnected with the previous moment or the following one. Monarchy alone, in Montesquieu's account, belongs to history in the sense that change for it means not a discontinuous succession of homogeneous states but a continuous process resulting from the interaction and conflict of nonidentical internal elements. This, it might be argued, is the important aspect of Montesquieu's theory of monarchy, and not the purely formal matter of rule by a monarch or king. Now, while the "principle" of republicanism in the *Esprit des lois* is equality, and that of despotism is fear, the "principle" of monarchy, it will be remembered, is honor. And is not honor, from the philosopher's point of view, only an illusion founded on mere opinion? It is not surprising that some time before Gibbon, Montesquieu had argued that the important aspect of belief or religion from the point of view of the student of society, as distinct from the philosopher, is not its truth or illusoriness, but its social function:

> L'on peut chercher entre les religions fausses celles qui sont les plus conformes au bien de la société; celles qui, quoiqu'elles n'aient pas l'effet de mener les hommes aux félicités de l'autre vie, peuvent le plus contribuer à leur bonheur dans celle-ci. Je n'examinerai donc les diverses religions du monde, que par rapport au bien que l'on en tire dans l'état civil.[101]

These lines and many similar ones were certainly familiar to Gibbon.

The position of the wise and enlightened magistrate who knows that the emperor has no clothes but who believes at the same time in the value, indeed in the necessity, of the fiction that he has – who knows, in other words, that signs are necessary and valuable, even if what they signify cannot be shown to possess any reality – is analogous to the position in which Gibbon tells us he stood to his father and to the position in which Belisarius is said to have stood with respect to the "vacant space of the eternal city." Finally, it is analogous to the ironical yet respectful stance toward social and historical institutions that the narrator of the *Decline and Fall* appears to adopt and to invite or expect his readers to share.[102]

4

A liberal education and understanding

THE *Decline and Fall* PROBABLY OWES much of its continued, if diminished, popularity to the pervasive ironies that delighted contemporary readers. Irony may serve primarily critical or destructive ends, but it is not incompatible with a measure of attachment to its object, stemming from inability or unwillingness to substitute anything in place of the object of irony. In Gibbon's case, as in Montesquieu's, such attachment appears to have been neither unwilling nor unconscious. Both writers held themselves deliberately somewhat apart from the majority of the *philosophes*, who were their contemporaries or their friends, and from whom they differed above all in that they aimed not only to unmask but also to recuperate. What was unwarranted or absurd in the light of pure reason often turned out, for them, to be wise and even indispensable from the practical standpoint of social welfare and utility. That social activity might be directed toward nothing or founded on nothing and yet be productive of something was perhaps a paradox for the philosopher, but for the practical magistrate and the empirical student of history and society, it was abundantly demonstrable. All history, in a sense, was the product of absurd or illusory beliefs and motives.

The position of the magistrate is a delicate one, however, since he is, by Gibbon's own definition, himself a philosopher.[1] He must at the same time unmask "absurdity" and reconcile the reader to it by pointing out its hidden rationale. In the broadest terms, he must be sufficiently detached from a religious or providentialist idea of history to acknowledge that history must appear to the philosophical viewer as chaotic, meaningless, the work of blind passions and enthusiasms, and yet he must also be able to discern hidden regularities and a hidden sense in it. In Gibbon's own words, "There are few observers who possess a clear and comprehensive view of the revolutions of society, and who are capable of discovering the nice and secret springs of action which impel, in the same uniform direction, the blind and capricious passions of a multitude of individuals."[2]

The narrator of the *Decline and Fall* delights in exposing the chaotic

73

absurdity of history and of men's accounts of it. He often seems more interested in unmasking the illusoriness of human passions and the emptiness of the signs that inspire them, in the manner of most of the eighteenth-century *philosophes*, than in investigating the way signs work – and can be made to work – in human society, in the manner of Montesquieu. But if narrator and reader, discoursing urbanely and philosophically about events, often appear to stand over against them – as reason stands over against folly and the Heavenly City of the philosophers over against the worldly city of kings and commanders – the opposition is never absolute. Having been brought to a point of detachment from which he can view history "philosophically," Gibbon's reader is encouraged to consider the mechanisms of the passions by which men are governed and the positive value and function of signs as elements of social systems rather than as representatives of natures or essences.

The fundamental connection between irony and history writing for Gibbon is highlighted by the "memorable fable of the SEVEN SLEEPERS" reported in Chapter XXXIII. Seven noble youths of Ephesus fall into a deep slumber that lasts for 187 years. On awakening, they no longer recognize the "familiar aspect" of their native country and are continually "surprised" by what they see. Whereas most people fail to adopt a detached view of their world, the seven sleepers thus have one thrust upon them. "We imperceptibly advance from youth to age," Gibbon comments,

> without observing the gradual, but incessant, change of human affairs; and even in our larger experience of history, the imagination is accustomed, by a perpetual series of causes and effects, to unite the most distant revolutions. But if the interval between two memorable eras could be instantly annihilated; if it were possible, after a momentary slumber of two hundred years, to display the *new* world to the eyes of a spectator who still retained a lively and recent impression of the *old*, his surprise and his reflections would furnish the pleasing subject of a philosophical romance.[3]

Typically, the object of Gibbon's irony is "enthusiasm,"[4] "superstition," or intolerance – any total involvement in historical existence. Its form is usually that of elaborate circumlocution and contrived balance and order. The studied politeness and civility of the language, the abstractness and generality of the vocabulary are an essential part of the meaning. They affirm the value of urbanity, of cool and imperturbable detachment, and of deliberate, controlled, timeless elegance of form, against the ugly formlessness of uncontrolled passion and disorderly content; at the same time, they ensure that understanding will be reserved for an elite sufficiently educated and urbane to appreciate it and to find in its appreciation the confirmation of its superiority.[5] With Gibbon, as with Voltaire, an affectation of surprise at the absurdities of human belief is a significant feature of irony. But whereas the surprise is usually attributed, in the philosophical tale or "romance," to the pure critical intelligence of the outsider, the man without history or prejudice – Candide, Zadig, Micromégas, the Huron of *L'Ingénu* – who may in turn be the object of the narrator's ironical presentation, in historical writing it belongs immediately to the narrator, and depending on the latter's persona, it may be invested with a considerable measure of social content. The persona of the historian of the *Decline and Fall* is well defined, as we shall see, and has its own set of characteristics, which are not the same as those of the narrators of Voltaire's philosophical tales or of the historian of Charles XII, Louis XIV, and Peter the Great. The surprise expressed by the narrator of the *Decline and Fall* and expected from the reader is most prominently that of the polite, privileged, wellbred man of the world, whose refined intelligence and sense of decorum have been offended by some vulgarity or impropriety.

The specific character of Gibbon's irony in the *Decline and Fall* thus springs from two features of the text, one fairly general and one quite particular. Like other eighteenth-century ironists, the narrator continually assumes or points to a position of detachment and invites the reader to join him in it. At the same time, the persona the narrator projects and invites the reader to identify with as he achieves detachment has particular features. He is, for instance, not as sharp, playful, mobile, or irreverential as Voltaire's literary personae, but "judicious," "thoughtful," "prudent," "skeptical," and never "zealous," not even for philosophy.[6] He smiles, he does not laugh, at the absurdities of history. The adoption of a certain stance toward the world is thus both a condition of reading the *Decline and Fall* and the model of behavior proposed in it by the persona of the narrator.

The now familiar division of the historical or narrative text into *discours* (the dialogue of the narrator with the reader) and *histoire* (the actual narrative of events)[7] provides in itself the essential condition for what is commonly called dramatic irony: The narrator and the reader share knowledge that the characters themselves do not possess – in this case because they stand outside the time of the actors or characters and know the end of the story that the latter are living. Since *discours* plays an important part in the *Decline and Fall*, as in all eighteenth-century narrative – a significantly more important and certainly a more explicit one than in early nineteenth-century narrative, for instance – the reader is continually being detached from the story, buttonholed by the narrator, and engaged by him in commentary on or speculation about both the events of the narrative and the narrative itself. There is thus ample opportunity for the contemporary allusions, the contrasts, the parallels that underline on every page the superior ironical position of the narrator and the reader.

The notes are obviously a privileged place for discourse with the reader, for sharing information with him, for referring to works that imply common experiences (contemporary or near-contemporary authors such as Montesquieu, d'Herbelot, Tillemont) or for proposing experiences that the narrator would like to share, as in Chapter XII, where Gibbon puts in a good word for Adam's recently published *Antiquities of Spalato*. The notes also include, as is well known, many snide comments on the narrative itself,[8] particularly where religion is concerned, much criticism of sources, and a large number of personal references that consolidate the complicity of narrator and reader. In Chapter XL, for instance, a description of Armenia in the text is the occasion of a reference in the notes to the Swiss residence of the historian at the time of writing, that is to say in the present time of the *discours*: "In the mountainous country which I inhabit it is well known that an ascent of some hours carries the traveller from the climate of Languedoc to that of Norway."[9] The importance of the notes to the complete text of the *Decline and Fall* was acknowledged by Gibbon when, beginning with the third edition of Volume I in 1777, he acted on a suggestion of Hume to his printer Strahan and had them placed at the foot of the pages instead of at the end of the volume.

But the narrative itself is full of nods and asides to the reader. Contemporary allusions, temporal expressions, such as "now," "at this time," "modern," whose reference point is the present moment of enunciation, or verb tenses commonly used in ongoing conversation with an interlocutor, rather than in formal narrative (the present, the future, the compound past), mark the time of *discours* as opposed to that of *histoire* and engage the complicity of the reader with the narrator. The Antonine Wall, we are told, stood "at a small distance beyond the *modern* cities of Edinburgh and Glasgow," which reader and narrator may be expected to know of, but which the Romans of the age of the Antonines obviously could not. The interior of Dalmatia, similarly, "is *still* infested by tribes of barbarians." The country south of Trebizond "rises into dark forests and craggy mountains, as savage, though not so lofty as the Alps and the Pyrenees." "Canada, *at this day*, is an exact picture of ancient Germany."[10] The names of ancient cities are translated into those known to narrator and reader: "Chryopolis, or as it is *now* called, . . . Scutari"; "Beroea, or, as it is *now* called, . . . Aleppo, in Syria."[11] Saint Sophia in Constantinople is described from the point of view of the narrator and the reader: "The architecture of St. Sophia, which is *now* converted into the principal mosque, has been imitated by the Turkish Sultans, and that venerable pile *continues to excite* the fond admiration of the Greeks, and the more rational curiosity of European travellers. The eye of the spectator is disappointed by an irregular prospect of half-domes and shelving roofs."[12] In a reference to the Greek colony of Naples, the time from which it is being recollected is conveyed by the addition of a phrase and the use of a compound past: "Naples, which *has swelled* to a great and populous capital. . . ." The Maronites, followers of "a saint or savage of the fifth century . . . *still* enjoy, under their Turkish masters, a free religion and a mitigated servitude." In Mecca and Medina, "a family of three hundred persons, the pure and orthodox branch of the caliph Hassan . . . *still* retains, after the revolution of twelve centuries, the custody of the temple and the sovereignty of their native land." To the west, "in its present decay, Cairoan *still* holds the second rank in the kingdom of Tunis," while to the east, the populous capital of Bagdad, which at the time of the narrative could have sent "eight hundred thousand men and sixty thousand women" to attend the funeral of a popular saint, has "*now* dwindled to a provincial town."[13]

   Gibbon's frequent contrasting of "then" and "now," the time referred to in the narrative and the time of the discourse, reinforces the complicity of reader and narrator as privileged observers of the historical scene. At the same time, the emphasis placed on the shrinkage or depletion of reality between then and now has the effect common to all uses of the traditional *ubi sunt* topos of reminding the reader of the transitoriness of all historical existence, including his own. The theme of decline had been given a new immediacy in Gibbon's time by the contemporary debate – itself an episode in the continuing quarrel of the Ancients and the Moderns – on the relative populations of the ancient and the modern worlds. Though Gibbon's position in the debate is characteristically uncertain – at times he appears cautiously favorable to the Ancients, at times he seems to support the Moderns, at times he merely refers neutrally to Hume, Wallace, and Montesquieu, the leading spokesmen in the controversy – he invariably ascribes to the great centers of Roman imperial civilization a larger population than they held in his own time. Here decadence is unmistakable, and Gibbon's text evokes in words the images of desolation and ruin much favored by contemporary artists:

The *present* citizens of Palmyra, consisting of thirty or forty families, *have erected* their mud-cottages within the spacious court of a
magnificent temple.[14]
A miserable village *still* preserves the name of Salona; but so late
as the sixteenth century the remains of a theatre, and a confused
prospect of broken arches and marble columns, continued to attest
its ancient splendour.[15]

At Lambesa,

> a Roman city, once the seat of a legion, and the residence of forty
> thousand inhabitants [,] the Ionic temple of Aescalapius *is encom-
> passed* with Moorish huts; and the cattle *now graze* in the midst of
> an amphitheatre, under the shade of Corinthian columns.[16]

As for Carthage,

> in the beginning of the sixteenth century the second capital of the
> West was represented by a mosch, a college without students,
> twenty-five or thirty shops, and the huts of five hundred peas-
> ants. . . . Even that paltry village was swept away by the Spaniards
> whom Charles the Fifth had stationed in the fortress of the Go-
> letta. The ruins of Carthage *have perished*; and the place might be
> unknown if some broken arches of an aqueduct did not guide the
> footsteps of the inquisitive traveller.[17]

As he contemplates the ruins of Roman grandeur, the historian associates the reader with him in the recognition that their world too, the present
world from which they look out together on the spectacle of the past – and
Gibbon is partial to the theatrical image[18] – will also pass. Spectators themselves become part of the spectacle of history, like the small contemporary
figures in eighteenth-century views of classical sites and monuments. In the
Decline and Fall, Constantius, the son of Constantine, looking with aston-
ishment, on the occasion of a brief visit to the former capital of the world,
upon "the awful majesty of the Capitol, the vast extent of the baths of
Caracalla and Diocletian, the severe simplicity of the Pantheon, the massy
greatness of the amphitheatre of Titus, the elegant architecture of the theatre of Pompey and the Temple of Peace, and above all, the stately structure of the Forum and column of Trajan," is in his turn the object of a later
viewer's contemplation.[19]
If he is to avoid becoming the inert object of another vision, the specta-

tor cannot be content with the provisional and precarious privilege that his location in time affords. He must try to preempt time's inevitable victory over him by standing back from his own present existence. Likewise, if the narrator's judgments on the events and personalities of his narrative are to have authority and credibility, they may not appear to be those of the historian as an historical being, but must present themselves as neutral and impartial. In a note on Saint Augustine, Gibbon describes the path that the ideal reader must strive to follow:

> The church of Rome has canonised Augustin and reprobated Calvin. Yet, as the *real* difference between them is invisible even to a theological microscope, the Molinists are oppressed by the authority of the saint, and the Jansenists are disgraced by their resemblance to the heretic. In the meanwhile the Protestant Arminians stand aloof and deride the mutual perplexity of the disputants. . . . Perhaps a reasoner still more independent may smile in *his* turn when he peruses an Arminian Commentary on the Epistle to the Romans.[20]

The balance of parallelisms and antitheses here (Augustine/Calvin, Molinists/Jansenists, canonised/reprobated, oppressed by . . . saint/disgraced by . . . heretic) is apparently resolved by a third term, the Protestant Arminians, who stand aloof and deride both parties. But the Arminians are in turn observed by a "reason still more independent." The reader, in short, must always be ready to step back with the narrator in an infinite regress from total historical engagement toward a point of absolute neutrality or disengagement, which must ultimately, it would seem, lie outside the bounds of history.

Such a position is constantly indicated by the historical parallels that are so common in Gibbon. To perceive the relationships among the varied historical phenomena being observed and compared, the reader must situate himself at a point beyond all of them, beyond even his own contemporary world. Only from such an ideal perspective can he hope to survey the immense stage of history and to recognize the repertory of roles and actions whose recurrence in innumerable different combinations provides it with both consistency and variety. Sometimes the comparisons are explicit and elaborate. In the struggle between the Romans and the Goths in the fourth century, "the triumph of Stilicho was compared by the poet [Claudian],and perhaps by the public, to that of Marius; who, in the same part of Italy, had encountered and destroyed another army of barbarians; . . . and posterity might erect a common trophy to the memory of the two most illustrious generals, who had vanquished on the same memorable ground, the two most formidable enemies of Rome."[21] Six centuries after the destruction of Carthage by the younger Scipio, the city again meets the same fate at the hands of the Vandals.[22] More frequently, Gibbon's parallels are telescoped into brief metaphorical phrases. Spain, for instance, "was the Peru and Mexico of the old world." Odin is "the Mahomet of the North," Carthage "the Rome . . . of the African world," Colchis "the Holland of antiquity." Ali, the son of Abu Taleb and the companion of Mahomet, is "the faithful Aaron of a second Moses," Aikbah the Saracen a "Mohammedan Alexander."[23]

The historical metaphor is favored also by Thierry, Macaulay, Mommsen, and other nineteenth-century historians, but whereas for them it serves usually to bring the past vividly to life by making it seem as vital as the reader's present, in Gibbon's historical writing, as in Voltaire's, the purpose and the effect obtained are the opposite: to suggest the permanence of roles and functions underlying the apparent profusion of historical phenomena and visible only to the eye of the philosopher, to reveal constants and universals while not depriving phenomena of their concrete existence. If the first step in the making of the philosophical historian or the philosophical reader of history is the defamiliarization of history, the breaking of continuities, and the perception of change and difference, the second is thus the recognition of permanent features in the shifting patterns of change.

At the same time, however, that the narrator proposes withdrawal from historical engagement as the condition of the reader's transformation into a *philosophe*, he also points to the impossibility of total withdrawal and the foolhardiness of attempting to achieve it. To challenge our human condition is madness, the narrator implies, and leads inevitably to an enslavement to illusion no less drastic than the enslavement of those who live wholly within the world of history. The Stoic is as fanatical in his way as the most ambitious of princes. Candide, Zadig, and the wise Quaker of the *Lettres philosophiques*, it will be recalled, all take up residence just outside the city, to which they remain connected in vitally important ways, while at the same time ensuring their distance and detachment from it; and in the same way Voltaire himself settled at Ferney, far from Paris, with which he nevertheless maintained frequent and uninterrupted contact, and close to Geneva, from which he was careful to separate himself by a frontier. In the same way, the historian of the Roman Empire settled in Lausanne, as he reminds his reader in the notes, far from the hurlyburly of London politics and social life, with which, nevertheless, through his stepmother, the Holroyds, and his publisher, he kept in constant touch, while in the city of his adoption he remained an outsider who might decide to leave at any point. The philosopher, in short, does not place himself outside history. Disengagement is achieved not by withdrawing from history but while remaining in it, not by attempting to refuse historical roles but by assuming them, playing them consciously like an actor, and, above all, varying them and moving nimbly from one to another. Thus Gibbon is alternately, and with equal facility, a British patriot and a loyal Swiss. The philosopher is never out of history, but he is never completely identifiable with any historical role or position; he seems always ready to change position without notice, and thus, while always situated somewhere, is never fully situated anywhere. He offers himself to the world, one might say, as a sign, not a nature or essence, thereby both assuming and exploiting that space between the sign and the thing that was widely acknowledged – even as it was deplored – to be characteristic of the historical world.

Certain formal features peculiar to the historiographical text reinforce the philosophical historian's position of simultaneous engagement and disengagement. In historiographical narrative, as opposed to fictional narrative, the *histoire* of the text is given as faithfully representative of a history (a time, a sequence, a series of happenings existing outside the text); correspondingly, the narrator of the historiographical work, unlike the narrator of a fictional work, is given as the representation of a historical or a real-life author whose name appears on the title page. The *discours* of the historiographical narrator is thus offered as a faithful representation in writing of the speaking of a real historical person at a particular moment in real historical time.[24] Indeed, to the extent that certain fictional texts attempt to achieve an effect of immediacy and to erase the signs of their own "literariness," they often present themselves in the same manner and aim to pass as historiographical texts, while at the same time ensuring, in most cases, that a small number of contradictory signals will make their fictional character still perceptible to the attentive reader. Nevertheless, the relation of the narrator of an historiographical work to its author is no more one of simple representation than is the relation of the events narrated in the text to "real" events outside the text.

In both cases the relation is one of signification, not representation. The author who seems to be represented by the narrator of an historiographical work is in fact signified by him. This is especially striking in the literary world of the eighteenth century, where "Gibbon" and "Voltaire" were indistinguishable from the various public myths created by their work, while in the case of Rousseau, the attempt to escape from signification toward representation led only to ever renewed acts of signification. Though the narrator of an historiographical work may be given as identical with the historical or "real" author, whereas fictional works distinguish ontologically between the two, the author is not, in sum, in either case a final reality or solid ground sustaining the narrator as his representation. The implied identity of narrator and author in the historiographical work is first and foremost a genre signal indicating to the reader how the text is to be classified and according to what conventions it is to be read. It thus resembles certain so-called metalinguistic signals in everyday speech – statements such as "This is a true story" or, alternately, "This is a good story" – which, aiming to affect the listener's reception of a message rather than constituting part of it, may appear to be outside the system they are commenting on, but which are in fact themselves messages of a special type within that sign system. The peculiarity of the historiographical text, in short, is that it offers itself as representative while remaining no less subject to the constraints of language than any other text; the peculiarity of the historiographical narrator is that he claims to found his discourse in a transcendant extratextual "voice," which is itself signified by the text. The *philosophe*'s stance of simultaneous identification with his historical roles and distance from them is thus curiously reflected by the historian, inasmuch as the latter both identifies himself with his literary mask and remains distinct from it, becoming in the end, as a public, historical figure, himself a mask, the creation of his narrator and his text rather than their model.

Discours and *histoire*, in other words, retain a categorial aspect in historiographical works as in fictional ones. While they may be given as representations of a reality outside the text, they continue to function as structuring elements within the text. The figures of the narrator and the reader in Gibbon's text point to a location outside the text, in historical reality, but they are also, as in fictional works, timeless functions of the narrative. In this sense they can never be overtaken by the passage of time, because the time of *discours*, in which as characters or personae they are situated, is unrelated and impervious to chronological time. It never passes into history, but remains always itself, an eternal grammatical present, from which a story is narrated and commented upon. Every reader of the *Decline and Fall* reoccupies, in the act of reading, the same impregnable position, and so finds himself in the same situation as Gibbon's philosopher, at once in history and out of it.

The problem of the philosopher's – that is, the historian's and the reader's – relation to history is touched upon in the *Decline and Fall* in a considerable number of exemplary self-contained episodes that develop the popular eighteenth-century theme of the life of retirement. Tacitus, the senator, enjoying "with elegance and sobriety his ample patrimony of between two and three million sterling" at the time he was called on to assume the imperial throne, is a somewhat idealized version of those eighteenth-century Englishmen to whose admirably tended estates Gibbon, in Hampshire and elsewhere, had been a frequent visitor. When the "ungrateful rumour" of his impending promotion to the most powerful position in the Empire reached him, Tacitus "sought the retirement of one of his villas in Campania," and only "reluctantly obeyed the summons of the consul to resume his honourable place in the senate."[25] The aged general Vetranio, "beloved for the simplicity of his manners," is graciously pardoned after his defeat by the sons of Constantine and withdraws to Prusa, where he "lived six years in the enjoyment of ease and affluence," advising his benefactor to follow suit, "to resign the sceptre of the world, and to seek for content (where alone it could be found) in the peaceful obscurity of a private condition."[26] In yet another finely drawn episode, adapted from Procopius, Gelimer, the defeated King of the Vandals, answers an invitation to give himself up to the mercy of Justinian by recalling the vicissitudes of all historical existence and extolling the life that is led on its fringes:

> "I am not insensible," replied the king of the Vandals, "how kind and rational is your advice. But I cannot persuade myself to become the slave of an unjust enemy, who has deserved my implacable hatred. *Him* I have never injured either by word or deed; yet he has sent against me, I know not from whence, a certain Belisarius, who has cast me headlong from the throne into this abyss of misery. Justinian is a man; he is a prince; does he not dread for himself a similar reverse of fortune? I can write no more; my grief oppresses me. Send me, I beseech you, my dear Pharas, send me a lyre, a sponge, and a loaf of bread."

Gibbon's translation of Procopius's text transforms the old Vandal king into an eighteenth-century gentleman filled with notions learned from Ecclesiastes, the Stoics, and the Epicureans. When he finally does surrender and is led captive through the streets of Constantinople, Gelimer sheds not a tear, but "his pride or piety derived some secret consolation from the words of Solomon, which he repeatedly pronounced, Vanity! Vanity! All is vanity!"[27]

In a significant number of cases, however, the traditional contrast between *rus* and *urbs*, the *vita contemplativa* and the *vita activa*, the private life and the public life, is complicated, as it is in Voltaire and other eighteenth-century writers, by an implied contrast between the productive and historically useful labor of the obscure private citizen (the bourgeois or commoner) and the absurd, destructive activity of powerful public figures at the center of the world's stage. Though he may stand on the sidelines, in other words, the philosopher has by no means attempted to withdraw from history or from worldly activity. Diocletian in his retirement employed his leisure hours "in building, planting and gardening" and maintained that "if he could show Maximian the cabbages which he had planted with his own hands at Salona, he should no longer be urged to relinquish the enjoyment of happiness for the pursuit of power."[28] If Diocletian resembles Candide, Galerius, a few pages later, announces the Faust of Part II of Goethe's poem.

> Wisely relinquishing his view of universal empire, he devoted the remainder of his life to the enjoyment of pleasure and to the execution of works of public utility, among which we may distinguish the discharging into the Danube the superfluous waters of the lake Pelso and the cutting down the immense forests that encompassed it: an operation worthy of a monarch, since it gave an extensive country to the agriculture of his Pannonian subjects.[29]

The contrast between public affairs and the power struggles of the great on the one hand, and the "useful occupations" of "millions of obedient subjects" on the other is explicit,[30] and Gibbon seems almost to regret, as Voltaire and most of the Romantic historians claimed to do, that the historian is exclusively occupied by the former.[31] Unlike Voltaire and the Romantics, however, he does not actually challenge this practice of history writing, but holds, on the contrary, that the private, uneventful lives of the "millions" are unsuitable material for historical narrative, which can find an appropriate – that is, narratable – subject matter only in wars and public affairs. In the modern world, where there is separation of princes and commoners, rulers and ruled, public and private persons, Gibbon observes, the historian's attention will be concentrated on the narrow circle of the great public figures, and it is only in archaic societies, where such a separation does not exist, where private life is not distinct from public affairs – in "petty republics" and "the state of freedom and barbarism" – that all the members of a society will have equal claim on the historian's attention:

> Wars, and the administration of public affairs, are the principal subjects of history; but the number of persons interested in these busy scenes is very different according to the different condition of mankind. In great monarchies, millions of obedient subjects pursue their useful occupations in peace and obscurity. The atten-

tion of the writer, as well as of the reader, is solely confined to a court, a capital, a regular army, and the districts which happen to be the occasional scene of military operations. But a state of freedom and barbarism, the season of civil commotions, or the situation of petty republics, raises almost every member of the community into action, and consequently into notice.[32]

The work of the historian himself, however, is closer to the productive labors of the "millions" than it is to the "restless motions"[33] of his characters, the principal actors on the stage of history. In a note in which, in characteristic Enlightenment manner, he criticizes the "detractors of human life" on the grounds that "their expectations are commonly immoderate, their estimates . . . seldom impartial," Gibbon claims that he himself is not discontented with his lot. But if life is not a vale of tears, he explains, happiness does not lie on the highroads of history. The historian, as "spectator of the great World,"[34] is happier than his hero: "If I may speak of myself (the only person of whom I can speak with certainty), *my* happy hours have far exceeded, and far exceed the scanty numbers of the caliph of Spain, and I shall not scruple to add, that many of them are due to the pleasing labour of the present composition."[35]

The historian serves, in many ways, like the gardener, as a model of the productive bourgeois citizen. He is not outside history or inactive in the world; nor, on the other hand, does he occupy the center of the stage. He is situated on the edge of history, as it were, laboring obscurely but usefully to create patches of order in the chaos surrounding him and trying to show how uncontrolled and often destructive enemies may – without violence – be tamed, domesticated and turned to beneficial ends, how nature may be cultivated. The relation between the historian and the bourgeois was not lost on Walter Bagehot, who emphasized in his essay on Gibbon "the practical ability required to write a large book, and especially a large history." Bagehot resorts easily to the metaphor of economics to describe the historian's activity:

Long before you get to the pen, there is an immensity of pure business; heaps of material are strewn everywhere; but they lie in disorder, unread, uncatalogued, unknown. It seems a dreary waste of life to be analyzing, indexing, extracting works and passages, in which one per cent of the contents are interesting, and not half of that percentage will ultimately appear in the flowing narrative. As an accountant takes up a bankrupt's books filled with confused statements of ephemeral events, the disorderly record of unprofitable speculations, and charges that to that head, and that to this, – estimates earnings, specifies expenses, demonstrates failures; so the great narrator, going over the scattered annalists of extinct ages, groups and divides, notes and combines, until from a crude mass of darkened fragments there emerges a clear narrative, a concise account of the result and upshot of the whole."[36]

The efforts of history's heroes – artfully associated in the reader's mind with criminals – to impose order on the world inevitably end in death and destruction. Virtually nothing remains after the noise of battle dies away or the "ferment of controversy" subsides. The prize always escapes: "the grave is ever beside the throne; the success of a criminal is almost instantly followed by the loss of his prize." A similar fate attends the writings of those who have associated their pens with the ambitions of the great: their "verbose folios . . . slumber by the side of their rivals."[37] The useful, though often less immediately striking products of industry, on the other hand – among them the histories of conquests and other criminal activities, as told by historians – have a chance of enduring and increasing human well-being. Whereas those who strive for power and mastery are rarely more than the unseeing instruments of the natural forces and passions that rule them, the historian expands the scope of human self-determination by providing the large and comprehensive view that is the condition of man's control of his environment. To the mere succession of kings and commanders, the endlessly renewed pattern of triumph and defeat, the historian opposes the stability and permanence of his own achievement:

> Many were the paths that led to the summit of royalty: the fabric of rebellion was overthrown by the stroke of conspiracy, or undermined by the silent arts of intrigue: the favourites of the soldiers or people, of the senate or clergy, of the women and eunuchs, were alternately clothed with the purple: the means of their elevation were base, and their end was often contemptible or tragic. A being of the nature of man, endowed with the same faculties, but with a longer measure of existence, would cast down a smile of pity and contempt on the crimes and follies of human ambition, so eager, in a narrow span, to grasp at a precarious and short-lived enjoyment. It is thus that the experience of history exalts and enlarges the horizon of our intellectual view. In a composition of some days, in a perusal of some hours, six hundred years have rolled away, and the duration of a life or reign is contracted to a fleeting moment: the grave is ever beside the throne; the success of a crimi-

nal is almost instantly followed by the loss of his prize; and our immortal reason survives and disdains the sixty phantoms of kings who have passed before our eyes, and faintly dwell on our remembrance.[38]

Perhaps it was not only vanity, as his enemies charged, that made Gibbon feel pleased that a prince of Prussia or a natural son of the Empress of Russia had come to Lausanne to see him and had treated him with deference and respect.[39] In the honor paid them by the great, both he and Voltaire, who held an even more distinguished court at Ferney, may well have thought they could discern the outlines of a rival order to the order imposed on the world by the great and the powerful — an order that could subsist without either the ideological foundation of transcendent origins or the material support of armies.

If the act of reading the *Decline and Fall* in itself places the reader in an ironical position with respect to the heroes and masters of the world and their glorious *gesta*, the persona of the narrator proposes the concrete model, which the reader is hardly free to reject, of a detached philosophical observer. No hero is more fully developed in Gibbon's history than the persona of the narrator himself, no character approaches the narrator as a model for the reader. Historical figures, good and bad, admirable or contemptible — and even the best are found wanting in some respect — come and go in the thousands of pages of Gibbon's epic narrative, but the historian himself is a constant presence. On almost every page, in the text or in the footnotes, he makes his appearance to address the reader, to discuss sources with him, to evaluate conflicting evidence, to comment on or offer a judgment of the events and personages of the narrative. With his quiet assurance, his temperate decisions, his wise caution, his dispassionate good sense, and his polite wit, he dominates the shifting scene and is the single stable feature in a world given over to change, the principal unifying element in a text that embraces countless episodes only loosely held together by chronology and theme.

Gibbon's narrator is no merely formal figure reducible to his function as storyteller. In the course of his frequent interventions he presents himself to the reader with well-defined traits of character and intellect. He defines himself as a "modern historian" committed to the principles of historical criticism elaborated by the generation of Pierre Bayle,[40] as "prudent," "judicious," "candid," "accurate," "impartial," as "attached to no party, interested only for the truth and candour of history, and directed by the most temperate and skilful guides" – in sum, as "a philosopher."[41] Since he "views . . . with an impartial eye" and exercises "the impartial severity of modern criticism,"[42] he is zealous for no party, not even that of reason, and is not blinded in his evaluation of historical testimony by "the zeal of the philosophic historian for the rights of mankind."[43] Philosophy is not, for him, a cause; it is not a party. On the contrary, as wisdom lies between the extremes,[44] philosophy is the middle term between belief and incredulity.[45] It is a critical, skeptical temper,[46] always free of partisan passion. The philosopher scrutinizes everything, including his own principles and prejudices, "with *calm* suspicion,"[47] even if he can do no more than establish an ironical distance from them.[48] Though he sometimes presents himself, in characteristic Enlightenment fashion, as a "stranger,"[49] thus ensuring his standing among his more urbane and critical readers, the prudent "historian of the Roman empire,"[50] just as he is neither incredulous nor believing, is neither a pure cosmopolitan nor a zealous patriot. He accepts his own historicity and announces clearly that he is British; but this historical attachment is acknowledged with urbanity and courtesy, as though to reassure the reader that, although he cannot and would not wish to repudiate it, he cannot be blinded by it. The Germans, he confesses at one point, "possess a stronger, and, if we may use the expression, a more domestic claim to our attention and regard" than the Scythians;[51] likewise mention of the Saxons prompts the comment that it is a "name in which we have a dear and domestic interest";[52] but if he excuses the pages devoted to the British Isles after the departure of the Romans on the grounds that "an Englishman may curiously trace the establishment of the barbarians from whom he derives his name, his laws, and perhaps his origin," the motives of the Englishman are complemented by those of the "historian of the empire," who "may be tempted to pursue the revolutions of a Roman province till it vanishes from his sight."[53] In sum, if "it is the duty of a patriot to prefer and promote the exclusive interest and glory of his native country; . . . a philosopher may be permitted to enlarge his views, and to consider Europe as one great republic, whose various inhabitants have attained almost the same level of politeness and cultivation."[54]

As he steers a middle course between incredulity and belief, between the zeal of the patriot and the indifference of the fanatical *philosophe*, the historian also establishes himself in a middle ground between erudition, antiquarianism, or mere chronicle, on the one hand, and rhetorical history, based on imitation of the ancients, on the other, between scholarly investigation of traditions, institutions, or topographical problems, and narrative history.[55] He is still close enough to the rhetorical tradition to be able, for instance, to borrow a battle scene found in an ancient historian and apply it with equanimity to a completely different battle in his own narrative.[56] Obviously the battle scene, for Gibbon, is still a "set piece," a rhetorical exercise rather than a scholarly reconstruction. On the other hand, unlike some contemporary historians who made a point of denigrating erudition, he is not only immensely learned, but proud of it, displaying his vast reading copiously and acknowledging with satisfaction his debt not only to ancient sources, but also to recent scholars such as Tillemont or d'Herbelot.[57] In addition to a narrative, the *Decline and Fall* is a vast essay in critical bibliography, and the numerous discussions both of sources and of modern historical writings were no doubt intended to reassure the reader that his urbane and elegant guide to the history of Rome was as well informed as the most industrious antiquarian. Without adopting either the manner or the narrow objectives of a pedant, Gibbon was in a position to take fellow historians to task for faulty scholarship. Voltaire, Mably, Montesquieu and Robertson, for instance, had been too quick to crown Charlemagne "with the praises of the historians and the philosophers of an enlightened age" and had failed to study the historical materials as thoroughly as they should – not only the agreeable writings of modern historians (and Gibbon can show how carefully he keeps abreast of contemporary historiography by citing Gaillard's *Histoire de Charlemagne* of 1782, a work "laboured with industry and elegance" by "a man of sense and humanity"), but the less enjoyable "original monuments of the reigns of Pepin and Charlemagne in the fifth volume of the Historians of France."[58]

It is not enough, in short, to write well or with good sense. At various points in the narrative Gibbon intervenes to distinguish with care between history and romance and to insist that rhetoric alone will not make a historian. At the same time, there is no question of rejecting art altogether, as the "honest Tillemont" did. It is characteristic that in an essay on the Latin historians Gibbon identifies "style," along with "facts" and "reflections," as an essential component of the historical text.[59] Like Voltaire, he is convinced that, properly handled, modern historical writing is destined to take the place of classical epic.[60] "A plain narrative of facts," he assures, can turn out to be "more pathetic than the most laboured descriptions of the epic poets."[61]

Gibbon's criticism is thus not pedantic: It is that of a philosopher, a connoisseur of literature, an observer of human nature. The historian of the *Decline and Fall* does not grovel in the minutiae of erudition, nor, however, does he ignore or reject them. He includes them and at the same time claims to rise above them. Moreover, his position as both judge and utilizer of all that was done before him establishes both his familiarity with the work of his predecessors and his superiority to it. The antiquarian, the compiler, and the annalist remain inferior species that exercise themselves on detail and are incapable of selection, order, and the large overview.[62] D'Herbelot's *Bibliothèque orientale*, for instance, "is an agreeable miscellany ... but I never can digest the alphabetical order."[63] Even the historian's generous acknowledgement of his indebtedness to modern orientalists, on account of his ignorance of Arabic, is tinged by satisfaction at being able to reassure the reader that in erudition too he has avoided excess and remains an urbane man of the world and thus an appropriate mentor and friend.[64]

The maintenance of a relation of compatibility and confidence between himself and the reader is, indeed, an essential concern of the historian throughout the *Decline and Fall*. In the Autobiography Gibbon tells that he disliked polemical or adversary situations: "I should shrink with terror from the modern history of England, where every character is a problem, and every reader a friend or an enemy."[65] The historian, in Gibbon's conception of him, must win the reader's trust in his honesty, his reliability, his good sense, his commitment to common values; and he must make the reader feel that trust will never be abused. Much effort is expended on reassuring the reader of the narrator's scrupulous regard for truth and his repudiation of every temptation to use the power of language and imagination for purposes of manipulation. As we saw, the historian continually weighs the evidence before the reader's eyes, as though to show him all his cards, whether this activity is relegated to asides in the footnotes or is allowed to interrupt the narrative flow itself.[66] At the same time, he continues to consider it his duty to provide an absorbing narrative.[67] In other words, his concern for the reader is such that he wishes at the same time to entertain and please him, and to reveal his hand to him, so that the reader will be a kind of partner rather than a victim or object of manipulation. The reader is ideally neither a master commanding his servant, the narrator, to entertain him, nor, in contrast, the dupe of the servant's wiles. Gibbon's aim is, as it so often is, to avoid radical oppositions by adopting a rhetoric in which writer and reader will stand – or at least will seem to stand – to each other not as master and servant in a relation of competition and conflict, but as partners in a relation of complicity, albeit one whose rules are laid down by the writer. In Gibbon's own life these two stances can perhaps be associated with parliamentary oratory, which he shrank from engaging in, and salon conversation, at which he excelled.

The reader of the *Decline and Fall* is presented in the text – and this is therefore the role that the actual reader is invited to fill – as the mirror image of the narrator. Like the latter, he is "prudent," "judicious," "philosophical," "curious."[68] The reader of history, like the writer of it, is preeminently someone who would subscribe to the principle put forward in Chapter XV, that "the acquisition of knowledge, the exercise of our reason or fancy, and the cheerful flow of unguarded conversation, may employ the leisure of a liberal mind."[69] And it is to him that the historian appeals indirectly when he declares of this or that "idle and extravagent opinion" that it "was rejected with contempt by every man of a liberal education and understanding,"[70] or recounts of the Christians, for instance, that they "exacted an implicit submission to their mysterious doctrines, without being able to produce a single argument that could engage the attention of men of sense and learning."[71] Men "of a liberal education and understanding," "men of sense and learning," "men of wit and learning,"[72] such are the historian and his reader alike. The "we" that so often occurs in the text is not only a grammatical variant of the equally common "I"; it embraces the "patient reader" for whose well-being the historian throughout expresses his concern.

Gibbon's discovery of a void at the heart of the world order does not imply, for him, that order will or should collapse or that absolute freedom will or should replace absolute authority. Indeed, he is careful to set up guardrails against the vertigo of liberty. If signification is not an unproblematic, two-term relation between a sign and a referent, the relation between the two aspects of the sign itself – the signifier and the signified – is not a necessary or natural one either. Traditionally however – and especially in conservative cultures – it is considered paramount that this relation be controlled, since communication and social order are seen to depend on its strict regulation. Deviation within recognized limits is tolerated as "connotation," but it is rejected unhesitatingly as "nonsense" or "madness" when it becomes "excessive." Perhaps it is only in our own time that a resolute effort has been made to throw over all such constraints, along with other instrumentalities of "oppression" and "authority," in the name of the "liberation of the signifier." It would be very surprising if Gibbon, with his horror of democracy, his elaborate deference, and his great need of control and decorum, had ever dreamed of such a state of linguistic democracy. On the contrary, the maintenance of communication and social order among those admitted to the insight that there may be no prior objective foundation for the meanings men make is a matter of great concern to him. The whole thrust of his ironical discourse is to force the reader's effective compliance with his language and his system of meanings and values[73] and at the same time to make him feel that this compliance was freely granted and to give him the impression that there are only two possible meanings – the one controlled by the code of the uninitiated multitude, the other controlled by the code of the initiated, the people of "liberal education and understanding." It is thus not the order of society (or of communication) itself that Gibbon seeks to loosen; it is only, for the initiated, the idea that it is based on a transcendental reality. Among the enlightened – the narrator and his reader – who are party to the "dangerous secret"[74] that authority is not naturally continuous with a sacred origin, order and communication will be effectively secured, he appears to hold, by recognition and acceptance of the pure sign character of authority. As for the others, their beliefs and superstitions, being useful, are best left undisturbed. The community constituted by Gibbon and his readers can thus be thought of as mediating between a rigidly stable world in which signs cleave to the things they signify and are virtually one with them, so that order and communication rest on the belief that they are rooted in nature or the will of the gods, and no disagreement or diversity of opinion is possible (the ideal of the Roman Republic or small city-state), and an unregulated world of infinite interpretation, in which the arbitrariness of the link between the signifier and the signified itself has been exposed (the anarchy of democracy in a large and diverse state). It is a kind of constitutional monarchy in which, though the sign has been detached from any necessary link to the thing it signifies, there is still no complete disjunction of signifier and signified; in which authority, in sum, rests on a tacit common agreement to accept it, and the pleasures of freedom and the privacy of persons are reconciled, for a few, with the benefits of order and the public weal.

5

Order and perspicuity

GIBBON'S DESIRE TO AVOID the extremes of pure narrative and pure dissertation – that is, of the text that is too concerned with the reader and, in its eagerness to please him, also treats him as an object of manipulation, and of the text that is not concerned with him enough and manifests its disregard of him by depriving him of his pleasure – creates a number of compositional problems for him. Characteristically, the discussion of these problems occupies many pages and actually contributes to producing the desired relation with the reader. As the narrator reaffirms his respect for the reader and his acknowledgment of the latter's justified expectations,[1] he also points out that he is prevented on occasion, by the very respect he owes the reader, from pleasing him as he would like. It is his refusal to be anything other than absolutely openhanded with his reader, he explains, that forces him to sacrifice the even flow of the narrative, which he knows his reader would like and which he would like to be able to offer him: "We might content ourselves with relating this extraordinary transaction, but we cannot dissemble how much, in its present form, it appears to us inconsistent and incredible."[2]

In another instance, the narrator interrupts his account of the progress of Christianity in the Empire to tell the reader that he cannot, unfortunately, hope for a simple, straightforward account: "The number of its proselytes has been excessively magnified by fear on the one side, and by devotion on the other . . . ; as we are left without any distinct information, it is impossible to determine, and it is difficult even to conjecture, the real numbers of the primitive Christians."[3] Even where the narrative flow of the upper part of the text is preserved, the reader may be warned in a footnote below that the apparently sure account rests on conjectures: "I owe it to myself and to historic truth to declare that some *circumstances* in this paragraph are founded only on conjecture and analogy. The stubbornness of our language has sometimes forced me to deviate from the *conditional* into the *indicative* mood."[4] The reader can hardly harbor ill will toward a storyteller who takes him unreservedly into his confidence and refuses to delude him, even if it sometimes means depriving himself of the satisfaction of presenting a picturesque and entertaining story:

> I have purposely refrained from describing the particular sufferings and deaths of the Christian martyrs. It would have been an easy task, from the history of Eusebius, from the declamations of Lactantius, and from the most ancient acts, to collect a long series of horrid and disgusting pictures, and to fill many pages with racks and scourges, with iron hooks and red-hot beds, and with all the variety of tortures which fire and steel, savage beasts and more savage executioners, could inflict on the human body. These melancholy scenes might be enlivened by a crowd of visions and miracles destined either to delay the death, to celebrate the triumph, or to discover the relics of those canonised saints who suffered for the name of Christ. But I cannot determine what I ought to transcribe, till I am satisfied how much I ought to believe.[5]

The uncertainties and the lacunae of the historical record are not the only obstacles in the narrator's path. Sometimes it is difficult to find any significance in the information we do possess and to give it the form of a coherent action. At such moments, history may seem to mark time: Battles are fought, towns besieged "with various and doubtful success"; neither one side nor another gains a decisive victory in the course of "campaigns that were not productive of any decisive or memorable events."[6]

Nevertheless, the historian's aim remains to provide the reader with a coherent and intelligible account of the history of the Roman Empire – of its "decline and fall." The discovery of the obscurities of history and of the obstacles to our understanding of it only enhances the desire for "order and perspicuity," which Gibbon gives again and again as the aim of all his labor as an historian,[7] and the search for order and perspicuity in history is indistinguishable for him from the search for an orderly and perspicuous narrative. To be intelligible to the reader, an event or a character, whether historical or fictional, must be part of a story. The rules and conventions of classical narrative are thus, for Gibbon, the rules of historical composition. The historian agrees with Richard Hurd that "[epic] poetry is an imitation of history," from which it deviates only "for the sake of making the fable one, connected, marvellous, heroic, and answering to our notions of justice." But ordering of the narrative is common both to the imitation of history in epic verse and to that which is carried out in the "plain narrative" preferred by Gibbon. A proper relation of parts to whole, the subordination of each episodic element to the point where it is "proportionate with its importance and degree of connexion with the principal subject," is also, according to Gibbon, "the rule of history."[8] He invokes it as the guiding principle of his own work. Faced, in Chapter XLVIII, with a vast, shapeless mass of materials for the history of the Byzantine empire, he is determined that "this scope of narrative, the riches and variety of these materials" will not be "incompatible with the unity of design and composition." The central theme will be the history of Constantinople itself, and all the rest will be arranged as subordinate episodes. "The excursive line may embrace the wilds of Arabia and Tartary", but "the historian's eye shall always be fixed on the city of Constantinople."[9] It is, in short, the order and continuity of classical narrative itself – obstructed by both the chaotic abundance and the scarcity of the historical record – that guide the historian in the weaving of his history: "The confusion of the times, and the scarcity of authentic materials, oppose equal difficulties to the historian, who attempts to preserve a clear and unbroken thread of narration. Surrounded with imperfect fragments, always concise, often obscure, and sometimes contradictory, he is reduced to collect, to compare, and to conjecture."[10]

What is given as the "design" of Chapter XVI, on the attitude of the Roman government to the Christians – "to separate (if it be possible) a few authentic as well as interesting facts from an undigested mass of fiction and error, and to relate, in a clear and rational manner, the causes, the extent, the duration, and the most important circumstances of the persecutions to which the first Christians were exposed"[11] – can be taken *mutatis mutandis* as the design of the entire History. It is for the sake of the "order and perspicuity" of the narrative and in order not "to oppress the memory and perplex the attention of the reader"[12] that the historian carries out a rigorous selection among the chaotic and obscure materials that press upon him.[13] His task is to spare the reader the labor of searching for order in the abundance of individual phenomena by selecting for him only those that have already been identified as having significant consequences and that can acquire meaning from their place in a chain; for "the tedious detail of leaves without flowers and of branches without fruit, would soon exhaust the patience and disappoint the curiosity of the laborious student."[14] The "tedious repetition," he declares in another place, that would be the consequence of a series of histories of individual towns or families, "would fatigue the attention of the most patient reader."[15] This tedium of the mere unconnected particular is the enemy the historian must continually combat in order to secure for the reader the order and perspicuity, the intellectual and esthetic well-being, that are the principal object of his reading. Writing of "the tedious negotiations that succeeded the synod of Ephesus" and that "are diffusely related in the original Acts . . . ," the historian is confident that "the most patient reader will thank me for compressing so much non-sense and falsehood in a few lines."[16]

The goal of "order and perspicuity" imposes other compositional choices that the writer discusses freely with his reader. At the beginning of Chapter XLVIII, for instance, he explains that with the disintegration of the Empire his own narrative is also in danger of disintegrating into formlessness – in itself an arresting suggestion that there may be a relation between political order and the order of narrative. Unless he alters the tempo and the degree of detail, he declares, the reader, instead of being enlightened and entertained, will be uncomfortably confused and mystified:

> Should I persevere in the same course, should I observe the same measure, a prolix and slender thread would be spun through many a volume, nor would the patient reader find an adequate reward of instruction or amusement. At every step as we sink deeper into the decline and fall of the Eastern empire, the annals of each succeeding reign would impose a more ungrateful and melancholy task. These annals must continue to repeat a tedious and uniform tale of weakness and misery; the natural connection of causes and events would be broken by frequent and hasty transitions, and a minute accumulation of circumstances must destroy the light and effect of those pictures which compose the use and ornament of a remote history. From the time of Heraclius the Byzantine theatre is contracted and darkened: the line of empire, which had been defined by the laws of Justinian and the arms of Belisarius, recedes on all sides from our view. . . .[17]

In Chapter XVII it is the interruption of the narrative flow by a lengthy account of Roman law that the narrator feels constrained to justify to his reader:

> This variety of objects will suspend, for some time, the course of the narrative; but the interruption will be censured only by those readers who are insensible to the importance of laws and manners, while they peruse, with eager curiosity, the transient intrigues of a court, or the accidental event of a battle.[18]

In this characteristic passage the historian at once defers to the reader and prescribes his role. Clearly, the role the reader is called upon and indeed obliged to play, if he continues to read, is that of the writer's double – a person of moderation and multiple sympathies, sensitive to the (feminine) pleasure that narrative procures, yet also capable of the more sober (masculine) satisfactions of reflection and understanding.

Most frequently the historian intervenes to explain that "order and perspicuity" require that he play a more active role in the construction of the narrative than that of a humble annalist:

> As the Roman empire was at the same time and on every side, attacked by the blind fury of foreign invaders, and the wild ambition of domestic usurpers, we shall consult order and perspicuity by pursuing not so much the doubtful arrangement of dates as the more natural disposition of subjects.[19]

Later, at the beginning of Chapter XVII, the age of Constantine and his sons is said to be "filled with important events; but the historian must be oppressed by their number and variety, unless he diligently separates from each other the scenes which are connected only by the order of time. He will describe the political institutions that gave strength and stability to the empire before he proceeds to relate the wars and revolutions which hastened its decline."[20]

"Order and perspicuity" are not, in short, immediately perceived; they are not given in the material, but proposed by the reason that contemplates and evaluates the material. Another favorite phrase of Gibbon's – "clear and rational"[21] – confirms the intimate connection of order, clarity, and reason. Whereas the early nineteenth-century historian claimed to find reason *in* history and for this reason aimed to reduce his own presence in his text to a minimum so that history might appear to speak, as it were, out of its own mouth, the eighteenth-century historian finds himself in front of a world that remains essentially foreign and obscure to him but that he cannot help trying to render intelligible. "Il faut cultiver notre jardin," in Voltaire's famous phrase. Unlike his nineteenth-century successor, he does not lay his ear piously to history, attempting to hear its muffled voices and to decipher its secret or lost languages. His is not an art of divination, but a combination of criticism and rhetoric, an art of analysis, conjecture, and composition. The historian is not the mouthpiece, the priest, or the minister of history: He takes pride in his own compositions. "Perhaps the Arabs might not find in a single historian," Gibbon claims, "so clear and comprehensive a narrative of their own exploits as that which will be deduced in the ensuing sheets."[22] History writing for Gibbon is literally Enlightenment – a constant struggle to extend the light of reason and understanding and to reduce the domain of chaos and obscurity by establishing the smoothness of continuity and connection in the place of fragmentariness and absurdity. The historian Mascou, for instance, is praised for having illuminated the "dark and doubtful" retreat of the Goths from Italy and "illustrated and connected the broken chronicles and fragments of the times."[23] Like the work of civilization in general, the historian's work can never be completed. Some obscurities are obdurate, some ruptures cannot be sealed. "It is impossible," the historian has to confess, "to fill the dark interval of time which elapsed after the Huns of the Volga were lost in the eyes of the Chinese, and before they showed themselves to the Romans."[24] The aim of historiography, however, is to sew together into a harmonious and extensive design as many of the pieces and patches of the historical record as possible, or, to borrow an image from Gibbon himself, to make a "tesselated pavement" from the fragmentary records and testimonies of the past.[25]

As enlightenment is a continuous process, the historian does not simply give the reader the end product of his reflection but tries to make him to some extent party to the work itself, to its difficulties and choices. In the end, moreover, enlightenment concerns the mind more than it concerns the world outside the mind. It is in our minds – the mind of the historian and the mind of his reader – that obscurities are to be illuminated and fragments (which, by definition, are absurd and irrational) woven together into a connected, coherent, and rational whole. The desire to hold this created order together, to shore it up against the perpetual danger of disintegration, accounts for the great frequency in the *Decline and Fall* of the narrator's interventions to outline what he is about to do, to recapitulate what he has done, and to enumerate or tabulate, usually under Roman-numeral headings, the points to be made or the points just made.[26]

The eighteenth-century historian's acceptance of his own role in the creation of history – in the sense not of events themselves but of the consciousness of them – and above all, in the creation of "order and perspicuity," makes his relation to his rhetoric a very different one from that of the early Romantic historian. Conceiving himself as a mediator or seer, the latter could not have a comfortable relation to the rhetoric that patterns his narrative – and Romantic historians do, despite their repudiation of them, make extensive use of traditional rhetorical devices such as parallelism, antithesis, and alliteration. To the Enlightenment historian, on the other hand, the order of rhetoric was an essential instrument in man's – and in his own – general ordering activity. He had no reason to wish to conceal it. On the contrary, it carried his message very effectively: the human language by which historical phenomena were grasped, appropriated, and transformed, was a highly and evidently ordered and patterned one. Order and perspicuity in Gibbon's text are found not only at long range in the structure of the narrative, but at close range too in the patterning of words, sentences, and paragraphs. Though history may resemble a wilderness, being "little more than the register of the crimes, follies, and misfortunes of mankind,"[27] the historiographical text is a garden of patterned and smoothly flowing discourse. The immense sense of accomplishment, of order, balance, and control that the *Decline and Fall* conveyed and still conveys to its readers, the sense of a veritable conquest of the amorphous and the undefined and of a triumphant achievement of definition, is due in no small measure, as every critic has acknowledged, to the architecture of Gibbon's prose.[28]

Gibbon uses all the devices of classical rhetoric, but the inescapable impression of order and control seems principally due to the pervasiveness of abstraction and various forms of parallelism. Examples of alliteration – in initial, medial, and final positions – and of rhythmic parallelism are found on every page:

of the *d*útiĕs   and
of the *d*ángĕrs   of the supreme rank[29]

the *pl*eásures of *s*énse
the *pŏl*ýgămў ŏf the *p*átrĭărchs
the *s*ĕráglĭŏ   of *S*ólŏmŏn[30]

the *pr*ŏmótĭŏn of those who had *p*úrchăsed at their hands the *p*ówĕrs of ŏ*pp*réssĭŏn[31]

those whŏ   *r*ĕfúse   the *s*wórd
     mŭst   *r*ĕnoúnce   the *s*céptre[32]

i*ñ*s*p*íre   the love   of vírtŭe or
*r*ĕstráin   the im*p*etuosity of *p*ássĭŏn[33]

the *bl*eak and *barr*en   hills   of Scythia and
      the *fr*ozen   *ban*ks   of the E*lb*e and Danu*be*[34]

the dangerous secret of the *w*ealth and *w*eakness of the empire[35]

a *pu*ny *st*ature and a *pus*illanimous *sp*irit[36]

*s*oure*d* by *s*olitu*d*e[37]

the *d*ark and *d*oubtful me*d*ium of a translation[38]

*s*upernatural or *s*ordid motives[39]

the *p*ains and *p*enalties of the The*od*osian co*d*e[40]

acting the part of a *m*usician or a *m*onarch[41]

the *s*ense, or rather the *s*ound, of a *s*yllable, was *s*ufficient to di*st*urb
the pea*c*e of an empire[42]

We know that the way his text sounded was extremely important to Gibbon, and many of the sound patterns in the *Decline and Fall* are in fact more intricate than the forms of alliteration quoted above. The following passage makes use of both submerged and suspended alliteration and is bound together by the repetition and interweaving of *f, i, o, p, r, s,* and *t* in various combinations (*pr, rt, st, sti, sit, ro, or, ri, ir*); there is, in addition, as in the passages cited, some use of assonance (vo*w*s; b*ou*nds; p*ow*ers; f*ou*ndations; s*a*cred; h*ai*l; hum*a*ne; Saturn*a*lia):

> Some of the most sacred festivals in the Roman ritual were destined to salute the new calends of January with vows of public and private felicity; to indulge the pious remembrance of the dead and living; to ascertain the inviolable bounds of property; to hail, on the return of spring, the genial powers of fecundity; to perpetuate the two memorable eras of Rome, the foundation of the city and that of the republic; and to restore, during the humane licence of the Saturnalia, the primitive equality of mankind.[43]

Assonance and rhythmic repetition, along with alliteration, are again prominent in the following short passage, selected from among many similar ones:

> as that feeble prince was destitute of personal merit either in peace or war;
> as he feared his generals and distrusted his ministers . . .[44]

Repetition at the phonemic level (alliteration and assonance) is, of course, frequently an accompaniment of repetition at the syntactical level (parallelism), as almost all the examples already cited clearly show. It must be emphasized that such passages are not exceptional, but are the basic material of Gibbon's prose. Syntactical parallelism is everywhere, usually reinforced by some alliteration, assonance, or rhythmic repetition:

If the eyes	of the spectators	have sometimes been deceived by *f*raud,
the under-	of the readers	has much more been insulted by *f*iction[45]
standing		frequently

it was the well-earned harvest of *many* a *l*earned *c*onference,
of *many* a *p*atient *l*e*c*ture,
and *many* a *m*idnight *l*u*c*ubra*t*ion.[46]

Gibbon also makes much use of antithesis, a special form of parallelism, the effect of which is to set boundaries to the knowable and to reinforce the sense of orderliness by defining symmetrically opposite extreme limits. Again examples are found on every page, and may take the form of short phrases ("he had deliberated with caution, he acted with vigour"; "a chief who had learned to obey, and who was worthy to command"[47]) or extended paragraphs.

While parallelism may sometimes serve to create a semantic association between otherwise unrelated terms occupying the same syntactical or rhythmic position in each member of the parallel – as, for instance, between *idle* and *saints* in "Constantine too easily believed that he should purchase the favour of Heaven if he maintained the idle at the expense of the industrious, and distributed among the saints the wealth of the republic"[48] – in most cases, accompanied or unaccompanied by alliteration, it is the form itself that carries significance, reassuring the reader that order has prevailed over chaos, repetition over randomness, and the general over the particular, though the particular is in no case completely abolished by the general. Every repetition in the passages quoted also includes a variation.[49]

It might be objected that as a "philosophical" historian Gibbon is interested in determining general laws of history, and that these, rather than narrative, furnish the true order of history in general for him and of the *Decline and Fall* in particular. Gibbon does write, it is true, of general laws in history. A passage in the early *Essai sur l'étude de la littérature* (1761) is often quoted: "L'histoire est pour un esprit philosophique ce qu'était le jeu pour le marquis de Dangeau. Il voyoit un système, des rapports, une suite, là, ou d'autres ne discernoient que les caprices de la fortune."[50] Clearly, this passage does not mean that history derives its meaning and its order, as it did to a considerable extent for many nineteenth-century writers, from a divine providence working through it, so that reading and deciphering history are almost identical with reading and deciphering the mind and intentions of God – the basis of the sacerdotalism of the historian in the nineteenth century. It means no more than that retrospectively it is possible to discover regularities in what to contemporaries or to unphilosophical minds may seem like pure caprice. The point is made again later, at the close of Chapter XXVII of the *Decline and Fall*: "There are few observers who possess a clear and comprehensive view of the revolutions of society, and who are capable of discovering the nice and secret springs of action which impel, in the same uniform direction, the blind and capricious passions of a multitude of individuals."[51]

Yet Gibbon remains cautious, even skeptical, in the matter of theories and general laws of history, and he contrasts his own prudence with the "ingenious, though somewhat fanciful" contentions of Montesquieu,[52] whom he appears to enjoy faulting on points of fact as though to compensate for the praise accorded him as a generalizer and theorist. Such general laws as are formulated in the *Decline and Fall* have very little of the systematic character of Montesquieu's. In most cases they are no more than the kind of generalization – ranging from the commonplace or the proverbial phrase to the more sophisticated form of the maxim – that has traditionally served not only historians but also novelists as a means of explaining or "motivating" narrative action.[53] Some of these generalizations concern human nature or human behavior:

> It is always easy, as well as agreeable, for the inferior ranks of mankind to claim a merit from the contempt of that pomp and pleasure which fortune has placed beyond their reach.[54]

> The lower ranks of society are governed by imitation . . . [55]

> The timid are always cruel . . . [56]

> Honorarius was without passions, and *consequently* without talents . . . [57]

> It was natural enough that Genseric should hate those whom he had injured . . . [58]

Other are maxims of conventional political or economic wisdom:

> The use of the dagger is seldom adopted in public councils, as long as they retain any confidence in the power of the sword.[59]

> A difference of religion is always pernicious and often fatal to the harmony of the prince and people . . . [60]

> Agriculture is the foundation of manufactures; since the productions of nature are the materials of art.[61]

> Most of the crimes which disturb the internal peace of society are produced by the restraints which the necessary, but unequal, laws

of property have imposed on the appetites of mankind, by confining to a few the possession of those objects that are coveted by many.[62]

Famine is almost always followed by epidemical diseases . . . [63]

Such is the condition of civil society, that, whilst a few persons are distinguished by riches, by honours, and by knowledge, the body of the people is condemned to obscurity, ignorance, and poverty.[64]

it is easier to destroy than to restore.[65]

how much swifter is the progress of corruption than its cure . . . [66]

Sometimes, again, the generalization is essentially a familiar proverb. "Pride comes before a fall" appears in fancier garb as "rash presumption . . . is the forerunner of disgrace."[67]
Typically the maxim is built into the sentence structure as explanation or anticipation:

[Gildo] proudly reviewed an army of seventy thousand men, and boasted, with the rash presumption which is the forerunner of disgrace, that his numerous cavalry would trample under their horses' feet the troops of Mascezel.[68]

Such presumption was the natural cause of a shameful defeat.[69]

As the timid are always cruel, the mind of Constantius was inaccessible to mercy.[70]

In general, an implied law or regularity will often be found underlying the simplest statement, even where the law is not formulated as such. To the extent that it says more than "many merchants came to the country," the statement that "a country possessed of so many valuable objects of exchange soon attracted the merchants of the world"[71] is a condensed syllogism: Riches attract merchants; Istria was rich; Istria attracted merchants.

Gibbon's "laws" are thus not much more than the conventional wisdom of his time about human behavior, politics, economics, the order of the world. They are not discovered through reflection on history, as Montesquieu's were, and they are not intended to constitute a system. They are discontinuous items prior to the narrative that they serve only to "motivate." Montesquieu's goal, in short, was the constitution of a science of society, Gibbon's was to write a historical narrative of particular events. The order Montesquieu sought lay in a systematic set of laws of social and

political organization; indeed, he seems deliberately to avoid the order of
narrative. Even the Roman history is highly fragmented and is pointedly
entitled "*Considérations sur* les causes de la grandeur des Romains et de leur
décadence." The order Gibbon finds in history, on the other hand, is prescribed first and foremost by the order of narrative itself. The historian
nods respectfully in the direction of Montesquieu and the idea that fortune
is only a term for what we have not yet succeeded in reducing to law;
nevertheless, he seems less than fully committed to the eventual victory of
"science" over "fortune." Fortune is questioned but also affirmed, and Gibbon appears to hold that although general laws may prescribe the main
lines of development in history or lay down the general conditions within
which individual actions may occur, they cannot account for actual individual cases – rather as in our own time the science of linguistics describes
the conditions of meaningful utterance in any given language but does not
account for any specific utterance or *parole*:

> Such is the empire of Fortune (if we may still disguise our igno-
> rance under that popular name), that it is almost equally difficult
> to foresee the events of war, or to explain their various conse-
> quences. A bloody and complete victory has sometimes yielded no
> more than possession of the field; and the loss of ten thousand
> men has sometimes been sufficient to destroy, in a single day, the
> work of ages.[72]

Gibbon remains characteristically unable or unwilling to resolve, in favor
of either term, the dichotomy of the general and the particular, method
and observation, or, as Diderot put it, reporting a delightful fable told by
the abbé Galiani, "the cuckoo and the nightingale."[73] Order and perspicuity, for him and for his readers, are always in tension with the disorder and
obscurity of the particular, the fragmentary, and the merely episodic, and it
is the act of ordering, not the mere fact of order, that is the source of the
reader's satisfaction. The particular, the fragmentary, and the episodic must
therefore be preserved, even as they are contained within a framework of
order. For Gibbon, it seems, narrative mediates more effectively than scientific generalization between the two demands of intelligibility on the one
hand, and concreteness or openness to experience on the other. Not surprisingly, therefore, the narrator's affirmation that "order and perspicuity"
are the goals of the historian's activity is complemented by many references
to the narrative artist's need to reconcile in his work the two requirements
of "consistency" and "interest."
Unlike the author of romances, the historian, according to Gibbon, does

not invent stories: He forms his own narrative, like a mosaic or "tesselated pavement," by judiciously collating existing narratives:

> The writer who aspires to the name of historian, is obliged to consult a variety of original testimonies, each of which, taken separately, is perhaps imperfect or partial. By a judicious reunion and arrangement of these dispersed materials, he endeavours to form a consistent and interesting narrative. Nothing ought to be inserted which is not proved by some of the witnesses; but their evidence must be so intimately blended together, that it is reasonable to expect that each of them should vouch for the whole, so it would be impossible to define the boundaries of their respective property.[74]

The historical narrative, in other words, should conform with the rules of historiographical writing, which require that in history and in epic, as distinct from "romance," the elements of the fable, though not necessarily its total composition, be borrowed from or substantiated by a previous story or by previous stories generally held to be "true" in the case of epic, and validated by historical criticism in the case of history. The historian's own narrative is a means of ordering these items or fragments of narrative and welding them into a coherent whole, while at the same time respecting the individuality of each.

The two principles of "consistency" and "interest," which Gibbon identifies as those that should guide the historian in the construction of the historical narrative, are, however, not peculiar to history. They are those of classical narrative in general. Each is as necessary to the other as the *utile* and the *dulce* – "instruction and amusement," in Gibbon's words[75] – are necessary to each other in neoclassical poetic doctrine, "form" and "life" in the esthetics of Schiller, or, for that matter, the "normative" and the "functional" in some more recent writing on esthetics.[76] Consistency without interest ends in identity, or the elimination of the different elements among which consistency is to be found, and interest without consistency leads to absolute difference and consequently to unintelligibility and the elimination of interest. Consistency and interest, in short, must always be balanced against each other, and the tension between the two is the foundation of narrative. There can be no story without both consistency and interest.

Different writers or different ages may situate themselves closer to one pole than to another. It could be argued that chronicle, for instance, leaned more toward the pole of interest, while the historical narrative that emerged in the seventeenth and eighteenth centuries leaned toward the pole of consistency. The eighteenth-century novel, on the other hand, appears to have tried to place itself, like chronicle, nearer to the pole of interest. It is always a matter of emphasis, however, and any classical narrative will seek to satisfy the claims of both interest and consistency. Narrative form itself, in other words, is expected to resolve the dichotomy between the general and the particular, between the immobility of abstract order and the directionless mobility of concrete individuals. As the philosopher takes up his position neither wholly in the world nor wholly outside it, the philosophical historian places himself at a distance from both excess of information and dearth of information in order that his narrative may acquire form and intelligibility while avoiding arbitrariness and abstraction. "Let us read with method," Gibbon noted in 1761,

> and propose to ourselves an end to which all our studies may point. Through neglect of this rule, gross ignorance often disgraces great readers; who, by skipping hastily and irregularly from one subject to another, render themselves incapable of combining their ideas. So many detached parcels of knowledge cannot constitute a whole . . . Yet let us avoid the contrary extreme; and respect method, without rendering ourselves its slaves . . . Inconstancy weakens the understanding: a long or exclusive application to a single object hardens and contracts it.[77]

Gibbon's history is first and foremost an epic narrative – one that, like most such narratives, is a conglomerate of narratives strung onto a central sequence, which in the *Decline and Fall* is provided by the fate of the Empire. The emperors themselves, their wives, their children, their generals, their enemies, their enemies' wives, their enemies' children, their enemies' generals, and so on, are the heroes and heroines of innumerable subnarratives ranging in length from a few lines to a whole chapter and in most cases capable, in Gibbon's own words, of furnishing "the subject of a very entertaining romance"[78] or "a very singular subject for tragedy."[79] What they become, whether they are the product of an *amplificatio* or of an *abbreviatio*, depends largely on the total narrative design of the work. In the case of the *Decline and Fall* a close study of the narrative design would probably reveal a complex but orderly and balanced pattern similar to that of Gibbon's sentences and giving due weight to the twin principles of consistency (the central theme) and interest (the variations, digressive or "singular" stories verging on "romance"). Gibbon, as we saw, subscribed to the prevailing view of his age that a proper hierarchy among its elements was as essential to any narrative – historical or fictional – as a proper hierarchy among its elements was essential to a sentence or a state. Each episode, he declared in his commentary on Hurd's commentary on Horace, should be "proportionate with its importance and degree of connexion with the principal subject."

The art of the transition, of ensuring smooth passage from one narrative to another and motivating or justifying each subnarrative, is thus essential to the composition of the *Decline and Fall*. Characteristically, it is not, with Gibbon, an art of subterfuge. The joints or *charnières* are not concealed from the reader. On the contrary, they are often highlighted by metahistorical or metanarrative reflections – candid interventions by the narrator to win the reader's approval of his narrative practice. Almost invariably, narratives are introduced and justified on the ground that they are illustrative, be it of the character of a prince, of a situation, or of the human heart in general. Incidents, "however slight or simple," always "denote," in Gibbon's own words, something general.[80] "I should not be apprehensive of deviating from my subject," the narrator declares at one point, "if it were in my power to delineate the private life of the conquerors of Italy; and I shall relate with pleasure the adventurous galantry of Autharis, which breathes the true spirit of chivalry and romance."[81] The "exploits" of Manuel Comnenus I, despite their suspiciously legendary character – they "appear as a model or a copy of the romances of chivalry"[82] – deserve to be recounted, because they give an idea of the contemporary imagination and may tell us something about the emperor. Another set of adventures, considered more authentic, may be told because they concern a prominent member of the emperor's family, Andronicus Comnenus, "one of the most conspicuous characters of the age."[83] "The story of Paul of Samosata, who filled the metropolitan see of Antioch while the East was in the hands of Odenathus and Zenobia," is told because it "may serve to illustrate the condition and character of the times."[84] The "adventures" of Para, during the reign of Valens, illustrate the cynicism of the Roman government of the time and the decay of political morality.[85] The "spotless integrity" and "equal and inexorable justice" of Count Boniface, one of Valentinian's generals, are exemplified by an anecdote.[86] The persecution of the Carthaginians by the Vandal king Genseric is illustrated by two short tales of individual victims.[87] A story of adultery and revenge throws into relief the decline of morality under Valentinian and the debauchery of the emperor himself.[88] The account of an expedition by the Christian conquerors of Damascus "will equally display their avidity and their contempt for the riches of the present world,"[89] and a brief but striking anecdote recounting how a Moslem woman, during the seige of Damascus, buried her slain husband "without a groan, without a tear" and took up his arms to lead a successful attack against the Christians is justified as an illustration of the bravery, determination, and solidarity of the Syrians.[90] The appearance of any new character is almost invariably the occasion of a brief narrative of his life and one or more illustrative anecdotes.

In almost every case, however, the illustrative anecdote is also "singular," "striking and singular," or "singular and interesting," to use Gibbon's own expressions.[91] Amid the unrecorded evenness of repeated or routine events or actions, it stands out and was committed to memory because it was different or unusual. The modern historian picks it up and incorporates it in his own narrative not only because it throws light on the character of the age, but because, being unusual and different, it contributes to the interest of the work as much as it contributes to its consistency. Thus, while the anecdote may well convey some moral lesson or exemplify some vice or virtue, as Gibbon takes care to point out,[92] it is also, paradoxically, an account of a picturesque and unusual occurrence in which some human passion or energy is pushed to such an extreme that current norms of behavior are exceeded and the familiar character of people and events is suspended or inverted. The story of Athanasius, for instance, is introduced as an unusual instance of human energy and will: "We have seldom an opportunity of observing, either in active or speculative life, what effect may be produced, or what obstacles may be surmounted, by the force of a single mind, when it is inflexibly applied to the pursuit of a single object."[93] Like many of his contemporaries, moreover, who were attracted to popular tales, medieval tales, and the tales or pseudotales of Norse and Celtic bards because they found in them something of those elemental forces and passions that their own highly civilized age had suppressed, concealed, or distorted, Gibbon acknowledges that he turned gladly to antiquity because it allowed "a larger scope" for the great passions than "the smooth and solid temper of the modern world, which cannot easily repeat either the triumph of Alexander or the fall of Darius."[94] In the *Decline and Fall* there is more than one story that "might be deemed an incredible romance, if such a romance had not been verified."[95] Much of the narrative, however well authenticated, does indeed bear the mark of romance, of truth that is "stranger than fiction." "Am I writing the history of Orlando or Amadis?" the narrator pauses at one point to ask.[96] The *Decline and Fall* is the work not only of a critical historical scholar, but of an expert storyteller with a flair for selecting good story material and a penchant for tales of excess.

6

A *fair and authentic history*

TRANSFORMED INTO ART , "the vain and transitory scenes of human greatness" are saved from the jaws of time to become enduring illustrations of the motions of the human mind and heart. History, as it is presented in the *Decline and Fall*, is a spectacle for the edification and amusement of an audience of philosophers. Those who are still mired in the world of desire and illusion never learn from it.[1] But to the neutral, philosophical observer, "the experience of history exalts and enlarges the horizon of our intellectual view."[2] Indeed, in re-creating the past according to the rules of his art, the historian may have and give the impression of having tamed and cultivated it and even of having achieved a measure of mastery over it that no actor in it ever achieved.

If the *Decline and Fall* is presented to the reader as a lesson in "philosophie," it is also offered as an object of esthetic pleasure, a model of order and harmony, and a source of innocent entertainment. As we saw earlier, Gibbon does not downplay the rhetorical and literary aspect of his work. His language is ostentatiously contrived and "artificial." Even where it is fairly simple lexically and syntactically, it retains a highly formal character. There is no attempt to achieve the agility and vivacity, the effect of spontaneity and naturalness that characterized the writing of Diderot in French or of Sterne in English at about the same time. Against the background of these modern masks of naturalness, indeed, the formality of Gibbon's writing is thrown into sharp relief. The effect of his often-remarked predilection for abstract and Latin terms or for French turns of phrase, for instance, is to highlight the formality of the text and to make its language stand out before the reader as language, so that he cannot easily overlook it or read through it but remains at all times fully conscious of it.[3]

And yet, though it can and should be read "en philosophe," in Voltaire's words, and for the pleasure it affords, history is not, for Gibbon, the equivalent of a philosophical romance, as d'Alembert once suggested, or simply "un plus long conte," as Voltaire's friend Cideville wrote.[4] "The public," Gibbon maintained, "have some interest to know whether the writer whom they have honoured with their favour is deserving of their confidence; whether they must content themselves with reading the History of the Decline and Fall of the Roman Empire as a tale amusing enough, or whether they may venture to receive it as a fair and authentic history."[5] In short, whatever its value as a lesson in Enlightenment philosophy, as a stylistic model of order, or as entertainment, Gibbon insisted upon the specifically historical character of his narrative.

In claiming that the *Decline and Fall* was not a fiction, Gibbon could hardly have expected his readers to view it as a simple copy or reflection of past reality. Not the least of the History's lessons had been that the sign is always separated from its referent or meaning by a gap that interpretation cannot close. Both the impassable space between even the most authentic source and the events it reports or is used to establish and the inevitable rhetorical aspect of any historical narrative ensured that no history can ever be a simple image of reality. In what way then did Gibbon intend that his work be distinguished from a work of fiction?

Nothing in a statement of fact itself allows the reader to determine whether it is fictional or historical. There is a presumption that patently improbable statements are fictional, but what is improbable in the experience of one reading community obviously may be commonplace in the experience of another. To some extent, the whole genre of science fiction exploits this fluidity of the probable. The probability of a narrative is not, therefore, any indication of its status, the more so as fictional narrative has frequently aspired to seem probable. Normally, the reader looks for a signal that will tell him whether a text is to be classified as history or as fiction and how he is expected to read it.

In general, a fictional text, like language itself, outlines a meaningful structure that the reader is free to apply to his experience as he sees fit but that claims no specific referent in reality. For this reason, the narrator of a fictional narrative is always a mask.

The historical text, on the other hand, presents itself not only as meaningful, but as asserting something particular, and it inserts itself into a real context of exchange with the reader. That is why the narrator of a historical work identifies himself as a real person, just as an actual speaker, at the moment of speaking, assumes and fills the empty slot provided by the linguistic shifter "I." The discourse of reader and narrator in historiographical writing claims to be located in a specific historical context and not in that ideal realm outside the world of history that is evoked in the frame story of Boccaccio's *Decameron*. The historical text asks, in short, to be taken as a specific utterance in a specific context – one for which a specific referent is assumed, even if none is logically entailed. Correspondingly, whereas the fictional narrative does not compete with other fictional narratives – or, at most, competes with them to mobilize the reader's desire – the historical narrative may well aim to displace other narratives and to establish itself as authoritative.

The signal that tells a reader that a narrative is historical rather than fictional (the title, the notes at the foot of the page, the insertion of the text into a context of other histories) is clearly not sufficient to establish the authenticity or truth of the narrative or of the facts and events it relates. Though any statement of fact, one philosopher has argued, involves a prima facie assumption that the person making the statement, unless he has indicated that he is proposing a fiction, believes the statement has a referent in the real world, no referent is logically or necessarily entailed. Even as specific a statement as "The king of France is wise" requires, if no referent can be pointed to, that the listener determine for himself, on the basis of the general credibility of the speaker or on the basis of other evidence available to him, whether there is indeed anything in reality to which the statement can be applied. A speaker, in other words, takes a linguistic expression, which is in itself entirely meaningful, and inserts it into the specific context of an exchange with another user of the language; that user must make up his own mind whether the implied referent really exists or not.[6]

The status of the *Decline and Fall*, as Gibbon saw it, seems to have been analogous to the utterance "The king of France is wise." The utterance claims to be about a real person, but it cannot rest its claim on a direct relation between words and their origin and foundation in things any more than kings and governments can rest their claim to authority on a direct relation to a founding father. One of the central problems in the *Decline and Fall* – the problem of the foundation of truth and authority – thus reappears, in relation to the rhetoric and epistemology of history, as a central problem of the work, the problem of the truth and authority of the text.[7]

On the question of authority, Gibbon's position, though it is seldom expressly stated and is almost always embedded in the text of his narrative, seems to have been close to that of his friend and mentor David Hume.[8] "All authority of the few over the many," Hume wrote in one of his popular *Essays Moral and Political* (1741), is founded "in opinion" and "habit."[9] Though acquiescence in authority may be considered in some sense voluntary, it is not in any sense, in Hume's view, the deliberate engagement of an original contract by which the authority of the state is founded on a free act of will on the part of every individual member of it. Nor can the foundation of authority be traced to an original founder. No state can show a direct, unbroken line of descent from such an origin: "Almost all the governments which exist at present, or of which there remains any record in history, have been founded originally, either in usurpation or conquest, or both." [10] The Divinity itself is not a more solid foundation, as Providence justifies whatever is: "Whatever actually happens is comprehended in the general plan and intention of Providence; nor has the greatest and most lawful prince any more reason, upon that account, to plead a peculiar sacredness or inviolable authority, than an inferior magistrate, or even an usurper, or even a robber and a pirate." [11]

Authority, in short, for Hume, has no other foundation than custom and opinion. Though political parties cannot apparently support themselves "without a philosophical or speculative system of principles annexed to [their] political or practical one," so that one party traces government up to the Deity and the other traces it to "a kind of *original contract*," [12] philosophers may be expected to be more courageous. Yet their recognition of the "dangerous secret," to borrow Gibbon's phrase, [13] of the nature of authority should not lessen their obedience. For to reject authority as false, simply because there is nothing that the word "authority" can be said to represent, would be a dangerous naiveté. The social order would collapse under the strain of such criticism [14] as surely as the linguistic order and the possibility of communication among the members of a linguistic community would collapse if the users of a language were to refuse it on the ground that, as it is not a transparent image of a preexisting world of objects and events, and as the words in it are not necessarily or directly related to or representative of things, it is not true. In Hume's *Essays*, insight into the unfoundedness of authority does not lead to a rejection of authority; it leads rather to acceptance of it on a new basis, which may perhaps be characterized by Hume's expression "opinion of interest" – that is to say, "the sense of the general advantage which is reaped from government." [15]

Behind the various historical masks of authority, one might say, it is impossible, according to the author of the *Decline and Fall*, to discover any original founding authority. Such an original source of authority is at best signified by historical masks. It is not necessarily entailed by them, and nothing compels us to admit that its existence necessarily precedes the masks that signify it. In this sense, authority may appear as an invention of language and culture, and what is most often taken to be the foundation of a system of beliefs and behavior may be discovered to be itself part of that system – no longer the transcendental support of signs, but itself a sign.

A fair and authentic history

Gibbon's perception of the nature of authority did not tempt him – any more than Hume was tempted – to denounce it as a lie or a fraud. Likewise, his sense that historical narratives signify rather than reflect past reality and his acute awareness of the gap between the sign and its referent did not lead him to identify historical narratives with fictions. On the contrary, as the pious respect of sons in the *Decline and Fall* survives their insight into the infirmities of their fathers, the idea that history is essentially different from fiction survives the historian's insight into the gap between the sign and the referent. Though it may reveal discontinuities and gaps, history, for Gibbon, by its very nature is a healer: It continually appeals to authorities and never gives up the search for the path back to the origins. Like the monarch, the historian's text ultimately rests its own claim to authority on a legitimate line of transmission.

Gibbon's peculiar relation to authority may well have been the condition of his own writing. It is by no means implausible that to an individual who experienced himself as politically ineffectual, socially undistinguished, financially fragile, and physically unprepossessing the act of writing was impossible without the sanction of authority, and it may not be accidental that all Gibbon's work was in history rather than fiction. It is as though he could exercise his pen and his imagination only if he simultaneously affirmed his dependency on those who had preceded him – on the tradition – and on his commitment to truth. The criticism of authorities or sources is never a rejection of authorities or sources as such. In the end, moreover, Gibbon seems to have succeeded to some extent in achieving as a writer the reconciliation of desire with piety, the synthesis of independence and legitimacy, that is held up as an ideal in the History. The authorization to write, derived initially from the scrupulously authenticated sources and predecessors on which the narrative is founded, was transferred finally to the persona created by the narrative, the respectable "historian of the Roman empire." An appearance of continuity by a legitimate line of succession from the origin founds the historian's authority, in sum, as in the History it serves as the best foundation of the ruler's. In both cases, the philosophically minded reader may perceive the tenuousness of the line of transmission and the fragility of the foundation, but if he is a true philosopher he will accept the authority, on the understanding that it is not a Machiavellian mask for individual desire – that is, for disorder – but the instrument of an authentic attempt to accommodate individual desire to general order.

If the reconciliation of criticism and piety, of imagination and respect for truth, was the condition of Gibbon's writing, it was also, it appears, the

113

condition of the success of his work with the public. As recently as a few decades ago, an eminent classical scholar with a special interest in historical writing still held that it is impossible to tell whether Gibbon used the mask of learning to tell stories or used the mask of style to contribute to historical knowledge.[16] The historian himself observed with satisfaction that his book was "on every table, and almost on every toilette" while at the same time it had won the "approbation of my Judges" – the established senior British historians Robertson and Hume ("Dr. Robertson" and "Mr. Hume").[17] There seems little doubt that the *Decline and Fall* owed its remarkable popularity in considerable measure to its ability to appeal not only to two different classes of reader – "Men of letters, men of the world and . . . fine feathered Ladies; in short . . . every set of people except . . . the Clergy"[18] – but to two impulses within each reader. Gibbon's History could claim with equal plausibility to have served and diverted its readers like a woman and to have led them on the stony paths of science like a man. It allowed its readers to take their pleasures safely, as it were, without transgression or provocation, within a framework of general subservience to the authority of truth. It thus appealed readily to a public that, like the author himself, was at once enlightened and conservative, enthusiastic for liberty yet concerned to restrict the enjoyment of it.

Among contemporary readers Gibbon's History appears to have functioned in a manner very similar to the social mask. The wearing of a mask in the eighteenth century was widely considered to be not a deception but an inevitable feature of social life. Simplicity itself was most frequently viewed by an age raised on rhetoric as a mask or at best a fiction. Deception consisted not in wearing a mask but in attempting to conceal or deny that one was wearing one and that one's words and gestures were at all times subject to interpretation by listener or observer. The wearing of a mask was thus in no way inconsistent with honesty and a kind of candor.[19]

At the same time, the space between the mask and the person – both that between the signifier and the signified and that between the signified and the referent – could also be adroitly exploited as the space of a modest freedom. Discreetly, without any intention of disrupting the established relations of signifiers and meanings on which social order and communication were perceived to rest, it was possible to find in the inevitable gap between them a limited space for play. In Molière's *Misanthrope* or in the abbé Prévost's novels – notably *Manon Lescaut* and *Histoire d'une Grecque moderne* – such a space of play and the ambiguity of the sign on which it depends is perceived as a threat to the stable order of society. A conflict ensues, in which those (the men) who are in power and who control the social order seek to resolve the ambiguity of signs and to close the space between signifiers and meanings and are resisted by those (the women) who are not in power and for whom that space is the only means of emancipating themselves from a repressive order. By the middle of the eighteenth century, however, the old noble and patrician idea of the free, independent male – whether conceived of as feudal lord or as citizen – and therefore of the unfree female and slave, had been eroded by a form of social life that required everybody to subordinate his individual freedom to the order and well-being of the state.

The domestication of the old nobility and the old urban patriciate under Louis XIV resulted in the internalizing of social constraints among all members of society alike. All – no longer only women, but men also – must now seek the realization of their individual desires in the cracks of a system which is at once an obstacle to individual pleasure and the condition of it. To the degree that all benefit from the social order and are dependent on it, all have an interest in maintaining it; at the same time, the price of maintaining it would be too high if it did not provide within itself limited opportunities for the pursuit of pleasure and the exercise of imagination. This situation, which occupied Montesquieu throughout his life, is vividly illustrated by the popular novels of Crébillon *fils* and the comedies of Marivaux. In Marivaux's comedies, closure or definition of meaning is endlessly delayed because of the "feminization" – as contemporaries perceived it – of the male partner in the courtship, his refusal unequivocally to declare his desire, and the insistence of each partner that the other take responsibility for reading in – or into – ambiguous words or gestures a desire of which, if challenged, he or she can profess innocence. Crébillon's novels and Marivaux's comedies celebrate a world of variable and decorous play that prolongs itself indefinitely by revealing in every apparent act of closure or definition, such as the avowal of love or the moment of possession, a merely temporary stoppage that can be discovered in its turn to be a sign and recuperated as such by the players for their game.

In much the same way, it seems, Gibbon tried to secure the freedom of his masterpiece and to save it from the kind of definition that would have destroyed its principal virtue – the ability to provide pleasure or entertainment and the exercise of freedom and criticism within a general framework of decorum and respect for authority. He chose, in general, not to reply to attacks on the opinions said to be expressed or implied by the *Decline and Fall*, preferring to withdraw behind a mask of neutrality and placing responsibility for the ideas imputed to him on the shoulders of the reader. His response to Joseph Priestley when the latter attempted to goad him into an open debate on the subject of his religious beliefs was characteristic. Gibbon refused the challenge, held up the mask of "the historian, who, without interposing his own sentiments, has delivered a simple narrative of authentic facts," and refused responsibility for the opinions and beliefs (or disbelief) that Priestley – or any other reader – might impute to him. "You attack opinions which I never maintained"and "maintain principles which I have never denied," he declared.[20] There is no truth of his text, in other words, only opinion about it and interpretation of it.

Priestley showed he was well aware of the basic difference between himself and Gibbon – a difference strikingly similar to that which had earlier caused the celebrated quarrel of Rousseau and Hume – when he answered defiantly that, unlike Gibbon, he was proud to "hold no opinions, obnoxious as they are, that I am not ready both to *avow*, in the most explicit manner, and able to defend with any person of competent judgment and ability."[21] Like Rousseau, Priestley was not interested in maintaining the delicate balance of order and freedom that meant so much to Gibbon and his friends. As radicals and outsiders, no doubt he and Rousseau were not sensitive to the benefits of decorum. Both experienced it, on the contrary, as fundamentally oppressive. Both, therefore, sought to destroy it by reintroducing open debate and conflict. To the "manly" Priestley – as to the "citoyen" – the space between the word or sign and its meaning is a scandal. His aim is to close it, to ensure the transparency of the sign and the suppression of every uncertainty. No doubt he would have rejected, as Rousseau did, the imputation that his purpose was simply to institute a new order more in keeping with this own interests in place of the one from which he felt excluded. There is little doubt that transparency and open and public debate were associated, in his view, as they were in Rousseau's, with democratic freedom and equality. Yet Rousseau's notorious exclusion of women from the full enjoyment of civic rights should perhaps give one pause. Absolute transparency does seem to require, in history at least, the suppression or exclusion of difference, and it may quickly become indistinguishable from absolute terror.

Although Gibbon characteristically shrank from controversy and public debate about the precise views expressed in the *Decline and Fall* and refused to specify its meaning, he could not permit his general honesty and good faith as a historian to be impugned. The ambiguity of the sign, as we saw, was not the equivalent of deception or hypocrisy. As Priestley observed, Gibbon would not defend his principles, but he would defend his honor as a historian.[22] The complicity he enjoyed with his best readers and the reputation of his work required that his good faith and discernment be generally acknowledged. Readers could use his History at will, they could regard it, if they wished, simply as a repository of "striking facts and remarkable characters," in Lord Hardwicke's words.[23] But the honesty, judgment, and good faith of the historian and his scrupulous observance of the best rules of historical procedure had to be beyond question. The *Vindication of Some Passages in the XVth and XVIth Chapters of the History of the Decline and Fall of the Roman Empire*, published in January, 1779, in response to a critical pamphlet by Henry Davis, an Oxford B.A., was written in a style of invective that the urbane decorum of the *Decline and Fall* can hardly have led the victim to expect.

Gibbon gave his reasons for departing, on this one occasion, from his general policy of refusing controversy. Davis, he said, had attacked

> my credit as an historian, my reputation as a scholar, and even my honour and veracity as a gentleman . . . If I am indeed incapable of understanding what I read, I can no longer claim a place among those writers who merit the esteem and confidence of the public. If I am capable of wilfully perverting what I understand, I no longer deserve to live in the society of those men, who consider a strict and inviolable adherence to truth as the foundation of everything that is virtuous and honorable in human nature.[24]

The high moral tone may seem surprising, but it is a mask that Gibbon sometimes put on in order to reaffirm his commitment, whatever his skepticism about the origins and foundations of authority, to the order and decorum on which human society and civility appeared to him to be based.[25] It was entirely appropriate that he adopt a tone of moral outrage as he presented himself before the bar of public opinion to clear himself and his work of the charges brought against them and to have his standing as the "historian of the Roman empire" confirmed by the only source of authority he recognized.

Both as a son and as a writer, Gibbon's solutions seem strikingly similar: to avoid subservience without overtly challenging the order that prescribes it. While he exposes the natural or divine foundations of that order as "a vacant space," he continues to manifest his respect for it, in its emptiness, and thus attempts to ensure that the "dangerous secret" of the emperor's nakedness will be piously kept. As a guarantee of his fidelity, the son proclaims his lack of desire. The historian too presents himself as "neuter,"[26] without desire; he refrains from interposing his own sentiments and proposes only "a simple narrative of authentic facts." Gibbon's position, one might say, combines resentment and acceptance of dependency, the exercise of freedom and the protection of authority.

As an individual marked by infantile maladies and adolescent deviations and above all by the terrible secret flaw "circa genitalia," and as a citizen committed to the ruling Whig party, dependent on it for posts and pensions to supplement his insufficient income and eager to live down the earlier Tory affiliations of his family, Gibbon resembled more than he might have liked to think the eunuchs he pursued so unrelentingly in the pages of his great work. In the real world, his solutions were precarious and not very successful. He never did make a career through his political patrons, and it is difficult for a modern reader not to see that as a man, however well he succeeded in keeping up appearances, he was crippled from the beginning by his family and his upbringing. The History was the only achievement of a life of failure and renunciation. "Par le magique de cet art seducteur vous avez sû placer un Ecrivain inconnu à cotè des plus grands hommes," he replied to Suzanne Necker's praise of his History.[27] He was referring to what he called her art of exaggeration, but he could have made the same comment even more appropriately of his own "art séducteur."

Nevertheless, the *Decline and Fall* itself bears the marks of Gibbon's particular historical condition. It may be one of the last works in the epic tradition, as E. M. Tillyard and others have argued, but it lacks the ingenuousness of classical epic. Gibbon's strategy as a writer is the same as his strategy as a son: to achieve control while remaining submissive. The narrator of the *Decline and Fall* is ingratiating, infinitely cautious, and deferential. He seems never to dogmatize, pontificate, or in any way attempt to dominate his reader.[28] That "the public is seldom wrong"[29] was a neoclassical principle to which the historian adhered from the beginning of his career to the end. Yet it is the narrator, finally, who is always in control.[30] Without forcing or browbeating the reader, he coaxes and seduces him – or her – into complicity with him. Whatever obligations, loyalties, or beliefs the reader might have that are not compatible with the role prescribed for him must be abandoned in order that reader and narrator may be joined in playful partnership. The reading situation, as Gibbon constructs it, is a veritable Enlightenment Utopia, a model of the ideal society. The partners, though formally different, are at the same time identical, like the members of the countless parallelisms in the text, or nephew and maiden aunt in the idyllic childhood partnership evoked by the historian in his Autobiography. As he enters into complicity with the narrator, the reader is enlightened, relieved of the burden of historical definition or "prejudice." But the free partnership envisaged by the narrator is a decorous one from which everything rowdy or rebellious has been excluded and to which no suspicion of sedition may attach. There is none of the teasing and taunting that characterize the relations of reader and narrator in Diderot's *Jack the Fatalist*, for instance, and that reflect at the level of the *discours* the essentially political rivalry of Jack and his Master that is the principal theme of the *histoire*. The reader who seeks a more vigorous and "manly" exercise of criticism must address himself elsewhere than to the *Decline and Fall*, for it is impossible for him to read Gibbon's History without accepting the narrator's terms. If he balks at them, he must put the book down, withdraw, and cease to exist as a reader or to fill the slot defined by the "you" to whom the narrator addresses himself.

As a text, the *Decline and Fall* excludes the noncomplicitous reader. The latter is the absolute other; he or she is beyond the pale. The worst reader of all is the one who, out of ignorance, malice, or resentment, not only refuses the code on which the complicity and understanding of reader and narrator is based, but also denounces it as subversive, thereby threatening the order and tranquillity that the text, whatever its complicitous ironies, seeks always to preserve. To accuse Jack of subversion, and thus implicitly to call on the master to reassert his authority by force, was to threaten a fragile, hard-won balance, from which Jacks and masters, sons and fathers stood equally to gain, since it promised to combine the opportunities of freedom with the security of order. Readers like Henry Davis are not only uncouth, they are dangerous and must be hounded back to the obscurity from which they ought never to have been permitted to emerge. Discourse and communication with them are neither desirable nor possible, as they do not observe the same laws or speak the same language as the narrator. Gibbon writes with undisguised contempt of Davis, presenting him as more animal than human:

> Every animal employs the note, or cry, or howl, which is peculiar to its species; every man expresses himself in the dialect the most congenial to his temper and inclination, the most familiar to the company in which he has lived, and to the authors with whom he is conversant; and while I was disposed to allow that Mr. Davis had made some proficiency in ecclesiastical studies, I should have considered the difference in our language and manners as an unsurmountable bar of separation between us. Mr. Davis has overleaped that bar, and forces me to contend with him on the very dirty ground which he has chosen for the scene of our combat.[31]

Davis, of course, is still not being addressed here. The "you" corresponding to the "I" of the speaker is still the like-minded, elegant, and complicitous reader, who is now being invited to serve as judge in the case, to exonerate the narrator from the charge of sedition, and to restore the status quo by pronouncing the sentence of exclusion and disgrace that the speaker, as prosecuting attorney, advocates. Davis, in short, does not qualify as a "you," a reader, or even a person. He is what the elegant French society of the time referred to as "une espèce."

While exposing the infirmities of the authority figures of history, the narrator, as we saw, admires the pious gesture by which the veil is discreetly drawn over them again. Father and son, authority and subversion are reconciled ideally by a mutual nonaggression pact. The violence that the son has shrunk from using or arousing against the father and that the narrator has banished from his relation to his reader is not eliminated, however. It resurfaces in the form of aggression against the outsider who dares to threaten the act of settlement by which peace was established between father and son. It matters little whether the outsider claims to be on the side of the son, or, as in the case of Davis, on the side of the father. Any disturbance of the delicately balanced status quo deserves to be put down, any incitement to disorder to be censored. The decorous complicity of narrator and reader, with its harmonious reconciliation of order and freedom, is thus seen to be a limited and exclusive one and to require the strictest censorship and repression of all elements that for whatever reason have not found it acceptable or have not been included in it.

Like many other productions of the eighteenth century, the *Decline and Fall* is an ambiguous work: at once literature and history, an incitement to freedom and enlightenment and a lesson in political conservatism. Ideologically, it may reflect the compromise of 1688 and the condition of that considerable part of English society that was situated astride the world of commerce and the world of the landed gentry. Today's reader, however, will probably appreciate it not so much for the Augustan confidence and order it displays as for the failures and anxieties it cannot quite conceal. We may derive from it today the lesson that Gibbon derived from his reading of Roman history: that no time, however strong and confident it may appear to us, was ever whole, complete, secure, untouched by doubt, or ignorant of division and alienation. In addition, we may be led to reflect both on the achievement and on the limitations of that ironical outlook that has been so important an ingredient of the liberal temper since the eighteenth century.

Notes

ABBREVIATIONS USED IN THE NOTES

AEG   *The Autobiographies of Edward Gibbon*, printed verbatim from hitherto un-published mss., with an introduction by the Earl of Sheffield, ed. John Murray. London: John Murray, 1896.

DF   *The Decline and Fall of the Roman Empire*, 3 vols. New York: The Modern Library (Random House, Inc.), n.d.
This edition, which corresponds to the Everyman Library edition in England, although not the most scholarly, is the least expensive and the most readily obtainable text of the *Decline and Fall* at the present moment. Figures refer to chapter number, followed, in parentheses, by the volume and page in this edition.

LEG   *The Letters of Edward Gibbon*, ed. J. E. Norton, 3 vols. London: Cassell and Co., 1956.
Figures refer to the number of the letter, the date (day/month/year), and, in parentheses, the volume and page.

MJH   *The Girlhood of Maria Josepha Holroyd (Lady Stanley of Alderley), Recorded in Letters of Two Hundred Years Ago: from 1776 to 1796*, ed. J. H. Adeane. London, New York, and Bombay: Longmans, Green, and Co., 1896.

MW   *Miscellaneous Works of Edward Gibbon Esq.*, ed. John, Lord Sheffield, 2nd ed., 5 vols. London: John Murray, 1814.

PREFACE

1. G. M. Young, *Gibbon* (London: Peter Davies, 1932) – still arguably the best and the most elegant all-around study; R. B. Mowat, *Gibbon* (London: Arthur Barker, 1936); D. M. Low, *Edward Gibbon 1737–1794* (London: Chatto and Windus, 1937) – the standard biography to date. Sir Gavin de Beer's *Gibbon and His World* (London: Thames and Hudson, 1968) is handsome, informative, and generously illustrated, like other volumes in this series. None of these works pretends to be literary criticism, but they do all contain illuminating comments on Gibbon's writing.

2. Giuseppe Giarrizzo's *Edward Gibbon e la cultura europea del settecento* (Naples: Istituto Italiano per gli Studi Istorici, 1954) has not been translated and has suffered from its relative inaccessibility. It is an immensely erudite and important work that situates Gibbon in the world of historical learning and historical writing of the eighteenth century and interprets the History itself in the light of Gibbon's handling of the problems presented by the Empire, by Christianity, and by the Middle Ages. Michel Baridon's massive (940 pp.) *Edward Gibbon et le mythe de Rome: histoire et idéologie au siècle des lumières* (Paris: Honoré Champion, 1977) is thorough, richly documented, and, in the manner of French *thèses d'état*, apparently exhaustive. It offers detailed accounts of Gibbon's life, his early literary endeavors, and the political and intellectual context of the *Decline and Fall*, with sections on English political thought and polemics in the seventeenth and eighteenth centuries, Calvinism, Jansenism, Boulainviller and his school in France, the *philosophes*, the sociological and economic theories of the Scottish Enlightenment, and so on. In addition, Baridon undertakes to provide ideological and stylistic analyses of the text of the *Decline and Fall*. Somewhat unwieldy and lacking focus, Baridon's book is a treasure house of information and bibliography and an indispensable work of scholarship. David Jordan's far shorter *Gibbon and His Roman Empire* (Urbana: Univ. of Illinois Press, 1971) addresses a narrower range of questions – Gibbon's scholarship, the influence of Tillemont and Pascal on his thought and style, his relation to Bayle, Montesquieu, and the Enlightenment in general, and his debt to Tacitus, his principal model, in Jordan's view – but Jordan relates these questions more successfully than Baridon sometimes does to the text of the *Decline and Fall*.

Among studies by literary scholars, Harold Bond's *The Literary Art of Edward Gibbon* (Oxford: Clarendon Press, 1960) is a valuable, essentially descriptive account of Gibbon's rhetoric, which aims to show that the *Decline and Fall* can be read as an exercise in epideictic rhetoric, a "commemorative address on the fate of the Roman Empire"; Leo Braudy's *Narrative Form in History and Fiction* (Princeton: Princeton Univ. Press, 1970) contains an important chapter on Gibbon's narrative strategies. Surprisingly, Braudy's lead in approaching Gibbon's text from this angle seems not to have been followed.

J. W. Swain's *Gibbon the Historian* (London: Macmillan, 1966) and R. N. Parkinson's *Gibbon* (New York: Twayne Publishers, 1973) are general introductory studies, touching briefly on the literary aspect of the *Decline and Fall* as well as on biography and history of ideas. Two recent collections of essays marked the bicentenary of the *Decline and Fall* – one a number of *Daedalus* (Summer, 1976), subsequently published with minor revisions as *Edward Gibbon and the Fall of the Roman Empire*, ed. G. W. Bowerstock and Stephen K. Graubard (Cambridge, Mass.: Harvard Univ. Press, 1977), and the other a volume put out by the University of Lausanne under the title *Gibbon et Rome à la lumière de l'historiographie moderne* (Geneva: Droz, 1977). Both collections range widely over all aspects of the historian's life and work.

Chapter 1 title is from *AEG*, 346.

1. *AEG*, 35. In fact, the parish registers at Putney show that of five subsequent male children only one received the name of Edward (*Gibbon's Journal to January 28th, 1763*, ed. D. M. Low [New York: W. W. Norton and Company, n.d.], Introd., p. xxix). Gibbon apparently perceived or wished to give the impression of greater fragility than the documentary evidence warrants.
2. *AEG*, 270; *LEG*, 365 (2:133); *DF*, 2:420, 423.
3. To Dorothea Gibbon, *LEG*, 633, 3/v/86 (3:44).
4. *AEG*, 346.
5. *AEG*, 48; also 117.
6. *AEG*, 35–6, 45, 111, 156. In a letter to Sheffield concerning his estate, he refers to his mother correctly, no doubt, in the context, but with striking indifference: "I as little understand the want of my father's marriage settlement; with his first wife? She has been dead above forty years, and I am her sole representative" (*LEG*, 726, 13/vi/89 [3:154]).
7. *AEG*, 36.
8. *AEG*, 20, 217.
9. *AEG*, 46.
10. See Pierre-Paul Clément, *Jean-Jacques Rousseau, de l'éros coupable à l'éros glorieux* (Neuchâtel: La Baconnière, 1976), notably pp. 53–62.
11. *AEG*, 48.
12. See, in addition to the texts in *AEG*, the letter to Lord Sheffield on the occasion of Catherine Porten's death (*LEG*, 634, 10/v/86 [3:45–6]).
13. *LEG*, 634, 10/v/86 (3:46).
14. *AEG*, 48.
15. *LEG*, 634, 10/v/86 (3:46). See also *AEG*, 117: "She was truly my mother, she became my friend;" *AEG*, 241: "the nurse of my infancy, the friend of my youth . . ."
16. Recalling Gibbon's request to the Sheffields that they satisfy "a secret wish" of Aunt Kitty to sleep in Gibbon's bed (*LEG*, 595, 8/ix/83 [2:363]), Virginia Woolf hints at the repressed sexuality of the relation of nephew and aunt: "So while Aunt Hester lay with William Law in the grave, Aunt Kitty hoisted herself into the great four-poster with the help of the stool which the little man always used . . . The great historian, whose gaze swept far horizons and surveyed the processions of the Roman Emperors, could also fix them minutely upon a rather tedious old lady and guess her fancy to sleep in a certain bed. He was a strange mixture" ("Reflections at Sheffield Place," *Collected Essays* [London: Hogarth Press, 1968], vol. 1, p. 129).
17. *AEG*, 56.
18. *AEG*, 43.
19. To Dorothea Gibbon, *LEG*, 633, 3/v/86 (3:43).
20. *LEG*, 652, mid-September, 1787 (3:72).

21. *LEG*, 628, 1/x/85 (3:32–33). See also another letter to Sheffield (*LEG*, 626): "my style of living is enlarged by the encrease of my relative importance, an obscure batchelor in England, the master of a considerable house, at Lausanne." He often writes of the eminent visitors who came to call on him, as on a prince or a king, and he appears to have resembled at Lausanne his own portrait of his grandfather at Putney, "the oracle and tyrant of a petty kingdom" (*AEG*, 20). Lady Holland writes impatiently that "His whim arranged and deranged all parties. All, in short, were subservient to his wishes" (*The Journal of Elizabeth, Lady Holland: 1791–1811*, ed. the Earl of Ilchester [London, New York, Bombay, and Calcutta: Longmans, Green, and Co., 1908], vol. 1, p. 2). Other visitors also commented, more or less kindly, on Gibbon's decision to settle in a small Swiss town, where he could be a big fish in a small pond. Maria Holroyd, who was fond of the family friend, is among the less malicious. "I own my surprise is very great," she wrote her aunt in England, "that Mr. Gibbon should chuse to spend his days here rather than in England, for there does not appear to me anybody with whom he can converse on equal terms, or who is worthy to hear him . . . However, he is so much attracted to the Place and the People, that he cannot bear the slightest joke about them." Maria Holroyd also notes that though there is "a very pleasant set of French here, with whom lady Webster [the future Lady Holland] is very intimate," Gibbon has little to do with it: "but we live entirely with the Severys and Mr. G's set, which is certainly not equally pleasant" (letter of 23/vii/91 in *MJH*, 63). Maria Holroyd returned to the question of Gibbon's pronounced preference for the Swiss several times. On September 3, 1791, after describing the Swiss parties as "a continual scene of eating," she again mentions that "Mr. Gibbon dislikes the French very much, which is nothing but Swiss prejudice, of which he has imbibed a large quantity" (*MJH*, 73). A week later, reporting that Lally Tolendal, then at Lausanne,was a great raconteur, "engrossing the whole conversation," she adds: "He is a companion that would not suit Mr. Gibbon constantly, as he does not much like playing a second part. Vive les Suisses for that! who, when the 'King of the Place,' as he is called opens his mouth, (which you know he generally does some time before he has arranged his sentence), all wait in awful and respectful silence for what shall follow, and look up to it as an oracle!" (*MJH*, 77).

22. *LEG*, 627, 15/vii/85 (3:29). See also *AEG*, 343: "While the Aristocracy of Bern protects the happiness, it is superfluous to enquire whether it is founded in the rights of man."

23. *LEG*, 652, ?/ix/87 (3:71).

24. Gibbon had not always approved of the oligarchic government of Berne; see the Letter on the government of Berne, supposedly written by a Swedish traveller, in *MW* II, 1–32.

25. *LEG*, 627, 15/vii/85 (3:28); see also *LEG*, 804, 1/viii/92 (3:266): "Lord S is still and will ever continue the same active being, always employed for himself, his friends and the public, and always persuading himself that he wishes for leisure and repose . . . There are various roads to happiness, but when I compare his situation with mine I do not upon the whole repent that I have given the preference to a life

of celibacy and retirement. Although I have been long a spectator of the great World, my unambitious temper has been content with the occupations and rewards of study, and . . . my library [is] still my favourite room . . . ”

26. *AEG*, 162–3.

27. *AEG*, 309–10.

28. See n. 21 above (*MJH*, 77). Suard, whom Gibbon hoped to engage to translate the *Decline and Fall* into French, wrote: “Anxious to succeed and to please, he wished to command attention, and obtained it without difficulty by a conversation animated, sprightly, and full of matter: all that was dictatorial in his tone betrayed not so much the desire of domineering over others, which is always offensive, as confidence in himself . . . Notwithstanding this, his conversation never carried one away; its fault was a kind of arrangement, which never permitted him to say anything unless well” (cit. *AEG*, 202n.). The slight stiffness in Gibbon’s conversation, on which almost all contemporaries seem to agree, is probably another sign of his general timidity in relation to others and of his need to compensate for it by maximizing his control of the situation. It is as though the unpredictability of free-flowing conversation caused him some apprehension, so that he tried to introduce into conversation something of the control that he could exercise as a writer.

29. *AEG*, 316.

30. *AEG*, 336n.

31. *AEG*, 310. See also *LEG*, 452, to G. Deyverdun, 4/vi/79 (2:218): “Dans le Senat Je suis toujours demeuré tel que vous m’avez laissé, mutus pecus; mais vis a vis du public j’ai la plume assez babillarde.”

32. *AEG*, 158. In his Journal for May 16, 1762, Gibbon notes his pleasure at spending some time with Dorothea Gibbon: “I love her as a companion, a friend, and a mother” (*Gibbon’s Journal to January 28th, 1763*, p. 72). Over thirty years later, on the eve of his final journey to England, he writes Mrs. Gibbon, now a very old lady, of the happiness he anticipates at seeing “the maternal countenance of my most faithful friend” (*LEG*, 839, 8/v/93 [3:331]).

33. *AEG*, 272. See also *AEG*, 157: “He received me as a man and a friend; all constraint was banished at our first interview, and we ever afterwards continued on the same terms of easy and equal politeness.”

34. To Sheffield, *LEG*, 732, 25/vii/89 (3:164).

35. *MJH*, 62. His descendants describe Salomon de Sévery as genuinely religious, “plus qu’on ne l’était au dix-huitième siècle” (M. et Mme. William de Sévery, *La Vie de sociéte dans le pays de Vaud à la fin du dix-huitième siècle* [Lausanne: Georges Bridel; Paris: Fischbacher, 1911–12], vol. 1, p. 122).

36. *MJH*, 74. See also *Le Journal de Gibbon à Lausanne*, ed. G. Bonnard (Lausanne: F. Rouge, 1945), p. 48. In general, Maria Holroyd found that “dignity and frigidity” were the chief charactcristics of the de Sévery family.

37. To Lady Sheffield, *LEG*, 819, 10/xi/92 (3:298).

38. Gibbon took a special interest in young Wilhelm de Sévery, to whom he refers in letters to the parents as “notre fils” (e.g. *LEG*, 652), and who rewarded him

with "les plaisirs de père qu'il me fait éprouver" (*LEG*, 696). Gibbon persuaded the parents to allow him to bring Wilhelm to England with him so that he could learn English, be introduced to society, and complete his education, and he organized and supervised the young man's stay in England with great care. Benjamin Constant, de Sévery's cousin, was apparently jealous of this interest (de Sévery, vol. 1, p. 151). Wilhelm de Sévery figured prominently in Gibbon's will.

39.　Other relations would be worth exploring in greater detail. For instance, of Madame Bontems, the mother of a young diplomat Gibbon had met in London in 1762, he wrote a year later from Paris: "Madame Bontems . . . seems to have conceived a real motherly attachment for me. I generally sup there three or four times a week quite in a friendly way" (to Dorothea Gibbon, *LEG*, 43, 25/iii/63 [1:139]). Similarly in his Journal: "Elle m'aimait, j'etais son fils et son ami" (quoted by G. M. Young, *Gibbon* [London: Peter Davies, 1932], pp. 41–2).

40.　*AEG*, 150–2 (brackets appear in the original). A better-known version is on pp. 238–9.

41.　*LEG*, 34a, c. end April, 1759 (1:123); 47, 4/vi/63 (1:148). In a reference to an engagement to another suitor, which she had broken off, Suzanne Curchod wrote: "que m'importe la fortune? d'ailleurs ce n'est point à vous que je l'ai sacrifiée, mais à un être factice qui n'exista jamais que dans une tête romanesquement fêlée, telle que la mienne; car dés le moment que votre lettre m'a désabusée vous êtes rentré pour moi dans la classe de tous les autres hommes, et aprés avoir été le seul que j'ai jamais pu aimer, vous êtes devenu un de ceux pour qui j'aurois le moins de penchant, parce que vous ressemblez le moins à ma chymère céladonique." The allusion is to Celadon, the hero of the best known of all French romances, d'Urfé's *L'Astrée*. Rousseau's *La nouvelle Héloise* had appeared in 1760, and Suzanne Curchod's later letters – notably *LEG*, 512, 21/ix/63 – seem strongly influenced by its rhetoric of passion.

42.　*AEG*, 274–5.

43.　*AEG*, 29.

44.　To Catherine de Sévery, *LEG*, 829, 1/ii/93 (3:316); to Abigail Holroyd, *LEG*, 819, 10/xi/92 (3:296–8); also *LEG*, 586, 18/viii/83 (2:354); *LEG*, 666, 18/xii/87 (3:86–8); *LEG*, 836, 27/iv/93 (3:327–8).

45.　*LEG*, 762, 7/viii/90 (3:199).

46.　*LEG*, 179, 21/iv/72 (1:315).

47.　*LEG*, 43, 25/iii/63 (1:139).

48.　*AEG*, 11.

49.　*AEG*, 12, 17, 20.

50.　*AEG*, 20, 216.

51.　*AEG*, 217–28.

52.　*AEG*, 20.

53.　*AEG*, 31–2, 287–8, 382–3, 412–13. "A man to spend a fortune quietly" is Bagehot's epigrammatic description of Edward Gibbon Sr. (*Literary Studies* [London: J. M. Dent, n.d., Everyman's Library ed.], vol. 2, p. 4). See also Michel

Baridon, *Edward Gibbon et le mythe de Rome: histoire et idéologie au siècle des lumières* (Paris: Editions Honoré Champion, 1977), pp. 134–5.

54. *AEG*, 152.
55. *AEG*, 155.
56. *LEG*, 27, 24/viii/58 (1:106).
57. *LEG*, 62, 10/xi/64 (1:187).
58. *AEG*, 302–3. Similarly, he rejects "the trite and lavish praise of the happiness of our boyish years, which is echoed with so much affection in the world" and closes an important section in one of the drafts of the Autobiography with a ringing eulogy of freedom: "Freedom is the first wish of our heart; freedom is the first blessing of our nature; and, unless we bind ourselves with the voluntary chains of interest or passion, we advance in freedom as we advance in years" (*AEG*, 59, 61).
59. *AEG*, 306.
60. *AEG*, 288.
61. *AEG*, 413.
62. *AEG*, 288.
63. *AEG*, 53.
64. *AEG*, 85.
65. *AEG*, 134.
66. *LEG*, 51a, 21/ix/63 (1:159).
67. *AEG*, 238–9. The correspondence and the journals contain many references to the project of setting up house together – "songes de notre jeunesse, qui pourroient bien se réaliser" (*LEG*, 452, 4/vi/79 [2:218]; see also *LEG* 125, 2/xii/70 [1:268]; to Dorothea Gibbon, *LEG*, 455, 3/vii/79 [2:222]; *AEG*, 238; *Gibbon's Journal to January 28th, 1763*, pp. 82, 92–3; and *Journal de Gibbon à Lausanne*, p. 31).
68. *AEG*, 273.
69. To Dorothea Gibbon, *LEG*, 439, 7/i/79 (2:201): "The agreement of any friends to live together in the same house is a sort of Marriage." An enigmatic entry in the Journal for July 9, 1762 (*Gibbon's Journal to January 28th, 1763*, p. 92) gives an idea of the intimacy of Gibbon's relations with Deyverdun: "I finished my letter of eight pages to d'Eyverdun [he had begun it the day before], it is a kind of pleasure I have not had a great while, that of pouring out my whole soul to a real friend. *Why* I deferred writing and the *Schemes* I proposed to him are not to be trusted even to this paper." The letter in question has not been found; Deyverdun may well have destroyed it.
70. To Dorothea Gibbon, *LEG*, 610, 27/xii/83 (2:387); to Catherine Porten, same date, *LEG*, 611 (2:390).
71. To Catherine de Sévery, *LEG*, 631, Spring 1786 (3:41).
72. *AEG*, 340–1. The last sentence is rather elliptical; it appears to mean, "and if I had not thrown myself into study both before and after his death, I do not know if all my philosophy would have enabled me to overcome my grief." Gibbon's letters also contain many expressions of his grief at the death of Deyverdun and of his subsequent loneliness: "Je croyois être préparé mais ce coup m'a boulversé. Apres trente-trois ans – Adieu" (from a cryptic note to S. de Sévery announcing

the news of Deyverdun's death, *LEG*, 728, 4/vii/89 [3:156]); "The loss of a friend of five and thirty years is irreparable, and each day I feel the comfortless solitude to which I am reduced" (*LEG*, 739, 5/xii/89 [3:174–6]; see also *LEG*, 733, 9/ix/89 [3:165–8]; *LEG*, 759, 15/v/90 [3:190–3]; *LEG*, 819, 10/xi/92 [3:296–9] et passim). R. N. Parkinson, in *Edward Gibbon* (New York: Twayne, 1973), p. 25, has also observed that when he writes about Deyverdun Gibbon's language begins to approach that of the sentimental novels of the time.

73. *AEG*, 341. See also *LEG*, 784, to Dorothea Gibbon, 18/v/91 (3:226): "I sometimes feel, that like Adam I am alone in Paradise."

74. *AEG*, 341.

75. On S. de Sévery, *LEG*, 830, 9–18/ii/93 (3:317); on J. Necker, *LEG*, 393, 1/ix/77 (2:162); *LEG*, 394, 31/x/77 (2:163); *LEG*, 498, 26/ii/81 (2:264); *LEG*, 501, 1/vi/81 (2:267–9); *LEG*, 626, 13 and 21/iii/85 (3:26); *LEG*, 800, 4/iv/92 (3:253). The words most commonly used in relation to Necker are "amitié" and "devouement respectueux."

76. *LEG*, 439, 7/i/79 (2:201).

77. See n. 25 above. Virginia Woolf notes: "In Parliament Gibbon was dumb; in love he was ineffective. But his friend Holroyd was a member of a dozen committees; before one wife was two years in the grave he had married another" ("Reflections at Sheffield Place," p. 126). As a writer too, Holroyd was above all a practical man; Maria Holroyd viewed her father with affectionate despair as the producer of "horrid and illegible manuscripts" on the herring fishery or on the woolen manufacture (*MJH*, 11).

78. To Sheffield, *LEG*, 58, 18/v/64 (1:173); to Maria Holroyd, *LEG*, 790, 9/xi/91 (3:234); to Dorothy Holroyd, Sheffield's mother, *LEG*, 190, 17/vii/72 (1:323); to Sheffield, *LEG*, 836, 27/iv/93 (3:327).

79. To Sheffield, *LEG*, 732, 25/vii/89 (3:164). See also Virginia Woolf, p. 126: "But what tie was it that attached the downright, self-confident, perhaps loose-living man of the world to the suave, erudite, sedentary historian?"

80. To Lady Sheffield, 22/x/84, *LEG*, 623 (3:12).

81. So they are described in a silhouette taken in 1791 and preserved by Maria Holroyd among souvenirs of the family visit to Gibbon in Lausanne. Reproduced by Sir Gavin de Beer, *Gibbon and His World* (London: Thames and Hudson, 1968), opp. p. 101.

82. To Sheffield, *LEG*, 726, 13/vi/89 (3:153).

83. Ibid.

84. *LEG*, 867, 11/xi/93 (3:359). See G. R. de Beer, "The Malady of Edward Gibbon F.R.S., " *Notes and Records of the Royal Society of London*, December, 1949, 7:71–80. The parallel with Rousseau's strange *retention d'urine* is striking.

85. De Beer ("The Malady of Edward Gibbon, F.R.S.") provides an interesting illustration of Gibbon's careful attention to his persona. Having finally acknowledged the existence of his malady, he insinuated to Sheffield that it was caused by a *lues veneria* in his youth. De Beer shows not only that there was no connection between Gibbon's condition and any possible *lues*, but that Gibbon himself knew

there was not and that he invented the story – which none of the surgeons credited – in order "to perpetuate the picture of a man whose success was great with the ladies."

86.   *Gibbon's Journal to January 28th, 1763*, p. 136.

87.   Sheffield relates that when he saw Gibbon in London in 1787 he was alarmed by the "prodigious increase" the swelling had undergone since Gibbon's departure for Lausanne in 1783. "Those who have seen him within the last eight or ten years must be surprised to hear," he adds, "that he could doubt, whether his disorder was apparent." Whatever Gibbon thought others actually noticed, he would not permit them to give their observations social reality. His valet told Sheffield that Gibbon would not tolerate the least allusion to the subject "and never would suffer him to notice it" (*MW* II:414). A letter from Jean Huber, the painter and engraver, to Salomon de Sévery indicates that Gibbon's friends at Lausanne were also aware of his affliction and that there too there was a taboo on any discussion of it or reference to it (de Sévery, vol. 2, p. 5).

88.   Quoted by Sir Gavin de Beer, *Gibbon and His World*, p. 120. The passage in the Earl of Ilchester's edition of Lady Holland's Journal (vol. 2, p. 39) does not contain the second sentence. As the Earl of Ilchester declares in his Introduction that "some passages . . . have been omitted and others have been somewhat softened" on account of Lady Holland's well-known forthrightness of expression, the passage in question must be one of those referred to by Sir Gavin de Beer as having been discovered in Lady Holland's manuscript, which the Earl of Ilchester permitted him to see.

89.   *Dictionary of National Biography*, art. "Law, William."

90.   *AEG*, 18.

91.   *AEG*, 23. The allusion is to a tradition that Hester appeared as Miranda in Law's *Serious Call*.

92.   *AEG*, 83.

93.   It is worth recalling that at least two other leading antireligious figures of the Enlightenment had similar close relations to the world of religious experience. Voltaire's brother was a Jansenist convulsionary, and Diderot's brother was a pious abbé. Diderot himself may well have known the enthusiasm of religion in his youth.

94.   *AEG*, 204.

95.   On Gibbon's own testimony, *AEG*, 176.

96.   Beckford wrote *Vathek* in French and then collaborated with his friend, Rev. Samuel Henley, in translating it into English – a rare example of literary perversity worthy of the author. On Gibbon's attitude to Beckford, with some members of whose family he appears to have been acquainted (William Beckford Sr. preceded Gibbon at Westminster School, and Gibbon appears to have made the acquaintance of other Beckfords when he was at Westminster), who was his neighbour at Vevey in 1786, across the lake at Evian in 1792, and at Lausanne itself at the end of 1792, and who purchased his library after his death, see Ch. 6, n. 25 below.

97.   *AEG* 175; see also 134, 152.

98.   The editor of *LEG* several times draws attention to Gibbon's confusion of

English and French terms and expressions (*e.g.* 1:4, n. 6; 1:6, n. 2, n. 3). "I am now good protestant," the future master of English style wrote to Catherine Porten in February, 1755 (*LEG*, 3 [1:3]). Walter Bagehot over a century ago and G. M. Young more recently are among the few writers on Gibbon to have remarked on this striking linguistic phenomenon (Bagehot, *Literary Studies*, vol. 2, p. 18, and G. M. Young, *Gibbon*, pp. 16–18). With characteristic sharpness, Bagehot suggests that there may have been in the young exile "some wish to magnify his continental progress, and . . . to make his friends fear he was forgetting his own language."

99. "Epousez votre Etrangere, vous etes independant, mais souvenez-vous avant de la faire que vous etes fils et Citoyen." "Elle est Etrangére. Vous n'avez deja que trop de penchant pour les moeurs Etrangéres. La Langue de votre pays ne vous est plus connûe." Such were some of Edward Gibbon Sr.'s reflections to his son at the end of 1758, as Gibbon reports them in his letters to Suzanne Curchod (*LEG*, 27, 24/viii/58 [1:106]; *LEG*, 34, 23/ii/59 [1:121]).

100. To Suzanne Necker, *LEG*, 361, 26/xi/76 (2:129).

101. To Deyverdun, *LEG*, 574 (2:338); to Sheffield, *LEG*, 577, 10/vii/83, (2:342); to Lady Sheffield, *LEG*, 623, 22/x/84 (3:14) et passim. See also Maria Holroyd's remarks, n. 21 above.

102. *AEG*, 18.

2. THE PLENITUDE OF PATERNAL POWER

Chapter 2 title is from *DF*, XLIV (2:700).

1. *DF*, IX (1:189).
2. *DF*, XII (1:275).
3. *DF*, XVII (1:525).
4. *DF*, II (1:35–6).
5. *DF*, XXVI (1:932). See also 1:906.
6. *DF*, XXXVIII (2:419).
7. *DF*, XVII (1:540); *DF*, "General Observations" (2:438).
8. *DF*, XV (1:394). See also Rousseau: "Le faux est susceptible d'une infinité de combinaisons; mais la vérité n'a qu'une manière d'être" ("Discours sur les sciences et les arts," in *Oeuvres complètes* [Paris: Gallimard, 1959–69], vol. 3, p. 18).
9. *DF*, XI (1:272), XVI (1:497).
10. *DF*, XXI (1:691).
11. *AEG*, 47.
12. *DF*, XIX (1:603–4).
13. *DF*, XXII (1:727).
14. *DF*, XIX (1:623–4).
15. *DF*, XIX (1:608).
16. *DF*, VI (1:133).
17. *DF*, XXII (1:727).
18. *DF*, XXIII (1:761, 763).

19. *DF*, XXII (1:756).
20. *DF*, XII (1:278), XII (1:283), XIII (1:304–5, 313), XVI (1:449, 496), XIX (1:613), XXIV (1:799), XXVII (2:4), XXXVII (2:379), XLIII (2:651), XLV (2:729).
21. *DF*, XXII (1:732).
22. *DF*, XXII (1:744, 745), XXIV (1:829).
23. *DF*, L (3:114).
24. *DF*, XVII (1:548). Cf. Rousseau, *Du Contrat social*, Book 2, Chapter 9.
25. *DF*, I (1:9).
26. *DF*, XXXI (2:134). The roots of Gibbon's thinking here can be traced to Harrington and to a discussion, which was carried on throughout the late seventeenth and eighteenth centuries and to which John Toland and Fletcher of Saltoun made especially notable contributions, of the question of the relative merits of a militia and a standing army in republics and in modern monarchies; see the well-documented study by J. R. Western, *The English Militia in the Eighteenth Century: The Story of a Political Issue, 1660–1802* (London: Routledge and Kegan Paul; Toronto: Univ. of Toronto Press, 1965). Once again there are striking similarities between Gibbon and Rousseau; see the *Discourse on the Arts and Sciences*, the *Social Contract*, and the *Constitution of Corsica* on property conditions for "citizens" and "patriots." Gibbon's view of the Roman Republic was probably conditioned in part, like Rousseau's, by an idealized conception of "Swiss Liberty."
27. *DF*, XLVIII (2:866).
28. *DF*, XVII (1:543).
29. *DF*, I (1:9); also XXXI (2:138).
30. *DF*, XXXI (2:146); see also XLIV (2:708).
31. *DF*, XII (1:276).
32. *DF*, XLIII (2:667).
33. *DF*, VII (1:168).
34. *DF*, XLIV (2:707–8). While emphasizing the important differences of temperament and outlook that separated Rousseau and Gibbon and discounting any influence of the former on the latter – despite the presence in the library at La Grotte of a bust of the Genevan – Michel Baridon does acknowledge "un écho des accents célèbres de la seconde partie du Discours sur l'Origine de l'Inégalité parmi les Hommes" in the passage quoted here (*Edward Gibbon et le Mythe de Rome*, pp. 513–29, 645–6). The deeper affinities may be quite extensive, whatever the surface differences of conduct and attitude.
35. *DF*, XVII (1:521).
36. *DF*, XV (1:396, 441), XVI (1:451), XX (1:657).
37. *DF*, XVI (1:483).
38. *DF*, XVIII (1:562–3).
39. *DF*, XXVII (2:50), XXVI (1:941).
40. *DF*, XXXIX (2:460).
41. *DF*, XXVI (1:941).
42. *DF*, XXXIX (2:453); see also XXVI (1:804), XLI (2:542), XLVI (2:800), XLVIII (2:913).

43. *DF*, XLVIII (2:909).
44. *DF*, LI (3:136n). The "tumid" is from Longinus, *On the Sublime, III*.
45. *DF*, XLVI (2:800), XXXV (2:294n).
46. Both passages quoted from Gibbon's abstract, with remarks, of the first volume of Blackstone's *Commentaries on the Laws of England* (1767), in *The English Essays of Edward Gibbon*, ed. Patricia A. Craddock (Oxford: The Clarendon Press, 1972), p. 63. A few pages of the abstract, with abridged remarks, had been published in *MW*, V, 545–7.
47. *DF*, II (1:52).
48. *DF*, XXIII (1:760n).
49. *DF*, XXIII (1:761).
50. *DF*, XLIV (2:685).
51. *DF*, XLIV (2:681).
52. *DF*, XXI (1:675).
53. *DF*, XLIV (2:681). Rousseau – surprisingly, perhaps – had already indicated that the best state was one whose origins were lost in the mists of antiquity (Preface to *Discourse on Inequality*): that is, one in which rational principles and custom were not separate. Later, with Burke and Savigny, this attitude hardened into a conservative doctrine that stood in opposition to natural law and to all attempts to establish new and rational legal codes. Gibbon, however, maintains the position that the accretion of precedents is a *deformation* of the original simplicity of the law in that golden age before interpretation, when there was no breach between the principle and its application, as there was no breach between the word and its meaning, the signifier and the signified; consequently, he writes favorably of a complete remaking of the law from original principles. To him, in sum, a rational code of law would be equivalent to rediscovery of the original law.
54. *DF*, XLIV (2:684).
55. Ibid.
56. *DF*, XLIV (2:686).
57. *DF*, XLIV (2:687).
58. *DF*, XLIV (2:688).
59. *DF*, XLIV (2:689).
60. *DF*, XLIV (2:691).
61. *DF*, XLIV (2:690).
62. *DF*, XLIV (2:687).
63. *DF*, XLIV (2:691–2).
64. *DF*, XLIV (2:693).
65. *DF*, XLIV (2:728).
66. *DF*, XVII (1:533).
67. *DF*, XVII (1:536).
68. *DF*, XXXI (2:146); see also V (1:92).
69. The decline of Rome itself is typically represented as a feminization and is vividly illustrated in Gibbon's account of the marriage of Placidia, daughter of the

great Theodosius and sister of Honorius, to Adolphus, the victorious king of the Goths (*DF*, XXXI [2:175]).

70. *DF*, XXI (1:673), XIX (1:605), XIX (1:599).
71. *DF*, XLVIII (2:874).
72. *DF*, XIX (1:598).
73. *DF*, XIX (1:598, 598n).
74. *DF*, XXXII (2:195–6).
75. Ibid.
76. *DF*, XXXII (2:197).
77. *DF*, XLI (2:574), XLIII (2:645), XLV (2:735).
78. *DF*, XLIV (2:723).
79. *DF*, VI (1:128).
80. *DF*, XXXIX (2:447).
81. *DF*, XLVIII (2:902).
82. *DF*, L (3:118).
83. *DF*, IX (1:199).
84. *DF*, XXXIX (2:447).
85. *DF*, XLVIII (2:898).
86. *DF*, XLVIII (2:884).
87. *DF*, XLVIII (2:902–4).
88. *DF*, XXXIII (2:229).
89. *DF*, XXXVIII (2:395).
90. *DF*, XLVIII (2:882).
91. *DF*, XLV (2:741–3).
92. *DF*, XLI (2:582–4).
93. *DF*, XVI (1:485), XXXVII (2:352).
94. *DF*, XVI (1:485).
95. *DF*, XXI (1:696).
96. *DF*, XXXVII (2:353).
97. *DF*, XXXVII (2:355).
98. *DF*, XLVIII (2:866).
99. *DF*, XXXVIII (2:379).
100. Ibid.
101. *DF*, XXXVII (2:347).
102. *DF*, XXI (1:715).
103. *DF*, XXXVII (2:352, 353).
104. See *DF*, XV (1:396): "The religion of the nations was not merely a speculative doctrine professed in the schools or preached in the temples. The innumerable deities and rites of polytheism were closely interwoven with every circumstance of business or pleasure, of public or of private life; and it seemed impossible to escape the observance of them, without, at the same time, renouncing the commerce of mankind, and all the offices and amusements of society. The important transactions of peace and war were prepared or concluded by solemn sacrifices, in

which the magistrate, the senator, and the soldier were obliged to preside or to participate."

105. *DF*, XXI (1:715, 717).

106. *AEG*, 270. G. M. Young (*Gibbon*, pp. 59–60), points out that the site was in fact the Temple of Juno: Gibbon was misled by his source, Nardini.

3. THE VACANT SPACE OF THE ETERNAL CITY

Chapter 3 title is from *DF*, XLIII (2:639).

1. *DF*, I (1:1).
2. *DF*, III (1:61).
3. *DF*, III (1:70).
4. *DF*, XVII (1:526).
5. *DF*, III (1:62–3).
6. *DF*, III (1:63).
7. Ibid.
8. *DF*, XIII (1:332).
9. *DF*, VII (1:168).
10. *DF*, XII (1:279).
11. *DF*, XXIX (2:71).
12. *DF*, XVIII (1:577–8).
13. *DF*, X (1:220); *Lettres persanes*, LXXXIII.
14. *DF*, II (1:25).
15. *DF*, II (1:27).
16. *DF*, XI (1:250).
17. *DF*, XXIII (1:769). In general, "it is easier to destroy than to restore" (IX [1:268]).
18. *DF*, VII (1:145–6). See n. 98 below.
19. *DF*, XIV (1:345).
20. *DF*, XLVIII (2:922).
21. *DF*, XVII (1:529). See Gibbon's own comments in his correspondence on the government of the Pays de Vaud, then in the hands of the Bernese. In a letter to his stepmother (*LEG*, 627, 15/vii/85 [3:27–30]), he declares that he is pleased at having escaped from the politics of England to the order of Lausanne: "That incessant hurry of Politicks was indeed one of [the] things which disgusted [me] the most, and there is nothing pleases me so much in this Country as to enjoy all the blessings of a Good Government without ever talking or thinking of our Governors." See also *LEG*, 652, mid-September, 1787 (3:71).
22. *DF*, XVII (1:525). Similarly, "the political society of the ancient Germans *has the appearance* of a voluntary alliance of independent warriors. The tribes of Scythia . . . *assume the form* of a numerous and increasing family" (XXVI, 1:906; italics added). But it is by "a useful prejudice, which has obtained the sanction of time and opinion" and "produces the effect of truth" that the Tartars recognize

their chief or *mursa* as "the representative of their great father" and allow him, in that capacity, to exercise "the authority of a judge in peace and of a leader in war" (XXVI, 1:906).

23. *DF*, XV (1:440).
24. *DF*, XLIV (2:708).
25. *DF*, IV (1:75).
26. *DF*, XLIV (2:718). Similarly, the "unwelcome discovery of the antiquity and extent of the disease [of homosexuality]" (XLIV, 2:724–5).
27. *DF*, XLIV (2:708).
28. See, for instance, Rousseau, *Emile*, in *Oeuvres complètes*, vol. 4, pp. 526–30.
29. *DF*, XV (1:394).
30. *LEG*, 633, 3/v/86 (3:43). The "matinée à l'angloise" in *La nouvelle Heloise* (pt. V, letter 3) is probably the most celebrated literary image of the silent, ineffable contentment that the bourgeois opposes as an ideal to the noise of aristocratic military adventure and courtly intrigue.
31. *LEG*, 784, 18/v/91 (3:226).
32. *DF*, III (1:69).
33. *DF*, XXXI (2:183).
34. *DF*, XLVII (2:863).
35. *DF*, XLVI (2:785).
36. *DF*, XLI (2:549).
37. *DF*, XXXVI (2:301).
38. *DF*, XLI (2:547–8).
39. See n. 22 above.
40. See Lewis P. Curtis, "Gibbon's Paradise Lost" in *The Age of Johnson: Essays Presented to Chauncey Brewster Tinker* (New Haven: Yale Univ. Press, 1949), p. 82: "Gibbon often mocked or deplored the vagaries of religious perception; yet throughout his life he adhered implicitly to what was, in fact, a religious concept of society and government." This interesting comment is not, however, sufficiently nuanced.
41. See n. 27 above.
42. In the dedication "A la République de Genève" of the *Discourse on the Origin of Inequality* Rousseau declares: "J'aurois donc cherché pour ma Patrie une heureuse et tranquille République dont l'ancienneté se perdît en quelque sorte dans la nuit des tems" (*Oeuvres complètes*, vol. 3, p. 113). In the eighth of the *Lettres écrites de la montagne*, he insists that "il ne s'agit pas ici d'innover; il s'agit, au contraire, d'empêcher qu'on n'innove; il s'agit non d'établir de nouvelles Loix, mais de maintenir les anciennes. Quand les choses tendent au changement par leur pente, il faut sans cesse de nouveaux soins pour les arrêter" (Ibid., p. 847). Law must not be allowed to become simply an instrument in the hands of the rich and privileged, in this case of the Petit Conseil of Geneva, and Statute Law must not be allowed to overthrow the founding laws of the state:

> Alors toute la solemnité des Loix seroit vaine et ridicule, et . . . réellement l'Etat n'auroit point d'autre Loi que la volonté du petit Conseil, maître

absolu de négliger, mépriser, violer, tourner à sa mode les regles qui lui seroient prescrites, et de prononcer *noir* où la Loi diroit *blanc*, sans en répondre à personne. A quoi bon s'assembler solemnellement dans le Temple de Saint Pierre, pour donner aux Edits une sanction sans effet; pour dire au petit Conseil: *Messieurs, voila le Corps de Loix que nous établissons dans l'Etat, et dont nous vous rendons les dépositaires, pour vous y conformer quand vous le jugerez à propos, et pour le transgresser quand il vous plaira.*

43. William Blackstone, *Commentaries on the Laws of England*, Introd., Section 3, which is quoted from the fifth edition (Oxford: Clarendon Press, 1773), vol. 1, p. 76.

44. *Gibbon's English Essays*, ed. Craddock, p. 63.

45. Unlike Michelet's Roman legislator, who "se laisse pousser d'interprétation en interprétation hors de la loi écrite, marchant, traîné plutôt, et ne convenant jamais qu'il a marché" (Jules Michelet, *Origines du droit français* [Paris: Calmann Levy, n.d.], p. xcvi) – who is and should be, in short, himself the victim as well as the accomplice of illusion – Gibbon's legislator is fully conscious of his role, and he respects the law not out of religious awe but because he recognizes its social value and utility. There is clearly an analogy between these two contrasting ideas of the legislator on the one hand and the Enlightenment and Romantic conceptions of the narrator on the other.

46. *DF*, XII (1:274).

47. Gibbon's position may seem to have been adumbrated in many respects by the radical Augustinian thinkers of the seventeenth century, such as Pascal. Yet Pascal's reaffirmation of the *hidden* God, of the immense gap between the human and the divine, devalues the human while leaving the divine intact. In revealing that human authority is a matter of signs, Pascal argues that the signs should still be obeyed for the sake of peace; the motive for obedience, however, is not human well-being but the conditions necessary to the pursuit of the spiritual life. In the end, it is the goal of salvation that sanctions whatever human arrangements best promote it. For Montesquieu and Gibbon, on the other hand, no truth, authority, or absolute origin remains, even on the other side of an unbridgeable divide, to contrast with the human order and reveal it as incomplete.

48. *DF*, II (1:27).

49. *DF*, XL (2:493).

50. *DF*, L (3:68).

51. Ibid.

52. *DF*, XLIV (2:667).

53. *DF*, XL (2:494).

54. *DF*, XL (2:495).

55. *DF*, XXXIV (2:254).

56. *DF*, XXXV (2:287).

57. *DF*, XXI (1:675).

58. See, for instance, the account of the Ichthyophagi on the shores of the Persian Gulf in Chapter L (3:59) or that of the life of the Moors in Chapter XLI (2:546).

59. *DF*, XXXIV (2:254).

60. *DF*, XXXVIII (2:407).

61. *DF*, XL (2:522).

62. Jacques Derrida describes a somewhat similar attitude to the spoken word in Rousseau: "L'éloge de la parole vive . . . compose et s'organise avec son contraire: une méfiance sans cesse ranimée à l'égard de la parole dite pleine . . . La parole que Rousseau a élevée au-dessus de l'écriture, c'est la parole telle qu'elle devrait être ou telle qu'elle aurait dû être." Derrida refers to *Social Contract*, ch. XX ("Relation of languages to Governments"), "un éloge de l'éloquence ou plutôt de l'élocution de la parole pleine, une condamnation des signes muets et impersonnels; argent, tracts ("placards"), armes et soldats en uniforme" (*De la Grammatologie*, [Paris: Editions de Minuit, 1967], p. 199).

63. *DF*, XL (2:474–6). See also on Constantine, XVIII (1:566–8).

64. *DF*, XLII (2:587, 589).

65. *DF*, XL (2:476, 477). In a curious comment in his travel journal, Gibbon observes that, although Carlo Emmanuele III of Savoy is in general a good administrator, his reign has been spoiled by the consequences of his remorse at having arrested and imprisoned his father Vittorio Amadeo II. "Malheureusement pour lui, son père est mort dans ses prisons. Une demarche qui peut cependant se justifier [Vittorio Amadeo, having abdicated in favor of his son, suddenly announced his intention of reclaiming the throne] a produit deux mauvais effets sur le caractère du Roi. Il lui inspire des remords et une melancolie qui l'ont jettè dans la petite devotion, en meme tems que ce souvenir lui donne une jalousie de son fils qui les rend malheureux tous les deux" (*Gibbon's Journal from Geneva to Rome*, ed. Georges A. Bonnard [Edinburgh and London: Nelson, 1961], p. 18).

66. *DF*, XLIV (2:689).

67. *DF*, XLIV (2:691).

68. *DF*, XLVII (2:837).

69. *DF*, XLIII (2:660).

70. *DF*, XLIII (2:659).

71. *DF*, XL (2:480–2).

72. *DF*, XL (2:483, 485).

73. *DF*, XL (2:484).

74. *DF*, XLII (2:611).

75. *DF*, XLIII (2:639).

76. *DF*, XLI (2:583–4).

77. *DF*, XLV (2:740–1).

78. *DF*, XLIV (2:697). Mommsen may have had Gibbon in mind when, in an account of *patria potestas* that is distinguished from Gibbon's by its matter-of-factness and its avoidance of pathos and value judgment, he roundly declares that wife

and child "were not things, but persons" (*Roman History*, Book I, ch. 5 [Everyman Edition, vol. 1, p. 60]).

79. *DF*, XLIV (2:697).
80. *DF*, XLIV (2:696).
81. *DF*, XLIV (2:699).
82. *DF*, XLIV (2:698).
83. *DF*, XLIV (2:698).
84. *DF*, XLIV (2:697).
85. *DF*, XLIV (2:700, 701–2).
86. *DF*, XLIV (2:700, 702).
87. *DF*, XLIV (2:702).
88. *DF*, XXXV (2:278).
89. *DF*, XXXV (2:275).
90. *DF*, XXXVII (2:347).
91. *DF*, XLV (2:752).
92. *DF*, LII (3:245).
93. *DF*, XXII (1:752).
94. *DF*, XLIII (2:639). See also Chap. LII (3:244): "a city which even yet, in her fallen state, was revered as the metropolis of the Christian world."
95. *LEG*, 816, 8/xi/92 (3:288); *LEG*, 762, 7/viii/90 (3:194–9).
96. *DF*, XII (1:282).
97. *DF*, II (1:25–6).
98. Montesquieu had himself praised the tolerance of the Romans in religious matters in terms very similar to Gibbon's in an early paper read to the Académie de Bordeaux in 1716, "Dissertation sur la politique des Romains dans la religion." This essay was not published until 1799, but its essential ideas, considerably refined, are included in the *Esprit des lois*.
99. *DF*, II (1:28).
100. Ibid.
101. *Esprit des lois*, V, xxiv. See also the 1716 essay: "Ce ne fut ni la crainte ni la piété qui etablit la religion chez les Romains; mais la necessité où sont toutes les sociétés d'en avoir une" (*Oeuvres*, ed. D. Oster [Paris: Seuil, 1964], p. 39).
102. In his own career Gibbon had leaned at first more toward the position of the philosopher. He had condemned the oligarchic government of Berne in the name of the liberty and sovereignty of all citizens in the early Letter on the government of Berne (see above, Chap. 1, n. 23). Similarly, his remarks on Blackstone's *Commentaries*, composed on the appearance of the first volume in 1765, place him in a position that W. S. Holdsworth has shown to be quite close to that of Bentham several decades later ("Gibbon, Blackstone, and Bentham," *The Law Quarterly Review*, 52 [1936], 46–59). Gibbon's admiration for Blackstone concerned mainly the form and style of the work and the elegance with which Blackstone had presented "a rational system of English Jurisprudence, digested into a natural method, and cleared of the pedantry, the obscurity, and the superfluities which rendered it the unknown horror of all men of taste." Bentham awarded similar praise to Black-

stone, though in a tone of sarcasm, for having "taught Jurisprudence to speak the language of the Scholar and the Gentleman; put a polish upon that rugged science, cleansed her from the dust and cobwebs of the office . . . ; decked her out . . . to advantage, from the toilette of classical erudition, enlivened her with metaphors and allusions . . . " In 1765 Gibbon was only slightly less critical of the matter of the *Commentaries* than Bentham was to be, with far less politeness, years later. Like Bentham, he was impatient with the mysteries of the law, which Blackstone revered; he preferred enacted law (statute law) to unenacted law (common law); and he held that its usefulness in promoting human happiness is the best criterion of the expediency and value of a law, whereas Blackstone shared with Burke the view that "we ought to understand [the law] according to our measure; and to venerate when we are not able presently to comprehend." Likewise he criticized Blackstone's attempt to prove the continuity of lineal succession of the British monarchs from Egbert to James I – despite its being "suspended" from the Conquest till the accession of the latter – as mere mystification: "Such a suspension must be equivalent to a total extinction in the opinion of all but iure divino men" (*The English Essays of Edward Gibbon*, p. 52). By the time he came to work on the *Decline and Fall*, Gibbon had come, as we have seen, to entertain more respect for such "fictions" of authority.

4. A LIBERAL EDUCATION AND UNDERSTANDING

Chapter 4 title is from *DF*, XV (1:399).

1. *DF*, II (1:28).
2. *DF*, XXVII (2:45).
3. *DF*, XXXIII (2:242–3).
4. "Enthusiasm" extends, of course, as it does with Voltaire, to the "enthusiasm" of philosophy, i.e. metaphysics and theology; see, for instance, *DF*, XXI (1:677–8) on the divine attributes of the *Logos*.
5. E.g. *DF*, XXI (1:681): "A theology which it was incumbent to believe, which it was impious to doubt, and which it might be dangerous, and even fatal, to mistake . . . " On the rhetorical value of abstract terms in eighteenth-century discourse, see the late W. K. Wimsatt's outstanding early study of Johnson, *The Prose Style of Samuel Johnson* (New Haven: Yale Univ. Press, 1941), especially the section on "Style as Meaning."
6. *DF*, XXI (1:723). "Philosophy" and "philosopher," as used by Gibbon, have the meaning these terms had in the eighteenth century, especially in France.
7. On the categories of *discours* and *histoire*, which are by now fairly familiar in discussions of narrative form, see Emile Benveniste, "La Relation de temps dans le verbe français" (1959) in *Problèmes de linguistique générale* (Paris: Gallimard, 1966), pp. 237–50.
8. See, for instance, *DF*, XIX, n. 39 (1:609–10) on the "jealous artifices of Eusebia," as recounted in the narrative.

9. *DF*, XL, n. 132 (2:516–17).
10. *DF*, I (1:4); *DF*, I (1:21); *DF*, XL (2:516); *DF*, IX (1:188). Italics added. Likewise, the kingdom of Artaxerxes was "nearly equal in extent to modern Persia" (*DF*, VIII [1:177]); in the lower Auvergne "the inexhaustible fertility of the soil supplied [at the time of Childebert], and still supplies, without any interval of repose, the constant repetition of the same harvests" (*DF*, XXXVIII [2:414]).
11. *DF*, XIV (1:380); *DF*, XV (1:390). Italics added.
12. *DF*, XL (2:508). Italics added.
13. *DF*, XLI (2:560); *DF*, XLVIII (2:855); *DF*, L (3:128); *DF*, LI (3:188); *DF*, LII (3:230). Italics added.
14. *DF*, XI (1:268). Italics added.
15. *DF*, XIII (1:337). Italics added.
16. *DF*, XLI (2:551). Italics added.
17. *DF*, LI (3:190). Italics added.
18. E.g., "In the same year all the principal actors in this great revolution were removed from the stage" (*DF*, XXXVI [2:337]); "From the time of Heraclius the Byzantine theatre is contracted and darkened" (*DF*, XLVIII [2:866]).
19. *DF*, XIX (1:611).
20. *DF*, XXXIII, n. 30 (2:236–7).
21. *DF*, XXX (2:104).
22. *DF*, XXXIII (2:238–9).
23. *DF*, VI (1:139); *DF*, X (1:210); *DF*, XXXIII (2:239); *DF*, XLII (2:624); *DF*, L (3:119); *DF*, LI (3:187).
24. See the interesting article by Paul Hernadi, "Clio's Cousins," *New Literary History*, 7 (1976), 247–55: "The narrator of every work of fiction is, as part of the work, fictional . . . By contrast, the narrator of a historical work can be considered historical; the historian endorses the narrator's credibility to the point of turning the ontological distinction between the author and narrator of fiction as creator and creature into the psychological distinction between the historian's actual person and the person he would like to be or at least to appear. In other words, fictional narratives demand, historical narratives preclude, a distinction between the narrator and the implied author."
25. *DF*, XII (1:277).
26. *DF*, XVII (1:592).
27. *DF*, XLI (2:546–8); cf. Procopius, "The Vandalic War," in *History of the Wars*, Book IV, ch. vi, sections 27–84 (Loeb Classical Library ed., vol. 2, pp. 262–3).
28. *DF*, XIII (1:336).
29. *DF*, XIV (1:355).
30. Gibbon's contrast of the predatory great, on the one hand, and their productive subjects, on the other, may well be related to his hesitation, signalled earlier, between idealization of republican liberty and praise of Antonine well-being and happiness. Quite possibly, the historian's uncertainty reflects a tension in bourgeois political thinking at his time, which, on the one hand, extols liberty and the political

life of the citizen, and on the other, sets great store by the productiveness and happiness of the individual as private person. Within the latter perspective, political life can be viewed as a more or less necessary evil, and the state may appear not as the arena of the political activity and self-fulfilment of the citizen, but simply as a condition of individual productive activity and private happiness. The best state would then not necessarily be the most free, but might be the most conducive to the industriousness and well-being of the individual.

31.   See, for instance, *DF*, XL (2:498): "To the historians of [Justinian] a campaign at the foot of Mount Caucasus has seemed more deserving of a minute relation than the labours of these missionaries of commerce, who again entered China, deceived a jealous people by concealing the eggs of the silkworm in a hollow cane, and returned in triumph with the spoils of the East." For similar views in Macaulay and Carlyle see Fritz Stern, *Varieties of History* (New York: Meridian Books, 1956), pp. 84–6, 97–8; in Thierry, see my *Augustin Thierry and Liberal Historiography* (Middletown, Conn.: Wesleyan Univ. Press, 1976), p. 15. Rousseau complained that "l'histoire en general est défectueuse en ce qu'elle ne tient registre que de faits sensibles et marqués, qu'on peut fixer par des noms, des lieux, des dates . . ." (*Emile*, Bk. IV, in *Oeuvres complètes* [Paris: Gallimard, 1959–69], vol. 4, p. 529).

32.   *DF*, X (1:206).

33.   Ibid.

34.   To Dorothea Gibbon, *LEG*, 804, 1/viii/92 (3:266). In this letter Gibbon contrasts his own "road to happiness" by way of "a life of celibacy and retirement" with that followed by his friend Sheffield, "always employed for himself, his friends and the public." See also Ch. 1, n. 25 above.

35.   *DF*, LII, n. 55 (3:232).

36.   Bagehot, *Literary Studies*, pp. 33–4.

37.   *DF*, XLVII (2:814, 831).

38.   *DF*, XLVIII (2:922–3).

39.   *LEG*, 623, 22/x/84 (3:9–11); *LEG*, 624, 27/x/84 (3:17).

40.   *DF*, II (1:25); see also *DF*, XXXII (2:215): "a prudent historian will refuse to examine the *propriety*, till he has ascertained the *truth*, of the testimony of Arcadius. As it stands without a parallel in the history of the world, we may justly require that it should be attested by the positive and unanimous evidence of contemporaries. The strange novelty of the event, which excites our distrust, must have attracted their notice; and their universal silence annihilates the vain tradition of the succeeding age."

41.   *DF*, XXI (1:695); *DF*, XXI (1:722); *DF*, XXIII (1:756); *DF*, XXXII (2:215); *DF*, XXXVIII (2:403); *DF*, "General Observations" (2:439); *DF*, XLIII (2:660); *DF*, XLIV (2:669). Similarly, the praise of Aeneas of Gaza, "a cool, a learned, and unexceptionable witness, without interest, and without passion" (*DF*, XXXVII [2:377]).

42.   *DF*, XXXVII (2:377); *DF*, XXXI (2:188).

43.   *DF*, XXI (1:723).

44. *DF*, XXII (2:748): "the fundamental maxim of Aristotle, that true virtue is placed at an equal distance between the opposite vices."

45. *DF*, XXIII (1:781): "Such authority should satisfy a believing, and must astonish an incredulous mind. Yet a philosopher may still require the original evidence of impartial and intelligent spectators."

46. *DF*, XVI (1:477–8): "The first of these examples is attended with some difficulties which might perplex a sceptical mind."

47. It often happens in the *Decline and Fall* that "we are induced to suspect," and most frequently "our suspicions are confirmed" (*DF*, VIII [1:181]); but it is always "with calm suspicion" that "the philosopher . . . examines" even the most unlikely phenomena reported by the chronicler of the past (*DF*, XX [1:648]).

48. Hence the irony of the narrator's praise of d'Herbelot: "That learned collector has shown much taste in stripping the Oriental chronicles of their instructive and amusing anecdotes" (*DF*, LII, n. 80 [3:239]).

49. *DF*, XXI (1:695); *DF*, XXXVIII (2:403).

50. *DF*, XXXVIII (2:420, 423).

51. *DF*, IX (1:186).

52. *DF*, XXV (1:872).

53. *DF*, XXXVIII (2:423).

54. *DF*, "General Observations" (2:439). In the early letter on the government of Berne, supposedly by a Swedish traveller, Gibbon had already embraced the position he adopts here: "Non, mon cher ami, je ne veux point être cosmopolite. Loin de moi ce titre fastueux, sous lequel nos philosophes cachent une égale indifférence pour tout le genre humain. Je veux aimer ma patrie, et pour aimer il me faut des préférences: mais ou je me trompe, ou mon coeur est susceptible de plus d'une" (*MW*, II, 1–2).

55. In a note appended to a passage in which he decries the poverty of history among the "Asiatics," Gibbon discerns "two sorts of Arabian historians – the dry annalist, and the tumid and flowery orator" (*DF*, LI, n. 15 [3:136]). Needless to say, he rejects both.

56. The classical scholar E. Badian points out that in his battle accounts Gibbon uses actual passages of classical authors freely "as part of the description of any battle that recalls to [him] the one they originally describe. Thus Thucydides 7, 71 is imported into the battle of the Golden Horn of 1453 (*Decline and Fall*, ch. 68 . . .) and Xenophon's *Anabasis* is quoted at length in the description of Galerius's victory in 297 (*Decline and Fall*, ch. 13 . . .)" ("Gibbon on War" in *Gibbon et Rome à la lumière de l'historiographie moderne*, ed. Pierre Ducrey [Geneva: Droz, 1977], p. 111). In general, the thrust of Badian's essay is to emphasize "the purely literary nature of Gibbon's mind" (p. 111) and to demonstrate that the stylized accounts of war in the *Decline and Fall* "reflect . . . the artist's conception of his task, in a thoroughly Ancient way, as primarily an artistic rendering of what he perceived through a literary imagination" (p. 129). Other contributors to the volume in which Badian's essay appears also emphasize the literary and rhetorical aspect of the *De-*

cline and Fall. D. van Berchem considers that in stylizing his descriptions of war
Gibbon was not unusual but was simply following a classical convention that also
affected his sources, including those historians who had participated in military
actions: "Outre le fait que Gibbon aurait eu de la peine à découvrir des détails
réalistes dans ses sources, s'il en avait cherché, il faut rappeler qu'il obéit, sur ce
point, à une convention observable dans toute l'historiographie antique et qui se
perpétue, au moins jusqu'à son temps, dans l'historiographie moderne" (p. 133). T.
Zawadski argues that in the space of a few pages in Ch. XIV Gibbon attributes
different and even contradictory values and characteristics to the armored cavalry
of Maxentius: In his account of the battle near Turin, he describes the armor of the
cataphracti as "artfully adapted" to the motions of the bodies of horse and men, but
in his account of the battle at Pons Mulvius, forgetting what he had written earlier,
he refers to them as "unwieldy cuirassiers." The reason for the shift: to avoid
undesirable repetition in two closely situated battle descriptions. "Ainsi le principe
de variété a été conservé," Zawadski observes, "mais aux frais de l'exactitude et
même de la vraisemblance d'une description des événements militaires" (p. 157). At
the beginning of the volume, Sir Ronald Syme presents Gibbon as "one of the
successors of the humanist historians of the Latin Renaissance, with all their preoc-
cupation with style and the models of Antiquity," even as "the last of the classical
historians themselves" (p. 55). François Paschoud draws attention to what he judges
the literary rather than scientific or critical considerations that often determined
Gibbon's use of sources (pp. 242–3). Against these views, however, Arnaldo Momigliano continues to regard Gibbon as a modern historian, "The first in date of the
great historians of antiquity" (p. 62; see also the earlier essay, "Gibbon's Contribution to Historical Method," originally published in 1954, in Momigliano's *Studies in
Historiography* [London: Weidenfeld and Nicolson, 1966], pp. 40–55). In the present study I am trying to show that Gibbon did indeed play both cards – that of
rhetoric and that of modern criticism – in an effort to win and retain the respect,
confidence, and goodwill of his readers. He remains a classical writer in that he
continues to follow the classical rule of *placere et docere*, adapting it to the ideas and
values of an eighteenth-century audience.

57.   To eliminate Gibbon's notes, as some editors of popular editions have done,
is to alter completely the meaning of the work. In the same way, the omission of
Augustin Thierry's lengthy notes to his *Récits des temps mérovingiens* in a modern
popular edition of that work distorts the work dangerously; on the other hand, the
addition of a huge scholarly apparatus of notes to the 1839 Brussels edition of
Barante's popular *Histoire des Ducs de Bourgogne* (1st ed., 1824) produced a parallel
though opposite distortion.

58.   *DF*, XLIX, n. 96 (3:34).

59.   See, for instance, the brief evaluation of Procopius under the headings of
"his facts," "his style," and "his reflections" (*DF*, XL [2:478–9]).

60.   See my "History and Literature: Reproduction or Signification," in Robert
H. Canary and Henry Kozicki, eds., *The Writing of History: Literary Form and*

Historical Understanding (Madison: Univ. of Wisconsin Press, 1978), especially pp. 10–17. E. M. Tillyard discusses the *Decline and Fall* as an epic project, in *The English Epic and its Background* (London: Oxford Univ. Press, 1954), pp. 510–27, and the thesis of Harold L. Bond's book, *The Literary Art of Edward Gibbon* (Oxford: Clarendon Press, 1960), is that "in composing *The Decline and Fall*, Gibbon aspired to write and did in fact write an historical epic" (pp. 1–2).

    61. *DF*, XXI, n. 76 (2:153).

    62. In a section on Roman military organization under Constantine we find the following observation: "A more particular enumeration, drawn from the *Notitia*, might exercise the diligence of an antiquary, but the historian will content himself with observing that the number of permanent stations or garrisons established on the frontiers of the empire amounted to five hundred and eighty-three; and that, under the successors of Constantine, the complete force of the military establishment was computed at six hundred and forty-five thousand soldiers" (*DF*, XVII [1:540–1]).

    63. *DF*, LI, n. 16 (3:136).

    64. See also the blunter repudiation of erudition – as befits the purported "editor" and "translator" of a romance – in the dedicatory epistle to the Sultana Sheraa that precedes the text of Voltaire's *Zadig*. The complicity of the worldly (female) reader is ensured by the disparaging reference to "l'ancien chaldéen que ni vous ni moi n'entendons."

    65. *AEG*, 196.

    66. E.g. *DF*, VI, n. 63 (1:129); *DF*, VI, n. 68 (1:131); *DF*, XXXV, n. 31 (2:279); *DF*, "General Observations," n. 7 (2:441); *DF*, VII (1:158–9); *DF*, XI (1:272); *DF*, XIV (1:342); *DF*, XV (1:439); *DF*, XVI (1:454–5); *DF*, XVII (1:517); *DF*, XVIII (1:560) et passim.

    67. See A. Momigliano, "Gibbon's Contribution to Historical Method" in his *Studies in Historiography*, p. 51: "Indeed, it is Gibbon's specialty that we can never be quite sure whether he displays erudition for the sake of a good story or tells a good story as a contribution to learning . . . He is far more amusing than any other historian except Herodotus." See also n. 54 above.

    68. *DF*, XXVII, n. 10 (2:4); *DF*, XXVIII (2:55); *DF*, XXXI (2:139); *DF*, "General Observations," n. 7 (2:441).

    69. *DF*, XV (1:413).

    70. *DF*, XV (1:399).

    71. *DF*, XV (1:442).

    72. *DF*, XVI (1:449).

    73. See H. Bond, *The Literary Art of Edward Gibbon*, p. 144: Gibbon "narrates, comments, evaluates, and judges as he goes along; the dualistic unit of his prose is admirably suited to the multiplicity of his artistic intentions, for it enables him to tell the reader what is happening and how he should feel about it at the same time."

    74. *DF*, X (1:220).

5. ORDER AND PERSPICUITY

Chapter 5 title is from *DF*, VI (1:137).

1. Thus in Ch. LI the narrator introduces the story of the destruction of the library at Alexandria on the orders of the Caliph Omar, because, though he will argue that it is spurious, "I should deceive the expectation of the reader if I passed in silence the fate of the Alexandrian library, as it is described by the learned Abulpharagius" (3:176).

2. *DF*, XI (1:272).

3. *DF*, XV (1:439); similarly in Ch. XXX: "The scarcity of facts, and the uncertainty of dates, oppose our attempts to describe the circumstances of the first invasion of Italy by the arms of Alaric" (2:99).

4. *DF*, XXXI, n. 179 (2:190).

5. *DF*, XVI (1:501).

6. *DF*, XXXII (2:222). Other narrative historians have made the same point. Half a century later, the author of the immensely popular *Histoire des Ducs de Bourgogne de la Maison de Valois* would argue, exactly as Voltaire and Gibbon had done, that "l'histoire se divise en périodes naturelles, en drames, qui ont leur commencement, leur progrès et leur dénouement" (Prosper de Barante, "Des Oeuvres de Lemontey et du siècle de Louis XIV" [1830], in *Mélanges historiques et littéraires* [Brussels: J. P. Meline, 1835], vol. 2, p. 227). At the same time, Barante held that there were periods when, to the embarassment of the historian, "les événemens ne se rallient plus à un centre commun, et flottent incertains . . . où rien ne marche à un but . . . C'est qu'à de telles époques, . . . les événemens sont pour ainsi dire inutiles, et n'ont pas encore de signification" ("De l'histoire," ibid., pp. 23–4).

7. *DF*, VI (1:137); *DF*, X (1:222, 242); *DF*, XIII (1:307) et passim.

8. "On Mr. Hurd's Commentary on Horace," *MW*, IV, 125, 126.

9. *DF*, XLVIII (2:867).

10. *DF*, X (1:207).

11. *DF*, XVI (1:445); similarly, in Ch. XX: "I shall endeavour to form a just estimate of the famous vision of Constantine, by a distinct consideration of the *standard*, the *dream*, and the *celestial sign*; by separating the historical, the natural, and the marvellous parts of this extraordinary story, which, in the composition of a specious argument, have been artfully confounded in one splendid and brittle mass" (1:644).

12. *DF*, X (1:222).

13. E.g., *DF*, X (1:239): "To illustrate the obscure monuments of the life and death of each individual would prove a laborious task, alike barren of instruction and amusement"; *DF*, XI (1:252): "The general design of this work will not permit us minutely to relate the actions of every emperor after he ascended the throne, much less to deduce the various fortunes of his private life"; *DF*, XVII (1:516): "But we should deviate from the design of this history if we attempted minutely to

describe the different buildings or quarters of the city [Constantinople]"; *DF*, XXV
(1:893): "The splendour and magnitude of this Gothic war are celebrated by a
contemporary historian: but the events scarcely deserve the attention of posterity,
except as the preliminary steps of the approaching decline and fall of the empire."
The goal of order and perspicuity implies an ideal perspective on the material
equidistant from both excess and dearth of information, from both the partial and
chaotically detailed closeup view of the participant and the empty abstractions of
the remote spectator or philosopher (see n. 47 below). The use of metaphorical
terms linking historical narrative with *peinture d'histoire* and questions of artistic
perspective is widespread in the eighteenth century.

    14. *DF*, XXI (1:688–9).

    15. *DF*, XXVI (1:941).

    16. *DF*, XVII, n. 51 (2:824). The reader did, indeed, thank him for precisely this
reason. "Vous avez porté la lumière dans le chaos," he was told by the French writer
J. B. Suard, whom he had tried to interest in doing a French translation of his
work, "et vous avez suivi le fil caché des événements les plus bizarres dans ce
labyrinthe obscur où tous les liens qui unissent les hommes en société et toutes les
règles qui les dirigent étant rompues, les plus grandes révolutions paroissent ne
tenir qu'au caprice d'une multitude ivre, aux passions extravagantes de quelques
individus, ou à des combinaisons fortuites de circonstances" (*MW*, II, 183, letter
XCVI, 251176).

    17. *DF*, XLVIII (2:865–6).

    18. *DF*, XVII (1:521).

    19. *DF*, X (1:222).

    20. *DF*, XVII (1:505).

    21. *DF*, XVI (1:445).

    22. *DF*, VI (1:136).

    23. *DF*, XXXI, n. 132 (2:174).

    24. *DF*, XXVI (1:918); again in Ch. XXX: "The chain of events is interrupted,
or rather is concealed, as it passes from the Volga to the Vistula, through the dark
interval which separates the extreme limits of the Chinese and of the Roman geog-
raphy" (2:110).

    25. *DF*, XLIV (2:688).

    26. E.g., *DF*, X (1:222, 242); *DF*, XI (1:251); *DF*, XL (2:501) et passim.

    27. *DF*, III (1:69).

    28. See R. N. Parkinson, *Edward Gibbon* (New York: Twayne, 1973), pp. 117–25;
Michel Baridon, *Edward Gibbon et le mythe de Rome* (Paris: Champion, 1977), pp.
749–78; Harold L. Bond, *The Literary Art of Edward Gibbon*. Discussing Gibbon's
"frequent and varied use of balance and antithesis," Bond considers it "typical of
the mind that wishes to fix with some exactitude the ambivalence in human affairs"
(p. 152). Similarly, for Ian Watt, in the periodic sentence, which "reached its full
development . . . with Johnson and Gibbon . . . the effort is for the speaker or
writer to contain or stabilize order, in some way impose a pattern, on the miscellaneous multifariousness of experience and individual attitudes" ("The Ironic Voice,"

in *The Augustan Age*, ed. Ian Watt [Greenwich, Conn.: Fawcett Publications, 1968],
p. 108).

29. *DF*, IV (1:86).
30. *DF*, XV (1:392).
31. *DF*, XIX (1:599).
32. *DF*, XII (1:284).
33. *DF*, XV (1:392).
34. *DF*, XXXI (2:172).
35. *DF*, X (1:220).
36. *DF*, XVIII (1:582).
37. *DF*, XIX (1:601).
38. *DF*, XXI (1:691).
39. *DF*, XXVIII (2:52).
40. *DF*, XXVIII (2:62).
41. *DF*, XXXI (2:182).
42. *DF*, XLVII (2:834–5).
43. *DF*, XV (1:397).
44. *DF*, XIX (1:598). See also the following passages from Ch. XXII and Ch.
XXVIII respectively: "Whenever the spirit of fanaticism, at once so credulous and
so crafty, has insinuated itself into a noble mind, it insensibly corrodes the vital
principles of virtue and veracity" (1:733); "a bold, bad man, whose hands were
alternately polluted with gold and with blood" (2:57–8).
45. *DF*, XX (1:648).
46. *DF*, III (1:69).
47. *DF*, XIV (1:359); *DF*, XI (1:254). See also the end of Ch. V: "The contemporaries of Severus, in the enjoyment of the peace and glory of his reign, forgave
the cruelties by which it had been introduced. Posterity, who experienced the fatal
effects of his maxims and example, justly considered him as the principal author of
the decline of the Roman empire" (1:110); at the opening of Ch. XIII: "As the reign
of Diocletian was more illustrious than that of any of his predecessors, so was his
birth more abject and obscure" (1:303); in Ch. XX: "As he gradually advanced in
the knowledge of truth, he proportionably declined in the practice of virtue"
(1:654). Even darkness and uncertainty are delimited and brought into line by a
reduction of possibilities to two opposites ("the courage or the fear," "the piety or
the avarice," "artful or sincere," etc.)
48. *DF*, XX (1:663).
49. In the first of the two examples of syntactic parallelism quoted above, the
plural subject and verb of the first member of the parallelism is varied by a singular
subject and verb in the second member; in the second example, the preposition
"of," which introduces the first two members, is omitted from the third; in "the
pleasure of sense, . . . the polygamy of the patriarchs, . . . and the seraglio of Solomon" the rhythm of the first member is different from that of the second and third
members, which is almost identical (polygamy/seraglio, patriarchs/Solomon),

though even here there are slight variations in the joining words ("of the" as against "of").

50. "Essai sur l'étude de la litterature," sec. XLVIII, in *MW*, IV, 1–94.

51. *DF*, XXVII (2:45).

52. *DF*, VII (1:166). In Ch. IX, n. 54, "the brilliant imagination of Montesquieu is corrected . . . by the dry, cold reason of the Abbé de Mably" (1:198); in Ch. XXVI, n. 11, Montesquieu is described as having "used and abused the relations of travellers" (1:905). See also Ch. XXVII, n. 17 (2:51).

53. On the historian's laws, see Isaiah Berlin, *Historical Inevitability* (London: Oxford Univ. Press, 1954), pp. 51–4.

54. *DF*, XV (1:414).

55. *DF*, XX (1:655).

56. *DF*, XVIII (1:598).

57. *DF*, XXIX (2:90).

58. *DF*, XXXIII (2:240).

59. *DF*, XXV (1:869–70).

60. *DF*, XXXIX (2:464).

61. *DF*, II (1:48).

62. *DF*, IV (1:75).

63. *DF*, X (1:244).

64. *DF*, XV (1:440).

65. *DF*, XI (1:268).

66. *DF*, XI (1:271).

67. *DF*, XXIX (2:87).

68. Ibid.

69. *DF*, XLII (2:621).

70. *DF*, XVIII (1:598).

71. *DF*, XXXIX (2:464).

72. *DF*, XXXVIII (2:399).

73. *Lettres à Sophie Volland*, ed. André Babelon (Paris: Gallimard, 1938), vol. 1, pp. 151–3.

74. "A Vindication of some passages in the XVth and XVIth chapters of the History of the Decline and Fall of the Roman Empire," *MW*, IV, 568.

75. *DF*, X (1:239).

76. On the "normative" or structured and the "functional" or unstructured in esthetics, see Jan Mukařovský, "The Esthetics of Language," in *Slovo a Slovesnost*, 6 (1940), 1–27, rpt. in *A Prague School Reader in Esthetics, Literary Structure, and Style*, sel. and trans. by Paul N. Garvin (Washington: Georgetown Univ. Press, 1964), pp. 31–69.

77. "Extraits raisonnés de mes lectures," dated Dover, 14th March, 1761, *MW*, V, 209–10.

78. *DF*, XXI (1:713).

79. *DF*, XIV (1:370).

80. *DF*, LI (3:141).

81. *DF*, XLIV (2:720).
82. *DF*, XLVIII (2:913).
83. *DF*, XLVIII (2:914).
84. *DF*, XVI (1:483).
85. *DF*, XXV (1:888–90).
86. *DF*, XXXIII (2:229).
87. *DF*, XXXIII (2:240).
88. *DF*, XXXV (2:297).
89. *DF*, LI (3:155).
90. *DF*, LI (3:152).

91. *DF*, XXXIII (2:229); *DF*, XXXVIII (2:417); *DF*, XXV (1:888–9); *DF*, XXXIII (2:240). Sometimes an anecdote seems justified by its singularity alone, as when the story of the four score gladiators who killed their keepers and went on a rampage through Rome is introduced into the account of the orderly reign of Probus by the rather unconvincing phrase "We cannot on this occasion forget . . . " (*DF*, XII [1:290]). The significance of the anecdote in classical historiography is brought out by Hannah Arendt in an essay on "Natur und Geschichte" in *Fragwürdige Traditionsbestände im politischen Denken der Gegenwart: vier Essays* (Frankfurt a.M.: Europäische Verlagsanstalt, n.d.), pp. 47–80. Arendt observes that for the Greeks, the historical was identical with the singular, the unusual, the act or word that detached itself from the eternal patterns of nature. It was to such specifically human – as opposed to natural – phenomena that the ancient poets and historians wished to give immortality. Such a notion of the historical is strange to the modern scholar, she contends: "history no longer is for historical science that dimension of the past in which the deeds and sufferings of men are recorded, and our histories no longer relate the countless, varied stories that defined the life of men on earth from the very beginning. History is now, at least since Hegel, rather the huge, all-encompassing process in which every individual phenomenon emerges and disappears and in which each deed and each event acquires sense and meaning only by constituting an intelligible part of this single total process" (p. 69 [my translation]). Like other neoclassical narrative historians, Gibbon seems still to hesitate between two notions of the historical – that of the ancients, who find it in the detached, autonomous, self-contained incident, and that of the moderns, who find it in the general laws or, as with the Romantics, the overall process, by which the individual event is subsumed.

92. E.g., the "charity" of Bishop Acacius of Amida, which "shall not be lost in oblivion" (*DF*, XXXII [2:223]), or the lesson "intelligent observers" derive from the laughter of Gelimer brought before his captor (*DF*, XLI [2:547]).

93. *DF*, XXI (1:697).
94. *DF*, XLVIII (2:923).
95. *DF*, XXXII (2:219).
96. *DF*, LIX (3:493).

6. A FAIR AND AUTHENTIC HISTORY

Chapter 6 title is from "A Vindication of some passages in the XVth and XVIth chapters of the Decline and Fall of the Roman Empire," *MW*, IV, 521–2.

1. "The experience of past faults, which may sometimes correct the mature age of an individual, is seldom profitable to the successive generations of mankind. The nations of antiquity, careless of each other's safety, were separately vanquished and enslaved by the Romans . . . The same error was repeated, the same consequences were felt, and the Goths, both of Italy and Spain, insensible of their approaching danger, beheld with indifference, and even with joy, the rapid downfall of the Vandals" (*DF*, XLI [2:552]).

2. *DF*, XLVIII (2:923).

3. This feature of Gibbon's work may account for the somewhat unexpected appreciation of it by Borges. See his preface to a selection of extracts published in Spanish translation at Buenos Aires in 1961, in Jorge Luis Borges, *Prólogos, con un prólogo de prólogos* (Buenos Aires: Torres Agüero, 1975), pp. 68–74. Gibbon's contemporaries may have been less keenly conscious of the formal quality of his writing than were nineteenth-century readers such as Bagehot, who were used to a different rhetoric, or, *a fortiori*, readers of our own time. That they were aware of it, however, seems indicated by Sheffield's comment that Gibbon's private correspondence would reveal the historian to the public "in a new and admirable light" (*MW*, I, 227).

4. D'Alembert, "Réflexions sur l'histoire," *Oeuvres* (Paris: Bastien, an XIII [1805]), vol. 4, p. 195. Letter from Cideville to Voltaire, 17.iii.1754, in *Voltaire's Correspondence*, ed. T. Besterman, 107 vols. (Geneva: Institut et Musée Voltaire, 1956–65), no. 6507. Similar views are found in Rousseau. From Pierre Bayle and the Pyrrhonists, Rousseau also learned that

> il s'en faut bien que les faits décrits dans l'histoire ne soient la peinture exacte des mêmes faits tels qu'ils sont arrivés. L'ignorance ou la partialité déguisent tout . . . Mettez un même objet à divers points de vüe, à peine paroîtra-t-il le même . . . Combien de fois un arbre de plus ou de moins, un rocher à droite ou à gauche, un tourbillon de poussière élevé par le vent ont décidé de l'événement d'un combat sans que personne s'en soit apperçû? Cela empêche-t-il que l'historien ne vous dise la cause de la defaite ou de la victoire avec autant d'assurance que s'il eut été par tout? . . . N'avez-vous jamais lû Cléopatre ou Cassandre, ou d'autres livres de cette espéce? Je vois peu de différence entre ces Romans et vos histoires, si ce n'est que le romancier se livre davantage à sa propre imagination, et que l'historien s'asservit plus à celle d'autrui; à quoi j'ajoûterai si l'on veut que le premier se propose un objet moral, bon ou mauvais dont l'autre ne se soucie guéres.

Thus, while history seems as "controuvé" as fiction, Rousseau prefers the latter because it at least has a moral end and because it is more likely to invent after nature: "On me dira que la fidelité de l'histoire interesse moins que la vérité des moeurs et des caractéres; . . . car après tout . . . que nous font des faits arrivés il y a deux mille ans? On a raison si les portraits sont bien rendus d'après nature; mais si la pluspart n'ont leur modéle que dans l'imagination de l'historien, . . . si mon élêve ne doit voir que des tableaux de fantaisie, j'aime mieux qu'ils soient tracés de ma main que d'une autre: ils lui seront du moins mieux appropriés" (*Emile*, Bk. IV, in *Oeuvres complètes*, vol. 4, pp. 527–8).

    5. "A Vindication of some passages in the XVth and XVIth chapters of the Decline and Fall of the Roman Empire," *MW*, IV, 521–2.

    6. See the classic article by P. F. Strawson, "On Referring," *Mind*, 59 (1950), 320–44. Meaning, according to Strawson,

> is a function of the sentence or expression; mentioning and referring and truth or falsity, are functions of the use of the sentence or expression. To give the meaning of an expression . . . is to give *general directions* for its use to refer to or to mention particular objects or persons; to give the meaning of a sentence is to give *general directions* for its use in making true or false assertions. It is not to talk about any particular occasion of the use of the sentence or expression. The meaning of an expression cannot be identified with the object it is used, on a particular occasion, to refer to. The meaning of a sentence cannot be identified with the assertion it is used, on a particular occasion, to make. For to talk about the meaning of an expression or sentence is not to talk about its use on a particular occasion, but about the rules, habits, conventions, governing its correct use, on all occasions, to refer or to assert. [p. 327]

Thus,

> To say, "The King of France is wise" is, in some sense of "imply," to *imply* that there is a king of France. But this is a very special and odd sense of "imply." "Implies" in this sense is certainly not equivalent to "entails" (or "logically implies"). And this comes out from the fact that when, in response to the statement, we say (as we should) "There is no king of France," we should certainly not say we were contradicting the statement that the king of France is wise. We are certainly not saying that it's false. We are, rather, giving a reason for saying that the question of whether it's true or false simply doesn't arise. [p. 330]

See also Strawson's *Introduction to Logical Theory* (London: Methuen, New York: John Wiley and Sons, 1951), pp. 188–9.

    7. The question of the *truth* of historical narratives and of the possibility of ever having true knowledge of the past had been a live issue among scholars in the

post-Cartesian climate of ideas at the end of the seventeenth century. By Gibbon's time, historical Pyrrhonism in its most radical form had been rejected, after having given rise to several important scholarly controversies, but a clear distinction had been drawn between historical truth and documentary authenticity and an epistemological distinction had been established, notably by Leibniz's friend Friedrich Bierling, between the certain truth of logical and mathematical propositions and the faith or belief underlying historical knowledge – *fides intellectus*, based on *revelatio humana*, and corresponding to *fides cordis*, based on *revelatio divina*.

8.   The theoretical question of authority is so complex, difficult, and fundamental to political and religious speculation that a layman cannot do more than scratch the surface of it. I found C. J. Friedrich, *Tradition and Authority* (London: Pall Mall, 1972) very helpful. Theodor Eschenberg, *Über Autorität* (Frankfurt A.M.: Suhrkamp Verlag, 2nd ed., 1976 [1st ed., 1965]) was a useful general guide to the various meanings of the term *auctoritas* in antiquity, the Middle Ages, and modern times. There is also an excellent general survey of the question by Leonard Krieger in *Dictionary of the History of Ideas* (New York: Scribners, 1968–74) vol. 1, pp. 141–62. Fritz Kern, *Kingship and Law in the Middle Ages*, trans. S. B. Chrimes (Oxford: Basil Blackwell, 1948), and E. H. Kantorowicz, *The King's Two Bodies* (Princeton: Princeton Univ. Press, 1957) were invaluable on the problem of authority in the Middle Ages; Kantorowicz, in particular, shows that the medieval fiction of the king as the invisible yet ubiquitous fount of authority, "not only incapable of doing wrong, but even of thinking wrong," survives with astonishing vigor in Blackstone's *Commentaries* (notably Bk. 1, Ch. 3). The intimate relation between authority, tradition, and religion, and the rootedness of the Roman concept of authority in a world view in which the present is bound by an unbroken bond to an original foundation in the past, to the original "founding fathers," are emphasized by Hannah Arendt in the essay "Was ist Autorität" (in *Fragwürdige Traditionsbestände im politischen Denken der Gegenwart: Vier Essays* [Frankfurt a.M.: Europäische Verlagsanstalt, n.d.], pp. 117–68, especially pp. 152–8). Arendt also underlines the incompatibility of authority and despotism on the one hand, and of authority and argument or debate on the other (p. 118). This aspect of authority seems particularly relevant to Gibbon, who was concerned to limit freedom but not to abolish it, and who wished to preserve authority – however unfounded – without having to defend or justify it by argument.

9.   "Of the First Principles of Government" (1741) in David Hume, *Essays Moral, Political and Literary* (London: Oxford Univ. Press, 1963), pp. 29–34. See also the essays "Of the Origin of Government" (not written until 1774, according to Mossner, *The Life of David Hume* [Edinburgh: Nelson, 1954], p. 553), pp. 35–9, and "Of the Original Contract" (first published in *Three Essays, Moral and Political* [1748] and included in the 3rd ed. of *Essays Moral and Political* [1748]), pp. 452–73, especially p. 461.

10.   "Of the Original Contract," p. 457.

11.   Ibid., p. 453.

12.   Ibid., p. 452.

13. *DF*, X (1:220).

14. While himself inclining to the view that the immense and increasing wealth of the monarch enhances his power, Hume produces the arguments of those who hold that the authority of the monarch is declining and that Britain is leaning more and more toward a republic:

> It may . . . be said that, though men be much governed by interest, yet even interest itself, and all human affairs, are entirely governed by *opinion*. Now there has been a sudden and sensible change in the opinions of men within these last fifty years, by the progress of learning and of liberty. Most people in this Island have divested themselves of all superstitious reverence to names and authority: the clergy have lost much of their credit: their pretensions and doctrines have been ridiculed; and even religion can scarcely support itself in the world. The mere name of *king* commands little respect; and to talk of a king as God's viceregent on earth, or to give him any of those magnificent titles which formerly dazzled mankind, would but excite laughter in every one. Though the crown, by means of its large revenue, may maintain its authority, in times of tranquillity, upon private interest and influence, yet, as the least shock of convulsion must break all these interests to pieces, the royal power, being no longer supported by the settled principles and opinions of men, will immediately dissolve. Had men been in the same disposition at the *Revolution*, as they are at present, monarchy would have run a great risk of being entirely lost in this Island. ["Whether the British Government inclines more to Absolute Monarchy or to a Republic," *Essays*, pp. 51–2]

15. "Of the First Principles of Government," ibid., p. 29. The view of authority outlined by Bertrand de Jouvenel (*Sovereignty: An Inquiry into the Political Good*, trans. J. F. Huntington [Chicago: Univ. of Chicago Press, 1957]) seems compatible, in many respects, with that of Hume and, if my reading is acceptable, of Gibbon. The original foundation of authority is "the natural ascendancy" of a single individual, according to de Jouvenel, but authority soon "became institutionalised by a complicity below the level of consciousness between leaders and led, who combined to stabilise a state of things, in itself unstable, which had proved beneficial. Though it was a natural ascendancy which founded the beneficial organisation, attachment to the latter has itself aroused a new regard for those who are its centre and symbol. They are now allowed an *induced ascendancy* as well, *which will henceforth sustain the natural ascendancy or make good its lack*" (p. 32 [italics added]). The successor, de Jouvenel continues, thus enjoys an induced authority. "Perhaps sceptics will say that there is superstition in the halo which is bestowed on the sovereign–successor and is the prop of his weakness. But it is this reflected prestige which keeps associations of men from dissolving on the disappearance of their founders." De Jouvenel insists, like Hannah Arendt, on the incompatibility of authority and power or the exercise of violence – a Roman tradition that finds

expression in Cicero, *De Legibus*, 3, 12, 28 and in Tacitus, *Germania*, XI – and argues that obedience to authority is voluntary, violence being necessary only where authority has broken down. The decline of authority in a state – "a great misfortune" – may be due to various inadequacies of the rulers, but also to "the destruction of the halo which upholds authority" (p. 33).

16.   Arnaldo Momigliano, "Gibbon's Contribution to Historical Method," p. 51. See Ch. 4, n. 67 above. The question of the *value* of Gibbon's work as history is clearly different from that of its character as history, although the two are not unconnected. As a historical work ceases to be valued as history, it will increasingly depend for its survival on whatever literary quality it may have. Gibbon himself was convinced that this is the destiny of historical writing ("Remarques sur les ouvrages et sur le caractere de Salluste, Jules Cesar, Cornelius Nepos, et Tite-Live," *MW*, IV, 430–1). Contemporary estimates of the value of Gibbon's history vary. In the "Bibliographical Appendix" to *Byzantium: An Introduction to East Roman Civilization*, ed. N. H. Baynes and H. St. L. B. Moss (Oxford: Clarendon Press, 1948), Norman Baynes judges that "Gibbon's masterpiece is still essential for the history of the Roman empire until the seventh century" (p. 392). More recently, however, Lynn White, Jr. concluded that "as history his work is almost unbelievably obsolete" (*The Transformations of the Roman World: Gibbon's Problem after Two Centuries* [Berkeley and Los Angeles: Univ. of California Press, 1966], p. 311). More recently still, François Paschoud argued that Gibbon is less critical, less reliable, and less useful to the contemporary scholar than Le Nain de Tillemont, and that the merits attributed to him by "Anglo-Saxon" readers are primarily literary (*Gibbon et Rome à la lumière de l'historiographie moderne*, p. 243). Michel Baridon also seems generally disposed to look for the present value of the *Decline and Fall* in its literary rather than its scientific qualities. His position is that

> Gibbon demeure essentiel pour la prospection des sources littéraires, mais qu'il fut dépassé de son vivant même par les sciences auxiliaires de l'histoire et par les théoriciens de l'histoire qui commençaient à mettre en oeuvre la causalité économique.

His final judgment of the *Decline and Fall* at the end of eight hundred scholarly pages is that it survives primarily as a literary work, with a residual value as history:

> Le *Decline and Fall* émerge ainsi comme une construction ambitieuse et originale qui ne satisfait plus l'historien d'aujourd'hui mais où le chercheur trouve toujours son compte et dont le caractère littéraire garantit un succès durable auprès du grand public. [*Edward Gibbon et le mythe de Rome*, pp. 828–9]

Borges was less equivocal about the destiny and the value of Gibbon's masterpiece:

De Quincey writes that history is an infinite or at least an indefinite discipline inasmuch as the same facts can be combined and interpreted in many ways. That observation dates from the nineteenth century; since then the interpretations have multiplied under the influence of the evolution of psychology, and unsuspected cultures and civilizations have been exhumed. Nevertheless, the work of Gibbon survives unharmed, and it is fair to conjecture that it will remain untouched by the vicissitudes of the future. Two causes combine to ensure that perduration. The first and perhaps the most important is esthetic; it is grounded in the spell that, according to Stevenson, is the indispensable and essential quality of literature. The other lies in the perhaps melancholy fact that at the end of time the historian is converted into history and it no longer matters to us only to know how Attila's camp looked: We also want to know how an English gentleman of the eighteenth century might have imagined it. There was a time when the pages of Pliny were read in search of exact knowledge; today we read them in search of wonders, and this change has not hurt the fortunes of Pliny . . . (*Prólogos*, p. 73 [my translation])

17. *AEG*, 311.
18. To Dorothea Gibbon, *LEG*, 334, 26/iii/76 (2:100).
19. Marivaux tells that he likes best those who "ne portent point leur masque, . . . ne l'ont qu'à la main, et vous disent: tenez, le voilà . . . J'aime tout à fait cette manière-là d'être ridicule; car enfin, il faut l'être et de toutes les manières de l'être, celle qui mérite le moins à mon gré, c'est celle qui ne trompe point les autres, qui ne les induit pas à erreur sur notre compte" ("L'Indigent Philosophe," 6 ème feuille, *Oeuvres complettes de M. Marivaux* [Paris: chez la Veuve Duchesne, 1781], vol. 9, p. 232).
20. To Joseph Priestley, *LEG*, 563, 21/i/83 (2:321).
21. *MW*, II, 268, letter CLXII, Priestley to Gibbon, 3/ii/83.
22. *MW*, II, 267–8. See n. 21 above.
23. *MW*, II, 254–5, letter CLII, Hardwicke to Gibbon, 20/ix/81, recommending material in the reigns of Justinian and Justin II to his attention.
24. *MW*, IV, 519–20.
25. Gibbon's well-publicized dislike of William Beckford, his neighbor on the shores of Lake Geneva and the purchaser of his library after his death, is illuminating in this connection. The son of a colorful and immensely wealthy Lord Mayor of London whose ardent support of Wilkes earned him the title "The Patriot," Beckford was forced to leave England after a homosexual scandal in 1784. He was Gibbon's neighbor at Vevey when his wife died giving birth to their second daughter in 1786, and in 1792 he was again living in close proximity to the historian, first at Evian on the other side of Lake Geneva, then at Lausanne itself. Thomas Whaley, who visited him at Evian before calling on Gibbon, reports that Gibbon deemed it "astonishing that any Englishman would visit a man who lay under such an imputation as B. did" (quoted by Sir Gavin de Beer, *Gibbon and His World*, p. 117, from

Buck Whaley's Memoires, ed. Sir Edward Sullivan, London, 1906). Gibbon's horror seemed comically excessive to Whaley and was probably provoked less by the fact of Beckford's homosexuality than by the scandal of it. Gibbon's dislike of Beckford, in short, was probably a deliberate signal of his acceptance of social convention, one that in this particular instance, moreover, he may have felt especially obligated to give. Beckford was never willing to make the kind of compromise with society that was Gibbon's ideal and that Beckford's father, "the Patriot," albeit in a very different way, had also disdained. The role he played was that of a rebel, an egotist. "What care I for Aristocrates or Democrates," he declared. "I am an – Autocrate . . . " (Letter to Lady Craven, 29/xi/1790, quoted by André Parreaux, *William Beckford, auteur de Vathek [1760–1844]: étude de la création littéraire* [Paris: Nizet, 1960], p. 42). Deliberately flouting conventions he despised, and mockingly wearing the mask of the hypocrite, Beckford did not conceal his homosexuality. Gibbon, in contrast, approached the very topic "with reluctance," dispatched it "with impatience," reproached Justinian with failing to distinguish, in his criminal code, between "the passive and active guilt of paederasty," and agreed with Montesquieu that "whatever is secret must be doubtful" (*DF*, XLIV [2:723–4]).

26. In Gibbon's usage the terms "neuter" and "neutral" remain virtually interchangeable and have not yet been assigned to particular spheres. Thus "Heaven was neuter in the quarrel" (*DF*, LIX [3:494]).

27. *LEG*, 361, 26/xi/76 (2:126).

28. Thus Horace Walpole could write him that of the many things he admired in him, his modesty was not the least: "How can you know so much, judge so well, possess your subject and your knowledge, and your power of judicious reflection so thoroughly, and yet command yourself and betray no dictatorial arrogance of decision. How unlike very ancient and very modern authors!" (*MW*, II, 154, letter LXXV, Horace Walpole to Gibbon, 14/ii/76).

29. *AEG*, 324. See also the "Avis au lecteur," dated "3 Février, 1759," in the *Essai sur l'étude de la littérature:* "Je tâcherai d'entendre l'arrêt du public et même son silence, et je ne l'entendrai que pour m'y soumettre" (*MW*, IV, 5).

30. Bond touches several times on the narrator's constant control of the reader in the *Decline and Fall*: "He measures precisely the degree of involvement he will permit his readers and the distance from which they are allowed to view the spectacle. Everywhere there is control . . . " (*The Literary Art of Edward Gibbon*, p. 88). He "narrates, comments, evaluates, and judges as he goes along; the dualistic unit of his prose is admirably suited to the multiplicity of his literary intentions, for it enables him to tell the reader what is happening and how he should feel about it at the same time" (p. 144).

31. *MW*, IV, 519–20.

Index

Index

Index

legitimacy, 55–8
Leo IV (pope), 68
Leontius (general of Justinian), 41
Leovigild (Gothic king), 29, 46
liberty, 52–3, 114–16, 119, 120
Locke, John, 19, 32
London, xvi, 4, 13, 27, 54, 80
Louis XIV (king of France), 8, 115
Low, D.M., ix, 121, 123
luxury, 59

Mably, Gabriel Bonnot de, 89, 148
Macaulay, Thomas Babington, xii, 80, 141
Magdalen College (Oxford), xv
Mandeville, Bernard de, 18
Marivaux, Pierre-Carlet de Chamblain de, 115, 155
Mascou (Johann Jakob Mascovius), 98
masculinity, 33, 34, 40, 41, 42–3, 47, 58, 64, 65, 97; *see also* femininity; sexuality
Maximin, 52
Maximus, 29
mercenaries, 31
metaphor, 80
Michelet, Jules, xii, 43, 136
Mohammed, 29–30, 43
Molière, Jean-Baptiste Poquelin, 114
Momigliano, Arnaldo, 143, 144, 154
Mommsen, Theodor, 80, 137
Montaigne, Michel de, 22
Montesquieu, Charles-Louis de Secondat, Baron de, 26, 27, 51, 57, 70, 73, 74, 77, 89, 102, 103–4, 115, 122, 138, 148, 156; *Esprit des Loix*, 57, 70; *Lettres persanes*, 26, 27, 51
Montolieu, Madame de, 10
Mowat, R.B., ix, 121

narrative and narrator, x, 75–9, 80, 81, 89, 90–1, 93, 94, 95–7, 98, 105, 106–7, 120, 136, 140
Narses, 29, 42
Necker, Jacques, xi, xv, 16
Necker, Suzanne (Suzanne Curchod), xi, xii, xv, 8–10, 13, 14, 16, 20, 21, 118, 126
neo-Platonists, 28, 35
Nerva, 49
Niebuhr, Barthold Georg, 30

origins, original, x, 27, 30, 36, 37, 40, 41, 53, 59–61
Oxford University, xv, 14, 19

parallelism, 79–80, 99, 100–1
Paris, 9
Parkinson, R.N., 122, 128, 146
Parliament, 6, 54
Pascal, Blaise, 122, 136
patricians, 49, 53
Pavilliard, M., xv
Petronius Maximus, 54

Philip, 50
Photius (stepson of Belisarius), 45–6, 61, 63
Placidia, 44, 45, 132–3
plebeians, 53
Pope, Alexander, 4
Porten, Catherine (his aunt), xi, 1–3, 5, 7, 12, 15, 17, 54, 123
Porten, James (his grandfather), 12
Priestley, Joseph, 115–16
primitivism, 59
Procopia, 44
Procopius, 38, 83, 143
property, 30–1, 32, 53
public/private dichotomy, 83–5
Pyrrhonism, 150, 152

reader, 90–1, 93–6, 98, 116–17, 118–19, 120, 156
religion, 115–16; authority, 26–7; Gibbon's experience of, 18–20; Rome, 28, 51–2, 69; *see also* Catholicism; Christianity
repetition, 100
Republic, 30, 31, 33, 39, 60; Empire and, 49, 50; fathers, 64–5; legitimacy, 55–6
Revolution of 1688, 120
rhetoric, x, 33, 34, 98, 99–101, 102–3, 106–8, 142–3; *see also* alliteration; assonance; irony; narrative and narrator; parallelism; reader; repetition
Robertson, William, 114
Roman law, 32, 34–5, 36–40, 61–2; family, 64; fathers, 64; justice, 51; *see also* justice; law
Rome, 22–3, 62–3, 68
Rousseau, Isaac, 2
Rousseau, Jean-Jacques, 2, 3, 22, 25, 26, 30, 32, 36, 53, 56–7, 81, 116, 130, 131, 132, 135, 141, 150; *Confessions*, 2, 22; *Contrat social*, 131, 137; *Discours sur l'origine de l'inégalité*, 135; *Lettres écrites de la montagne*, 56, 135; *Nouvelle Héloïse*, 10, 126, 135; *Rêveries*, 22
Rousseau, Suzanne, 2

Saint Augustine, 79
Saint Paul, 33
Sapor (king of Persia), 28
Savigny, Friedrich Karl von, 132
Schiller, Friedrich, 105
sexuality, 2, 3, 6–7, 9, 10–11, 34; authority, 18; language, 21; religion and, 19; Rome, 33; women, 44; *see also* femininity; masculinity
Sheffield, Lord, *see* Holroyd, John Baker
Sigismond, 45, 46
signs, 29, 36, 58, 59, 68–71, 91–2, 114–15, 116
slavery, 64
society, *see* civil society
sons, 61, 62–3, 65
Sophia, 63